Fiscal Sustainability in Theory and Practice

Fiscal Sustainability in Theory and Practice

A Handbook

Edited by

Craig Burnside

THE WORLD BANK
Washington, D.C.

© 2005 The International Bank for Reconstruction and Development / The World Bank
1818 H Street, NW
Washington, DC 20433
Telephone: 202-473-1000
Internet: www.worldbank.org
E-mail: feedback@worldbank.org

1 2 3 4 08 07 06 05

Cover: Photodisc Green/Getty Images

ISBN-10: 0-8213-5874-X   ISBN-13: 978-0-8213-5874-0
eISBN: 0-8213-5875-8   DOI: 10.1596/978-0-8213-5874-0

Library of Congress Cataloging-in-Publication Data

Fiscal sustainability in theory and practice : a handbook / edited by Craig Burnside.
     p. cm.
   Includes bibliographical references and index.
   ISBN 0-8213-5874-X (pbk.)
     1. Finance, Public—Handbooks, manuals, etc. 2. Budget—Handbooks, manuals, etc. 3. Fiscal policy—Handbooks, manuals, etc. I. Burnside, Craig.
   HJ141.F574 2005
   339.5'2—dc22
                                                      2005041485

Contents

v

Contents

Chapter 8

Craig Burnside, Martin Eichenbaum, and Sergio Rebelo

Chapter 9

Craig Burnside, Martin Eichenbaum, and Sergio Rebelo

Contents

Boxes

Figures

Tables

Contents

Book Title:
Preface

As the title suggests, this book is intended as an introduction to the theory of fiscal sustainability and the practice of fiscal sustainability assessment. It begins with an overview of the models and case studies presented and explains why topics such as contingent liabilities, external debt position, and fiscal federalism are not covered in detail.

This work evolved over time, as the need for a resource on fiscal sustainability analysis became apparent to the membership of the World Bank's Quality of Fiscal Adjustment Thematic Group (QFA TG). Fiscal sustainability has become a prominent issue in developing countries, and fiscal sustainability assessments have become an increasingly required component of macroeconomic analysis at the World Bank. Unfortunately, there was no single, basic source of information on this topic. Country economists new to this type of analysis could rely on sample work by other economists at the Bank or delve into scattered journal articles for the theoretical background. Frequently, however, work on fiscal sustainability analysis would be undertaken by hired experts from the Bank's Development Economics Research Group (DECRG) or Poverty Reduction and Economic Management, Economic Policy Group (PRMEP) or by outside academics.

I assumed leadership of the QFA TG in 2001, upon joining PRMEP. At that time, fiscal sustainability analysis was identified as a core area in which this group should provide leadership and support to economists working in the regional departments of the World Bank. The membership of the

QFA TG—which, despite its name, discusses a wide range of fiscal issues—agreed that the best way for the PRMEP group to provide this leadership and support was through training. To support that training, I embarked on a project to provide pedagogical resources on fiscal sustainability analysis. Those resources have come together in the form of this book.

For those who are unfamiliar with fiscal sustainability analysis, it is—at its core—the use of a simple set of tools to analyze a government's budget and debt positions. In its simplest form, this type of analysis leads to conclusions about the appropriateness of fiscal policy, which are often characterized in terms of the balance between revenue and expenditure given a government's debt level. As suggested above, many World Bank economists are familiar with fiscal sustainability analysis; the process has long been an important part of the Bank's economic and sector work. But for those who are less familiar with the subject, there has been no single reference work that explains it. This book seeks to fill that gap.

As is standard with any reference text, I should describe the intended audience. First, consistent with its original purpose, the book will serve as an integral part of the training courses in fiscal sustainability regularly offered by PRMEP (now known as PRMED) at the World Bank. These courses are aimed at economists who are unfamiliar with fiscal sustainability analysis but need an understanding of it in their daily work. Second, the book will serve as a useful reference work for all economists. A number of handy and standard formulas are presented in the book. Furthermore, many of the worked-out examples presented here can easily be replicated in other countries that collect sufficient data. Third, I hope that this book helps build a greater understanding of fiscal policy and the constraints faced by policy-makers. In particular, because many of these constraints are dynamic, a better understanding of fiscal sustainability by economists in developing countries may lead to greater pressure for better fiscal policy in these countries. Finally, I should point out that this book is not aimed at a research audience already familiar with the theoretical concepts described here: Most of the theoretical discussion in this book is neither new nor particularly advanced. Rather, the book collects and presents preexisting work from many sources in a single volume, and makes it accessible to economists with either an advanced undergraduate or a basic graduate level of training.

Please note that the opinions the authors express in this book are their own, and are not necessarily shared by the organizations with which they are, or have been, affiliated.

NA

Acknowledgments

In addition to the authors, many others who contributed to this book deserve special thanks. These include those who handled the necessary administrative details at various stages; the help of Duane Chilton, Debbie Fischer-Sturgess, Vivian Hon, Marketa Jonasova, and Sarah Lipscomb was invaluable. Upon my departure from PRMEP, stewardship of the book was taken over by the extremely patient Thomas Laursen, Elena Ianchovichina, and Nina Budina. Leadership support for the book was provided by Zia Qureshi, Yaw Ansu, and Vikram Nehru.

Thanks also to Stephen McGroarty and Janet Sasser in the Office of the Publisher at the World Bank, and to Kim Kelley, a consultant in that office. They smoothed the review and editorial processes, easing publication of an intricate book.

I also wish to thank three anonymous reviewers for their invaluable comments. Finally, I would like to thank the many students who have taken the fiscal sustainability courses offered by me at the World Bank since 2002. Their comments and suggestions have strengthened the final product considerably.

Contributors

Craig Burnside is the editor of this volume and the author or coauthor of chapters 1, 2, 3, 5, 6, 8, and 9. He is a professor of economics at Duke University in Durham, North Carolina, and a research associate for the National Bureau of Economic Research (NBER) in Cambridge, Massachusetts. He was previously a professor at the University of Virginia, a lead economist in the Poverty Reduction and Economic Management, Economic Policy Group (PRMEP) at the World Bank, and an assistant professor at the University of Pittsburgh and Queen's University. He received a Ph.D. in economics from Northwestern University in Evanston, Illinois.

Punam Chuhan, who contributed chapter 4, is a lead economist in the Global Monitoring Secretariat of the World Bank. Prior to joining the Bank in 1993, she worked as an economist at the Federal Reserve Bank of New York. She received a Ph.D. in economics from Georgetown University in Washington, D.C.

Martin Eichenbaum, a coauthor of chapters 8 and 9, is the Ethel and John Lindgren Professor of Economics at Northwestern University, a Fellow of the Econometric Society, and a research associate for the National Bureau of Economic Research. He has served as a consultant for both the Federal

Reserve Bank of Chicago and the World Bank. Previously, he was an associate professor at Carnegie Mellon University in Pittsburgh, Pennsylvania. He received a Ph.D. in economics from the University of Minnesota.

Norbert Fiess, who contributed chapter 7, is an economist in the Office of the Chief Economist of the Latin America and the Caribbean Region of the World Bank (LAC). Prior to joining the Bank he worked at Commerzbank AG and at the University of Strathclyde, in Glasgow, Scotland, where he earned a Ph.D. in international finance.

Yuliya Meshcheryakova, a coauthor of chapters 5 and 6, recently completed a Ph.D. in economics at Northwestern University. She was a research assistant in the World Bank's PRMEP group in 2001, and a consultant to the project that produced this book. She will soon begin work as a lecturer in the School of Economics and Finance at Victoria University of Wellington, in New Zealand.

Sergio Rebelo, a coauthor of chapters 8 and 9, is the Tokai Bank Distinguished Professor of Finance in the Kellogg School of Management at Northwestern University, a faculty research fellow of the National Bureau of Economic Research, a research fellow of the Centre for Economic Policy Research in London, and a consultant to the Federal Reserve Bank of Chicago. He previously was a professor at the University of Rochester, where he received a Ph.D. in economics, and at the Portuguese Catholic University. He also has served as a consultant to the Board of Governors of the Federal Reserve System, the International Monetary Fund, and the World Bank.

NA

Acronyms

ADF	Augmented Dickey Fuller (unit root test)
ARIMA	AutoRegressive Integrated Moving Average (time-series analysis model)
BEA	Bureau of Economic Analysis, U.S. Department of Commerce
BIS	Bank for International Settlements
BK	Baxter-King filter
BN	Beveridge-Nelson decomposition
CAB	current account balance
CEPR	Centre for Economic Policy Research (London)
CODELCO	Corporacion Nacional del Cobre (Chile)
CPI	consumer price index
CSF	Copper Stabilization Fund (Chile)
DSA	debt sustainability analysis
ECB	European Central Bank
EPI	export price index
EU	European Union
FDI	foreign direct investment
FRED	Federal Reserve Economic Data (Federal Reserve of St. Louis database)
FX	foreign exchange

FXR	foreign exchange reserves
GDI	gross domestic income
GDP	gross domestic product
GNI	gross national income
GNP	gross national product
G7	Group of Seven countries (Canada, France, Germany, Italy, Japan, United Kingdom, and United States)
HIPC	heavily indebted poor countries
HP	Hodrick and Prescott filter
ICOR	incremental capital output ratio
IDB	Inter-American Development Bank
IFS	International Financial Statistics
IIE	Institute for International Economics
IIP	International Investment Position statistics (IMF)
IMF	International Monetary Fund
INEGI	Instituto Nacional de Estadística Geografia e Informática (Mexico)
IPI	import price index
LAC	Latin America and the Caribbean region (World Bank)
LCU	local currency unit
NBER	National Bureau of Economic Research
NFA	net foreign asset position
OECD	Organisation for Economic Co-operation and Development
OLS	ordinary least squares
PEMEX	Petroleos Mexicanos (state oil company, Mexico)
PP	Phillips-Perron (test)
PPP	purchasing power parity
PRMEP	Poverty Reduction and Economic Management, Economic Policy Group
PSE	public sector enterprise
PV	present value
QFA TG	Quality of Fiscal Adjustment Thematic Group (World Bank)
TL	Turkish lira
UNCTAD	United Nations Commission on Trade and Development
VAR	vector autoregressive model
VAT	value-added tax

An Introduction to Fiscal Sustainability in Theory and Practice

Craig Burnside

H61 H63

E61 E32

This handbook is designed as an introductory guide to the analysis of fiscal sustainability. It explains the tools that can be used to analyze a government's budget and debt positions and thereby assess the appropriateness of its fiscal policy.

1   Themes

The book is organized around three themes: basic theory and tools for everyday use, the effects of business cycles on public finance and the role of fiscal rules, and crises and their impact on fiscal sustainability.

The first theme is central to the book's stated purpose of bringing the basic theoretical literature together, along with examples used to illustrate particular methods of analysis. The second and third themes develop the topic of fiscal sustainability further, by extending it to topics that have been at the forefront of policy discussions since the mid-1990s.

1

2   Omissions

Some important topics are omitted or not fully addressed. Among these are a broad discussion of contingent liabilities, debt management, a complete discussion of the sustainability of a country's external position, the role of uncertainty, and fiscal federalism.

In the case of contingent liabilities, this book does touch upon the subject under the theme of crises, where the role of contingent liabilities in the financial sector is explored. But the discussion is far from complete. Fortunately, there is an earlier World Bank-sponsored volume by Brixi and Schick (2002) that delves into that topic in considerable detail.

Similarly, one might have expected to find a chapter or two on debt management in a volume on fiscal sustainability. The government's debt portfolio implies risk, in the sense that future government outlays for debt service, expressed in real terms, depend on future realizations of uncertain variables. Debt managers deal with this risk, which clearly has implications for fiscal sustainability when loosely defined as the government's ability to meet its current and future obligations. Rather than discuss debt management, however, the authors have instead chosen to treat it as a specialized topic of its own, largely because there is an existing World Bank-sponsored volume by Jensen and Wheeler (2004) devoted to this subject.

The main focus of this book is on fiscal sustainability, that is, the sustainability of the *government's* finances, rather than external sustainability, which deals with a *country's* current and capital accounts as well as its external debt position. Chapter 4 describes some measures of vulnerability and touches upon the issue of external sustainability, but this is a subject unto itself that deserves its own volume.

Contingent liabilities are spending outlays that can arise in the future depending on uncertain outcomes. These liabilities can be explicit or implicit, whereas debt management deals with uncertainty related to the government's explicit liabilities. But uncertainty has more general implications for fiscal sustainability, because revenue and expenditure (other than on debt service and contingent liabilities) both lack perfect predictability. Some chapters address aspects of uncertainty, but its treatment is not comprehensive. This is partly a function of the fact that the literature on uncertainty in fiscal sustainability analysis is still evolving.

Finally, an important and nascent topic in the analysis of fiscal sustainability is fiscal federalism. This topic has relevance both for currency unions, in which monetary policy is centralized but fiscal policy is locally controlled subject to rules, and for countries with large and influential state governments. Again, the literature on this topic is active and evolving, and the subject matter could easily fill its own volume. Chapter 7 briefly discusses some of the relevant issues in its discussion of fiscal rules, but fiscal federalism is not discussed here in further detail.

3   Basic Theory and Tools

Chapter 2 begins by defining *sustainability*. The term suggests something akin to solvency. But for purposes of this book, a more precise meaning is needed. If a government is literally insolvent, this presumably implies that it is currently unable to service its debt. Determining whether a government is solvent or not, in that case, is trivial. We can simply look to see if a government is or is not defaulting on its debt. But the concept of insolvency used here refers to the government's inability to indefinitely maintain its current policies while avoiding default now or in the future. One aspect of analyzing fiscal sustainability is, therefore, assessing whether a government is insolvent—in this particular sense of the word.

To perform basic fiscal sustainability analysis, specific theoretical tools are needed, and these are discussed in chapter 2. Here mathematical representations of the government budget constraint are introduced, as well as what is most often referred to as a government's lifetime budget constraint. This chapter also explains the relationship between these concepts and the fiscal theory of the price level.

Chapter 2 uses the basic theory of the government budget constraint to derive results from the early literature on both the effects of government budget deficits and the coordination of monetary and fiscal policy.[1] The results presented in this chapter are important, and helpful, in interpreting the results of fiscal sustainability analysis. First, budget deficits need not be inflationary. Whether or not they are depends on how deficits are financed over a government's lifetime, as opposed to how they are financed during a particular period. Second, primary deficits that are not paid for by running primary surpluses in the future must inevitably lead to inflation or default. Third, lack of coordination of fiscal and monetary policies can lead to

1

perverse outcomes, in the sense that a "tough" monetary authority can, through its actions, worsen inflation outcomes if its actions are not coordinated with the fiscal authority.

Chapter 3 uses the theory described in chapter 2 to derive simple tools for conducting fiscal sustainability analysis, and illustrates these tools through numerous examples. The chapter begins by introducing the *long-run fiscal sustainability condition*, which is a steady-state version of the government's lifetime budget constraint. This condition describes the size of the primary surplus the government must run to maintain solvency given a particular degree of indebtedness, and given other assumptions that are made about policy and the economy. A government often has fiscal goals other than mere solvency. An additional tool that describes the size of the primary surplus needed to achieve a debt target within a particular time frame is also described in chapter 3. This tool is illustrated using a small case study of Bulgaria, where a level of debt suitable for entry into the European Union and adoption of the euro as its national currency are targets.

Chapter 3 also introduces the concept of *debt dynamics*, a tool that is used to understand the evolution of a country's debt stock over a historical interval of time. This tool is illustrated using case studies of Argentina and Turkey, and, in practical applied work, is helpful in drawing lessons about policy coordination using data from the fiscal, monetary, and national accounts. Debt dynamics show how the debt-to-GDP ratio is affected by real interest rates, exchange rate volatility, recessions, and expansions, as well as fiscal and monetary policy. Debt dynamics are also useful in making forward-looking projections that can be used to assess risks faced by a government stemming from its debt portfolio.

Finally, chapter 3 discusses issues in the measurement of debt. Much of the theoretical literature concentrates on examples in which debt is real, is rolled over period-by-period, and pays a constant real rate of interest. So this chapter considers which measure of debt—book or market value—is most relevant for a particular type of analysis.

Chapter 4 also focuses on the measurement of debt levels. It describes the types of debt instruments governments may have and how these are valued. The discussion then turns to the various debt indicators that are used in relatively casual assessments of sustainability or macroeconomic vulnerability. These include a variety of debt and debt-service ratios that are designed to capture a government's or in some cases, a country's vulnerability to solvency or liquidity problems.

4   Business Cycles and Fiscal Rules

Chapters 5, 6, and 7 turn to one of the two main subtopics discussed in this volume: business cycles and their effects on a government's budget. Chapter 5 discusses cyclical adjustment of measures of a government's budget balance. It describes the motivation for these adjustments, which is to identify what might be regarded as the *discretionary* component of fiscal policy. Modern tax systems imply that tax revenues are procyclical, since significant portions of the tax base (such as private income and personal consumption) are procyclical. Similarly, modern transfer programs tend to imply increased outlays during recessions, so that a portion of government expenditure is structurally countercyclical. These two facts imply that the budget balance has a natural tendency to move procyclically. One interpretation of this fact is that standard measures of the government's budget balance will tend to overstate the health of fiscal policy during expansions and understate it during contractions, hence the desire to adjust the budget balance for these effects. Chapter 5 shows that these adjustments have a theoretical motivation within the context of traditional Keynesian macroeconomic models.

Cyclicality of the government's budget relates to fiscal sustainability once the topic is broadened to include not only issues of government solvency, but also issues related to the optimality or desirability of particular government policies. Of particular interest are questions such as: Are the automatic stabilizers a government has in place sufficient? Does discretionary fiscal policy in a country help to dampen business cycles, or does it tend to exaggerate them?

Chapter 5 describes the methods that have been proposed for cyclical adjustment of the budget balance. These involve four steps: First, trends and cycles in measures of aggregate activity must be identified. Second, components of the budget data that should be regarded as being structurally sensitive to the business cycle must be identified and decomposed into trends and cycles. Third, the contemporaneous relationship between the cyclical components of real activity and the relevant budget data must be estimated. Finally, the budget data are "corrected" using the relationship identified in the third step.

Chapter 6 illustrates the tools described in chapter 5, using a detailed case study of fiscal policy in Mexico between 1980 and 2003. Since World War II, fiscal policy in industrialized countries has evolved to the point that it is viewed as *leaning against the wind*. This is for two reasons. First, automatic stabilizers—taxes tied to the level of real activity and transfers that are countercyclical—have become more important. In Keynesian models this implies a smaller multiplier mapping from changes in autonomous expenditure to output. Second, governments have attempted to use discretionary fiscal policy for countercyclical purposes. But in developing and industrializing countries, fiscal policy has not evolved in the same way; automatic stabilizers have tended to be weaker and discretionary policy, procyclical. Mexico serves as an interesting case study of this phenomenon.

Chapter 6 uses detailed fiscal data from Mexico to cyclically adjust the consolidated public sector's budget balance using the techniques outlined in chapter 5. It characterizes Mexico's automatic stabilizers, which prove to be quite weak, and the discretionary component of Mexico's budget balance, which over the sample period was countercyclical; that is, fiscal policy was procyclical. During expansions Mexico has tended to run discretionary deficits, while during recessions it has tended to run discretionary surpluses. Although this has exaggerated Mexico's business cycles to some degree, chapter 6 concludes that fiscal shocks did not play a primary role in driving real activity.

Chapter 7 discusses an emerging policy tool for dealing with procyclical fiscal policy: a *fiscal rule*. Fiscal rules have been introduced by governments for a number of reasons. They can be used to enhance a government's credibility and consolidate its debt, to ensure long-run fiscal sustainability (solvency), to minimize externalities among members of a federation, and to deal with any procyclical bias in fiscal policy.

Chapter 7 describes fiscal rules generally, and then turns to a discussion of Chile's fiscal rule, adopted in 2000 primarily to deal with a perceived procyclical bias in fiscal policy. The chapter describes the details of Chile's fiscal rule, which sets a target for the structural (or cyclically adjusted) surplus at 1 percent of GDP. Implementation of the rule and a preliminary assessment of its impact on the Chilean economy are also discussed.

5   Crises and Fiscal Sustainability

The final section of the book deals with crises, which can be considered the natural consequence of unsustainable policies on the part of a government. Earlier, we presented a simple definition of fiscal sustainability, which referred to the government's ability to maintain its current policies and satisfy its lifetime budget constraint without defaulting on its debt obligations. Chapter 8 explores a closely related issue: the sustainability of a fixed exchange rate regime. This chapter explains how we can think of the sustainability of a fixed exchange rate as dependent upon a government's ability to satisfy its lifetime budget constraint without reliance on inflation-related revenue.[2] Thus, the sustainability of a fixed exchange rate requires a stronger restriction on fiscal policy than the restriction required for mere fiscal sustainability.

In a simple model related to those described in chapters 2 and 3, chapter 8 shows that a fixed exchange rate regime will eventually collapse if a government's initial debt exceeds the present value of its future primary surpluses. This chapter also shows that a government's initial debt and current deficit are insufficient indicators of the likelihood of collapse by a fixed exchange rate regime, since this can be the consequence of either ongoing deficits (which are readily observable) or prospective deficits (that might, for example, stem from an anticipated bailout of a troubled financial system). Chapter 8 explains how the timing and consequences (for inflation and depreciation) of a crisis depend on the nature of a government's monetary policy response to the crisis.

The classic model described in chapter 8 emphasizes a government's choice, in the face of an unanticipated increase in its expenditure, between explicit fiscal reforms that would help it control inflation and maintain a pegged exchange rate, and increased seigniorage revenue, which is incompatible with maintaining a peg. In these models, the government finances its additional expenditure by printing more money. This, in turn, implies that it must abandon the fixed exchange rate and suffer higher inflation in the future. As recent crises have demonstrated, this model, though useful, has shortcomings. In many crises, governments facing big increases in their expenditure to bail out failing banks have abandoned fixed exchange rate regimes. These governments experienced big depreciations of their currencies, did not dramatically increase seigniorage revenue after the crisis, and yet have not suffered from high inflation.

Chapter 9 attempts to rationalize these findings. It does so by pointing out that the simple model of the government budget constraint used in the preceding chapters misses out on important real-world aspects of government budgets. This chapter shows that governments obtain revenue from sources other than explicit fiscal reform and seigniorage revenue. One can think of an explicit fiscal reform as the decision to raise tax rates, or the decision to purchase a smaller *quantity* of goods and services. But governments also obtain net revenue through implicit fiscal reforms or changes in

1

the value of government revenue and expenditure that are driven by changes in relative prices, not changes in quantities or tax rates. Governments also gain or lose revenue depending on the state of the economy, which they cannot control. By issuing debt in local currency rather than real debt, governments can also raise implicit revenue—if their policy decisions induce a depreciation of the currency.

Chapter 9 takes these aspects of government finance seriously and builds them into the theoretical model of the government budget constraint. It shows how the theoretical consequences of a crisis change with changes in the structure of the budget constraint. With an example calibrated to the experience of Korea in 1997–8, chapter 9 shows that a simple model of sustainable government finances can rationalize the inflation and depreciation outcomes observed in the wake of a recent crisis.

The results of the three case studies presented in chapter 9—of crises in Korea (1997–8), Mexico (1994–5), and Turkey (2001)—show that in all three cases, implicit fiscal reforms were an important factor in government financing after the crisis. This finding suggests that policy analysts would have reached incorrect conclusions about the likely consequences of these crises had they focused exclusively on the size of explicit fiscal reforms by the governments of these countries.

6   Application of These Tools

The methods and practice of fiscal sustainability analysis are constantly evolving. The methods currently used by international organizations (see, for example, IMF 2002 and 2003) represent simple extensions of the analysis presented in chapter 3 of this volume. A goal of this book is to enable readers to jump right into practical applications of these existing analytical tools—and that they will find themselves well placed to become consumers and critics of developments in this important area of fiscal policy analysis.

Notes

1. In particular, the chapter describes the results of Sargent and Wallace (1981) and Sargent (1983, 1985).
2. This should probably be considered as a minimum condition for the sustainability of a fixed exchange rate regime. Other problems faced by a

government, such as a liquidity crisis, might also force the abandonment of a fixed exchange rate.

References

Brixi, Hana Polackova, and Allen Schick, eds. 2002. *Government at Risk: Contingent Liabilities and Fiscal Risk*. Washington, DC: World Bank and Oxford University Press.

IMF (International Monetary Fund). 2002. "Assessing Sustainability." Washington, DC: IMF. http://www.imf.org/external/np/pdr/sus/2002/eng/052802.htm.

———. 2003. "Sustainability Assessments—Review of Application and Methodological Refinements." Washington, DC: IMF. http://www.imf.org/external/np/pdr/sustain/2003/ 061003.htm.

Jensen, Frederick H., and Graeme Paul Wheeler. 2004. *Sound Practice in Government Debt Management*. Washington, DC: World Bank.

Sargent, Thomas. 1983. "The Ends of Four Big Inflations." In Robert E. Hall, ed. *Inflation: Causes and Effects*. Chicago: University of Chicago Press for the National Bureau of Economic Research.

———. 1985. "Reaganomics and Credibility." In Albert Ando, Hidekazu Eguchi, Roger Farmer, and Yoshio Suzuki, eds. *Monetary Policy in Our Times*. Cambridge, MA: MIT Press.

Sargent, Thomas, and Neil Wallace. 1981. "Some Unpleasant Monetarist Arithmetic." *Federal Reserve Bank of Minneapolis Quarterly Review* 5 (3): 1–17.

Chapter 2

11-33

2

Theoretical Prerequisites for Fiscal Sustainability Analysis

Craig Burnside

H61 H63
E62 E52

To define fiscal sustainability analysis, it is useful to seek guidance from a dictionary. *Webster's*, for example, suggests using the adjective *sustainable* to describe something that can be kept up, prolonged, borne, and so forth. Or, the term might be used to describe a method of harvesting a resource so that the resource is not depleted or permanently damaged in the process.

When speaking of fiscal sustainability, economists are typically referring to the fiscal policies of a government. Of course, economists must make their definition of fiscal sustainability more precise than the dictionary definitions given above. But definitions such as these can guide their thinking.

The resource depletion analogy is not entirely appropriate here, because a government's resources are not that comparable to mineral or other physical resources. It does, however, suggest a concept of sustainability related to *solvency*. When speaking of *solvency*, economists refer to a government's ability to service its debt obligations without explicitly defaulting on them. One concept of fiscal sustainability relates to a government's ability to indefinitely maintain the same set of policies while remaining solvent. If a particular combination of fiscal and/or monetary policies would, if indefinitely maintained, lead to insolvency, these policies would be referred to as unsustainable. One role of fiscal sustainability analysis is to provide some indication as to whether or not a particular policy mix is sustainable.

2

Governments often change their policies if it becomes clear that they are unsustainable. Thus, the focus of fiscal sustainability analysis is frequently not on default itself—which governments tend to avoid—but rather on the consequences of the policy changes needed to avoid eventual default.

Even when a government is solvent and likely to remain solvent, its fiscal policies may be costly. Sometimes fiscal sustainability analysis will refer to the ongoing costs associated with a particular combination of fiscal and monetary policies.

This chapter develops the simple theoretical framework within which fiscal sustainability analysis is usually conducted. Several concepts are introduced: the single-period government budget constraint, the lifetime budget constraint, the fiscal theory of the price level, the no-Ponzi scheme condition, and the transversality condition. Later, in chapter 2, examples illustrate how these tools can be used to analyze and interpret data.

1   The Government Budget Constraint

The fundamental building block of fiscal sustainability analysis is the public sector or *government budget constraint*, which is an identity:

net issuance of debt = interest payments − primary balance
                        − seigniorage.   (1.1)

The net issuance of debt is gross receipts from issuing new debt minus any amortization payments made in the period.[1]

The identity (1.1) can be expressed in mathematical notation as

$$B_t - B_{t-1} = I_t - X_t - (M_t - M_{t-1}).$$ (1.2)

Here the subscript t indexes time, which is usually measured in years; B_t is quantity of public debt at the end of period t, I_t is interest payments, X_t is the primary balance (revenue minus noninterest expenditure), and M_t is the monetary base at the end of period t, all measured in local currency units (LCUs). The only subtlety involved in (1.2) is in associating the net issuance of debt (a net cash flow) with the change in a stock (the quantity of debt, B_t). To be sure that these objects are equivalent, precise definitions of the *quantity of debt* and *interest payments* are needed. To define the former, a decision must be made on how to value the government's outstanding debt obligations. To define the latter, debt service must be divided between amortization and interest. Precise definitions of debt and interest will not be explored until chapter 3.

But two clarifying statements should be made at this point. First, the debt and interest payments concepts should both be net; that is, debt should be net of any equivalent assets and interest should be payments net of receipts. Second, the analysis must fix on a particular definition of the government or public sector, since different measures of the variables in (1.2) would apply to different definitions of the public sector. For example, including seigniorage revenue (or change in the monetary base) in the definition implicitly defines the public sector to include at least the central bank, in addition to the central government. It is quite common to define the public sector as the consolidation of the central government, state and local governments, state-owned nonfinancial enterprises, and the central bank. Sometimes state banks are also included in the definition of the public sector, but more commonly they are not.

As shown in chapter 3, (1.2) is the fundamental building block for studying the evolution of a government's debt over time; this is more commonly referred to as the government's *debt dynamics*. But the flow budget constraint is also the first step in deriving the lifetime government budget constraint, which plays a crucial role in assessing a government's finances, interpreting its fiscal policies, and predicting the consequences of particular shocks to the economy for prices and exchange rates. To derive the lifetime budget constraint, one must first rewrite the flow budget constraint.

To begin, assume that time is discrete, that all debt has a maturity of one period, and that debt is real (in the sense that its face value is indexed to the price level) and pays a constant real rate of interest, r.[2] In this case (1.2) can be rewritten as

$$b_t = (1 + r)b_{t-1} - x_t - \sigma_t, \tag{1.3}$$

where $b_t = B_t/P_t$ is the end-of-period t stock of real debt, $x_t = X_t/P_t$ is the real primary surplus, and $\sigma_t = (M_t - M_{t-1})/P_t$ is the real value of seigniorage revenue.[3]

Rearranging (1.3),

$$b_{t-1} = (1 + r)^{-1}b_t + (1 + r)^{-1}(x_t + \sigma_t). \tag{1.4}$$

Notice that (1.4) can be updated to period t, implying that

$$b_t = (1 + r)^{-1}b_{t+1} + (1 + r)^{-1}(x_{t+1} + \sigma_{t+1}). \tag{1.5}$$

This can be used to substitute for b_t on the right-hand side of (1.4):

$$b_{t-1} = (1 + r)^{-2}b_{t+1} + (1 + r)^{-1}(x_t + \sigma_t) + (1 + r)^{-2}(x_{t+1} + \sigma_{t+1}). \quad (1.6)$$

Clearly, the same procedure could be used to substitute for b_{t+1} on the right-hand side of (1.6), and then for b_{t+2}, and so forth, in a recursive fashion. Hence, after several iterations one would obtain

$$b_{t-1} = (1 + r)^{-(j+1)}b_{t+j} + \sum_{i=0}^{j}(1 + r)^{-(i+1)}(x_{t+i} + \sigma_{t+i}). \quad (1.7)$$

Equation (1.7) provides a link between the amounts of debt the government has at two dates: $t - 1$ and $t + j$. In particular, the amount of debt the government has on date $t + j$ is a function of the debt it initially had at date $t - 1$, as well as the primary surpluses it ran and seigniorage it raised between these dates.

If one imposes the condition

$$\lim_{j \to \infty} (1 + r)^{-(j+1)} b_{t+j} = 0, \quad (1.8)$$

this reveals what is frequently called the government's *lifetime budget constraint*:

$$b_{t-1} = \sum_{i=0}^{\infty}(1 + r)^{-(i+1)}(x_{t+i} + \sigma_{t+i}). \quad (1.9)$$

Intuitively, the lifetime budget constraint states that the government finances its initial debt by raising seigniorage revenue and running primary surpluses in the future, whose present value is equal to its initial debt obligations.[4]

The lifetime budget constraint is a fundamental building block for a number of different tools and theoretical arguments developed in the literature and discussed in this volume. In the following section the lifetime budget constraint is used as a theoretical tool to discuss the effects of government deficits on inflation. This discussion will be closely related to the theoretical arguments made in Sargent and Wallace's (1981) *unpleasant monetarist arithmetic* paper and Sargent's papers (1983, 1985) on monetary and fiscal policy coordination. Later it will be shown that in the fiscal theory of the price level, (1.9) is reinterpreted as an equation that prices government debt.[5]

In chapter 3 the lifetime budget constraint is used to derive a simple tool for assessing fiscal sustainability: the long-run sustainability condition. How this can be used as the basis of formal statistical tests of (1.8) is also shown, as in Hamilton and Flavin (1986).

2 Fiscal and Monetary Policy and the Effects of Government Deficits

This section explores the effects of government deficits on inflation. The issue of fiscal and monetary policy coordination is also considered. At first, it may not seem obvious that these questions and concerns are closely related to fiscal sustainability. They are, however, intimately related. As argued in the introduction, it is possible that a government will violate (1.9) by defaulting on its debt obligations. Yet, in many cases, the role of fiscal sustainability analysis is not to point out concerns about default. Instead, the role of the analysis is to explain the macroeconomic consequences of alternative policies that happen to be consistent with (1.9). For example, the lifetime budget constraint can be satisfied by generating large primary surpluses. But it can also be satisfied by generating large amounts of seigniorage revenue. Obviously, these policies will have different consequences for macroeconomic outcomes; and the timing of when surpluses occur may be important as well.

It is time now to take a first step toward understanding the impact of different policy choices. As mentioned earlier, much of the discussion here is closely related to the arguments outlined in Sargent and Wallace (1981) and Sargent (1983, 1985). Begin by returning to the real version of the government budget constraint, (1.3):

$$b_t = (1 + r)b_{t-1} - x_t - (M_t - M_{t-1})/P_t.$$

Notice that this equation can be rearranged as

$$P_t(b_t - b_{t-1}) + M_t - M_{t-1} = P_t(rb_{t-1} - x_t). \qquad (2.1)$$

The right-hand side of (2.1) is the government's financing requirement: the nominal value of real interest payments plus the primary deficit. The left-hand side of (2.1) is the government's financing, which is a mix of net issuance of debt and net issuance of base money.

If one thinks of a fiscal authority (a legislature together with a ministry of finance) as the determiner of x_t, then given that rb_{t-1} is predetermined,

(2.1) appears to define the role of the monetary authority as that of debt manager: This entity chooses the financing mix between the government's debt and monetary obligations.

Price Level Determination

Conditional on a value for the price level P_t, one might think of the fiscal authority as choosing x_t and the monetary authority as choosing M_t and b_t, consistent with (2.1). Not surprisingly, however, the price level itself will be influenced by the monetary authority's choice. The link between the monetary authority's decisionmaking and the price level is usually made by writing down a model of money demand.

There are several models of money demand that might be used. For example, one might use the quantity theory of money, where the demand for real money balances is simply $M_t/P_t = y_t/v$. In this case, v represents a constant value for the velocity of money and y_t represents real GDP. Alternatively, a variant of the Cagan (1956) money demand representation might be used, where the demand for real balances depends negatively on the nominal interest rate: $M_t/P_t = Ay_t \exp(-\eta R_t)$, and R_t represents the nominal interest rate. One could also use any simple model of money demand that is consistent with the basic assumptions explained in a standard intermediate macroeconomics textbook—or perhaps choose a more complicated general equilibrium model. For the remainder of chapter 2, either the quantity theory or a variant of Cagan money demand will be used, mainly for analytical convenience. The qualitative findings derived with these assumptions would be robust to other specifications.

To obtain our first results on the effects of policy on the price level, take the Cagan money demand specification described above, assuming that: first, the transactions motive is constant, that is, $y_t = y$ for all t; and second, the nominal interest rate is just $R_t = r + E_t \ln(P_{t+1}/P_t)$. In this case:

$$\ln(M_t/P_t) = a - \eta E_t \ln(P_{t+1}/P_t), \qquad (2.2)$$

where $a = \ln(Ay) - \eta r$.

Notice that (2.2) represents a linear first-order difference equation in $\ln P_t$. If one treats M_t as an exogenous stochastic process controlled by the central bank, (2.2) implies the following solution for $\ln P_t$:

$$\ln P_t = -a + \frac{1}{1+\eta} \sum_{j=0}^{\infty} \left(\frac{\eta}{1+\eta} \right)^j E_t \ln M_{t+j}. \qquad (2.3)$$

It is important that P_t depends on the current money supply as well as the expected path of the money supply. If the interest semi-elasticity of money demand, η, is very small, say approximately 0, then the price level depends mainly on the current money supply: $\ln P_t \approx -a + \ln M_t$. But if η is very large, the discount factor in (2.3) will be close to 1, and the price level will to a large degree depend on what agents expect the money supply to be well into the future.

Government Deficits and Inflation

The solution for the price level, (2.3), is now used to ask whether government deficits are inflationary. The answer depends on how monetary and fiscal policies, together, are conducted. It will be shown that under different policy regimes deficits can have quite different implications for inflation.

   Regime 1. Suppose the government follows a regime in which it issues debt to finance deficits, and money is never printed:

$$M_t = M \text{ for all } t. \tag{2.4}$$

Under this regime, the lifetime budget constraint, (1.9), implies

$$b_{-1} = \sum_{t=0}^{\infty}(1 + r)^{-(t+1)}x_t, \tag{2.5}$$

so that the present value of the primary balance is the initial debt stock.

   In essence, if one abstracts from the stock of initial debt, the monetary policy $M_t = M$ for all t implies that running a primary deficit at time zero, $x_0 > 0$, forces there to be future primary surpluses in present value terms: that is, $\sum_{t=1}^{\infty}(1 + r)^{-(t+1)}x_t > 0$. In this policy regime monetary policy is rigid, and future fiscal policy must tighten if current fiscal policy becomes looser.

   Furthermore, and as a consequence of this, notice that inflation is zero in this regime: $P_t = e^{-a}M$ for all t. So running a deficit at time zero causes no inflation at time zero. This is precisely because agents in the economy understand the nature of monetary policy. They know that the deficit at time zero will not be monetized at time zero, or at any time in the future.

   Regime 2. In the previous example there is no connection between the current primary deficit and the inflation rate. Now imagine a policy regime in which the government never issues debt:

$$b_t = 0 \text{ for all } t. \tag{2.6}$$

Of course, in this setting the flow budget constraint, (1.3), implies

$$M_t - M_{t-1} = -P_t x_t. \tag{2.7}$$

Not surprisingly, this policy regime is much more likely to be one where there is a connection between the current deficit and current inflation. For example, in the extreme case where the interest rate elasticity is zero ($\eta = 0$), (2.3) and (2.7) imply that $P_t = e^{-a} M_{t-1}/(1 + e^{-a} x_t)$. This means that the smaller the primary surplus is, the higher today's price level is, given the value of M_{t-1}.

The important point here is that, under policy regime 2, the government prints money to meet its current financing need. This translates a short-run need for financing into inflation, something that does not occur under regime 1. Under regime 1, the government instead meets its financing needs through borrowing, and at some later date implements a fiscal reform that allows it to avoid using monetary financing.

Of course, in reality, there are all sorts of policy regimes that fit somewhere between these two polar cases. The important lesson from the simple analysis presented here is that the time-series correlation between deficits and inflation depends critically on the policy regime in question. In regime 1, deficits and inflation are uncorrelated: Inflation is always zero, no matter what the primary deficit is. In regime 2, primary deficits and the inflation rate are strongly and positively correlated.

Policy lessons. A lack of correlation between deficits and inflation might be naively interpreted as indicating that inflation is somehow driven by something other than the government's fiscal policy—and that it has a life of its own. It is important that policymakers not be misled into believing this. Even if it does not coordinate with the fiscal policymaker, the monetary authority can smooth the effects of fiscal policy on the price level by avoiding a monetary policy similar to the one shown in (2.7). However, the monetary authority cannot prevent inflation from occurring if the government is fiscally irresponsible.

To see this, notice that the central bank is always free to adopt a constant money growth rule, regardless of the government's choice for the path of x_t. Notice that if $\Delta \ln M_t = \mu$, it is easy to show that $P_t = e^{\mu \eta - a} M_t$ and, therefore, that $\Delta \ln P_t = \mu$. So the monetary authority can smooth inflation, avoiding the fluctuations in inflation that would be inherent in policy regime 2.

Despite its ability to *smooth* inflation, however, the central bank cannot *suppress* inflation if the fiscal authority is irresponsible. With constant

2

money growth, the flow of real seigniorage revenue is constant, allowing one to rewrite (1.9) as

$$\sigma + r \sum_{i=0}^{\infty}(1 + r)^{-(i+1)}x_{t+i} = rb_{t-1}.$$

The less fiscally responsible is the government, as measured by the annuity value of its future primary surpluses, $r\sum_{i=0}^{\infty}(1 + r)^{-(i+1)}x_{t+i}$, the larger σ must be. For the Cagan money demand function,

$$\sigma = \frac{M_t - M_{t-1}}{P_t} = e^{a-\mu\eta}(1 - e^{-\mu}). \qquad (2.8)$$

A simple graph of the relationship between σ and μ is found in figure 2.1. This graph indicates that as the government raises the money growth rate, it raises more seigniorage revenue (up to the point where $\partial\sigma/\partial\mu = 0$).[6] For other money demand specifications, σ will also increase in μ over some range.

Figure 2.1: Seigniorage as a Function of the Money Growth Rate

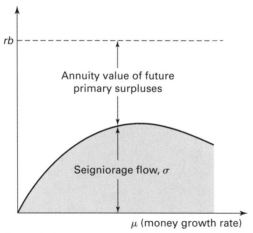

Source: Author.

Note: Under the assumptions listed in the text, the constant seigniorage flow is σ, given a constant money growth rate μ. Given a debt level, b, a particular annuity value of the future primary surpluses, we can calculate the required flow of seigniorage and, therefore, the required money growth rate, μ.

In conclusion, less fiscally responsible governments require more seigniorage revenue; therefore, they print money at a faster pace. Thus, when looking across countries one should expect to see higher inflation in countries with less fiscally responsible governments—as long as inflation and primary balances are measured over reasonably long horizons.

Coordination of Fiscal and Monetary Policy

The analysis of the previous section is now extended to the coordination of monetary and fiscal policy.[7] Earlier it was shown that for a given country, fiscal deficits and inflation need not be correlated with one another if the monetary authority chooses a constant money growth rule. Conditional on such a policy, the fiscal authority's choice for the path of the primary surplus was shown to determine the money growth rate and the inflation rate.

It is clear that one choice for the government and the central bank is to coordinate policy. They could agree on a desired inflation target, π, and the central bank could set the money growth rate consistent with π. The government, in turn, could ensure that its choice of the path for the primary surplus would be consistent with (1.9), given π.

Alternatively, it is interesting to consider the case of uncoordinated policy. In this case, as in Sargent and Wallace (1981), one could imagine a fiscal authority that chooses $\{x_t\}_{t=0}^{\infty}$ without regard to any coordinated policy goals. But the monetary authority attempts to do what most central banks do: fight inflation. Initially, the central bank fights inflation by setting a low value of the money growth rate. Eventually, however, in the world Sargent and Wallace imagined, the central bank must face the reality of the fiscal authority's dominance—and eventually accommodate the government's financing needs, by printing more money. Here, the consequences of such a policy are of interest.

To determine the implications of uncoordinated policy, it is helpful to adopt the quantity theory specification of money demand, so that $M_t/P_t = y_t/v$.[8] Assume that the transactions motive for money demand is constant, that is, $y_t = y$, so that real balances are also constant: $M_t/P_t = m = y/v$. In this setting, if money growth is constant at some rate μ, it is clear that the inflation rate will be $\pi = \mu$, and that the real value of seigniorage will be constant: $\sigma_t = \sigma$, where[9]

$$\sigma = \frac{M_t - M_{t-1}}{P_t} = \frac{(1+\mu)M_{t-1} - M_{t-1}}{(1+\mu)P_{t-1}} = \frac{\mu}{1+\mu} m. \qquad (2.9)$$

In order to model the central bank's initial desire to be tough on inflation, assume that from period zero to some period T, the bank sets the money growth rate to some arbitrary "low" value, μ. However, at date T, the central bank accepts the inevitable, that it will have to print more money to ensure the government's solvency. Therefore, from date T forward, the central bank sets the money growth rate to a constant, μ', consistent with satisfying the government's lifetime budget constraint.

With these assumptions one can easily solve for, and characterize, the path of inflation for $t \geq 0$. Assume, for simplicity, that the fiscal authority sets $x_t = x$ for all t, and that $x < rb_{-1}$. The second assumption implies that some seigniorage revenue will be required in order for the lifetime budget constraint to be satisfied.

Notice that the government's lifetime budget constraint as of period $T + 1$ is

$$b_T = \sum_{t=T+1}^{\infty} (1 + r)^{-(t-T)}(x_t + \sigma_t). \qquad (2.10)$$

Since $\sigma_t = \mu'm/(1 + \mu')$ for $t > T$, and $x_t = x$ for all t, (2.10) can be rewritten as

$$b_T = \frac{x + \mu'm/(1 + \mu')}{r}. \qquad (2.11)$$

Notice that if solving for μ' one obtains

$$\mu' = \frac{rb_T - x}{m - (rb_T - x)}. \qquad (2.12)$$

Clearly the higher the level of debt at date T, the higher μ' must be, since

$$\frac{d\mu'}{db_T} = \frac{rm}{[m - (rb_T - x)]^2} > 0.$$

The budget constraint rolled forward from period zero to period T is

$$b_{-1} = (1 + r)^{-(T+1)}b_T + \sum_{t=0}^{T}(1 + r)^{-(t+1)}(x_t + \sigma_t),$$

which can be rewritten as

$$b_T = (1+r)^{T+1}b_{-1} - \frac{(1+r)^{T+1}-1}{r}\left(x + m\frac{\mu}{1+\mu}\right).$$

Notice that

$$\frac{\partial b_T}{\partial T} = \ln(1+r)(1+r)^{T+1}\left[b_{-1} - \frac{1}{r}\left(x + m\frac{\mu}{1+\mu}\right)\right], \quad (2.13)$$

which is positive if the central bank sets μ low enough.[10] Also,

$$\frac{\partial b_T}{\partial \mu} = -\frac{(1+r)^{T+1}-1}{r}m(1+\mu)^{-2} < 0. \quad (2.14)$$

So the lower is μ, the more debt the government accumulates.

Together these results imply that the tougher the monetary authority is initially (the lower it sets μ), and the longer it is tough (the higher is T), the greater the stock of debt (b_T) will be when it finally recognizes the necessity of satisfying the government's need for financing. But the greater the stock of debt, b_T, the higher the inflation rate will eventually be.

The basic policy message that emerges from this discussion is that the tougher the monetary authority tries to be on inflation in the near term, the higher inflation will be in the long term. Having stably low inflation requires the coordination of fiscal and monetary policies.

Controlling Inflation

The discussion so far has described inflation as a problem that stems from loose fiscal policy. In particular, when the government sets its primary balance too low, so that

$$\sum_{t=0}^{\infty}(1+r)^{-(t+1)}x_t \ll b_{-1},$$

the central bank is forced, at some point, to print money. The logical consequence of printing money is inflation. This suggests that, in order for the government to reduce inflation, it must impose some degree of fiscal discipline. In a world with uncertainty, the government must not only impose fiscal discipline but it must also convince other agents that it will remain disciplined in the future.[11]

Policymakers frequently argue that inflation stems from other root causes, and that it is difficult for them to eliminate inflation once it becomes part of people's everyday lives. One often hears of the role played by private expectations. Although it is possible to construct examples in which outcomes can depend on self-fulfilling changes in agents' expectations, the role played by expectations is often overemphasized. As Sargent (1983) argues, the fundamentals, namely, fiscal policy, are often the important determinant of private expectations. In particular, if the government announces a credible policy regime change that involves a shift to a permanently better primary balance, inflation can be brought down, and quickly.

Sargent's argument is based on the shared experiences of Austria, Hungary, Poland, and Germany after World War I. All four countries ran large deficits after the war and experienced hyperinflations. All four countries used fiscal rather than strong monetary measures to end their hyperinflations. They renegotiated war debts and reparations payments, which represented a substantial part of their fiscal burdens, and they announced other fiscal measures to contain their budget deficits. However, even after the hyperinflations were over, the four governments continued to print money at a healthy pace for several months. By following this policy mix, all four governments quickly stabilized their price levels and exchange rates.

The lesson from these case studies is straightforward. In the face of credible fiscal reforms, private expectations of future money growth will adjust, and the price level and inflation will stabilize. While the example of the central European economies in the interwar period may not be perfectly analogous to today's developing and emerging market economies, the story is still valuable. If private expectations of inflation are entrenched in these markets, why are they entrenched? The theory presented here suggests that this must stem from fiscal difficulties—and that without fundamental steps being taken to correct fiscal imbalances, no monetary policy that attempts to control inflation can be successful indefinitely.

One issue not yet discussed is the political feasibility of fiscal reform. It is arguable that during periods of hyperinflation, disinflation is politically more feasible. The more dire the economic circumstances of a country, the more politically acceptable radical economic solutions may become. In less extreme inflationary environments, of course, political considerations may become more important, and the transition to a low inflation environment more difficult.

3 The Fiscal Theory of the Price Level

A branch of macroeconomic theory that has recently become more popular, the fiscal theory of the price level, differs in its interpretation of the government's lifetime budget constraint. In fact, this theory would not even admit that the equation (1.9) represents a constraint on the government.

Interpreting the Lifetime Budget Constraint

Return now to (1.9), and consider how it was obtained. Analysis began at the flow budget constraint, (1.3), which represents a simple accounting identity that holds under certain assumptions about the real interest rate and the structure of debt. From (1.3) an intertemporal equation, (1.7), was derived. If one imposed the condition (1.8), repeated here as

$$\lim_{j \to \infty} (1 + r)^{-(j+1)} b_{t+j} = 0, \tag{3.1}$$

then the lifetime budget constraint, (1.9), emerged.

Equation (3.1) is often referred to as a no-Ponzi scheme condition on the government. So imposing the lifetime budget constraint on the government's behavior is often thought of as being equivalent to not allowing the government to run a Ponzi scheme. However, as McCallum (1984) points out, if one considers theoretical settings in which optimizing households are the potential holders of government debt, any violation of the government lifetime budget constraint, (1.9), implies either that the households are not optimizing, or that they are violating a no-Ponzi scheme condition imposed on them. As Cochrane (2005) points out, the transversality (or no-Ponzi scheme) condition that we are familiar with from dynamic consumer problems is applied to households so that dynamic trading opportunities do not broaden the household budget set relative to having a single contingent claims market at time zero. So, it would appear that an additional constraint on the government is not needed to justify (1.9). And it would appear that this condition is the consequence of imposing rationality and a no-Ponzi scheme condition on households.

To see this worked through, let $x_t + \sigma_t = -k$, so that debt increases in each period by an amount

$$b_t - b_{t-1} = r b_{t-1} + k. \tag{3.2}$$

If $k > -rb_0$, then debt grows over time with

$$\lim_{t \to \infty} (1 + r)^{-t} b_t = b_0 + \frac{k}{r} > 0. \qquad (3.3)$$

In simple dynamic macroeconomic models this would immediately imply a violation of the type of transversality (or no-Ponzi scheme) condition that is usually imposed on households.

It is important to understand, however, that allowing the government's debt to grow fast enough so that (1.8) is violated also implies a violation of optimizing behavior on the part of households. Notice that the household's flow budget constraint will usually look like:

$$\text{income} - \text{purchases} = (1 + r)^{-1} b_t - b_{t-1}. \qquad (3.4)$$

Notice that, here, this means

$$\text{income} - \text{purchases} = k.$$

Clearly, this means the household is doing something suboptimal, since it is *voluntarily* giving up a constant stream of income that could be used to permanently increase its consumption. In essence, this is the nature of the argument in McCallum: that we need not think of the lifetime budget constraint as an additional constraint on the government.

Cochrane (2005) presents a much more general argument than McCallum's. And though his argument is more complex, Cochrane makes clear why one can think of the government budget constraint as an equation for valuing government debt rather than as a budget constraint. A similar but simple argument put forward by Christiano and Fitzgerald (2000) is now considered.

Fiscal Theory in a Nutshell

Christiano and Fitzgerald (2000) use a simple one-period model to describe the fiscal theory of the price level. Households enter the period with real claims on the government, b. Households demand end-of-period claims on the government, b'.

Clearly, households will not pick $b' > 0$, because the world ends at the end of period one. The argument is simple: Any household that demands $b' > 0$ is wasting resources (no matter the exact specification of its budget constraint). In essence, this is the same point made by McCallum (1984) in the context of a dynamic model.

If households were completely unconstrained in their choice of b', they would choose $b' = -\infty$. So $b' \geq 0$ is usually imposed. That is, households are not allowed to end life with unpaid debt. This constraint, in a one-period model, is the natural analog to the no-Ponzi scheme condition in a dynamic infinite horizon model. Since optimizing households will not choose $b' > 0$, and they are constrained to have $b' \geq 0$, it is clear that households will choose $b' = 0$ no matter what government policy is in the period.

In a one-period model, the government's budget constraint is simply

$$b' = b - x - \sigma, \tag{3.5}$$

because b now represents total claims on the government; that is, it represents principal *plus* interest. This is just a notational difference and is of no consequence for the arguments being made.

The fact that households will choose $b' = 0$ for any combination of government policies implies that the government budget constraint reduces to

$$b = x + \sigma. \tag{3.6}$$

Real debt. Suppose that one is in a world similar to the one described earlier, where government debt is a claim to real quantities of goods; that is, the value of b is fixed in real terms. This means that if the government chooses a "loose" fiscal policy (loose in the sense that $x \ll b$), it is clear that the monetary authority must provide the necessary "loose" monetary policy ($\sigma \gg 0$) to finance the government's debt payment.

Here the arguments made earlier in this chapter are presented in an incredibly simple form. If the government sets fiscal policy without regard to the price level or rate of inflation, the central bank must accommodate by printing money. When illustrated before, in a dynamic setting, there was an issue of timing. The central bank faced a choice between inflation now or later; but the central bank could not avoid printing money eventually in the face of loose fiscal policy.

Nominal debt. Now imagine, instead, that (as is the case for most of the debt issued by the United States government), the government's debt represents a claim to a certain number of units of local currency. Now the government budget constraint is

$$B' = B - P(x + \sigma). \tag{3.7}$$

Since, again, households will not want to hold government debt at the end of the period, assume that $B' = 0$. This implies that $B = P(x + \sigma)$, or

$$B/P = x + \sigma. \tag{3.8}$$

Notice, now, that the government and the central bank are free to choose any $x + \sigma$ combination subject to $x + \sigma > 0$. Given a policy commitment to x and σ, a beginning-of-period market for government debt will *induce* a price level P that satisfies the "government budget constraint." In this sense, the government is not constrained in its actions, and (3.8) does not represent a government budget constraint. Instead, (3.8) provides a way of valuing the nominal government debt issued in the previous period.

Relevance of the Fiscal Theory

The curious reader may wonder if the fiscal theory of the price level has any relevance to real-world policymaking. The astute reader may also wonder how there can be two equations determining the price level: the lifetime budget constraint and the solution for the price level derived from a money demand specification. The answers to these two questions are related. The basic relevance of the fiscal theory is established by the fact that many governments issue nominal debt. But the fact that the fiscal theory does not overdetermine the price level depends crucially on the assumption that some monetary policy rules do not specify an exogenous path for the money supply. In particular, according to some monetary policy rules, the money supply is endogenous.

Consider, for example, the case where money demand conforms to the Cagan specification shown earlier, so that $M_t = Ay_t \exp(-\eta R_t)P_t$, where y_t is real output, R_t is the nominal interest rate, and P_t is the price level. Suppose that output is constant, $y_t = y$, and that the central bank pegs the nominal interest rate at some value R. Clearly, this policy requires that whatever the price level P_t, the central bank must ensure that the monetary base is equal to $M_t = Aye^{-\eta R}P_t$. But notice that since this rule specifies the money supply in terms of the price level, this policy rule does not allow one to solve for the price level using (2.3).

This is where the government's lifetime budget constraint comes into play. Notice that real balances are constant and equal to $m = Aye^{-\eta R}$. If the real interest rate is some constant, r, the central bank's peg of the nominal interest rate also implies that the inflation rate must be constant and equal to $\pi = (R - r)/(1 + r)$. This implies that the real value of seigniorage is

$$\sigma = \frac{M_t - M_{t-1}}{P_t} = \frac{M_t}{P_t} - \frac{1}{1 + \pi}\frac{M_{t-1}}{P_{t-1}} = \frac{\pi}{1 + \pi}m. \qquad (3.9)$$

If one returns to the dynamic model where (1.9) must hold, notice that now

$$b_{t-1} = \sum_{i=0}^{\infty} (1 + r)^{-(i+1)} x_{t+i} + \frac{1}{r} \frac{\pi}{1 + \pi} m.$$

If the government's debt at the beginning of time t is denominated in units of local currency, and equals B_{t-1}, this means that

$$\frac{B_{t-1}}{P_t} = \sum_{i=0}^{\infty} (1 + r)^{-(i+1)} x_{t+i} + \frac{1}{r} \frac{\pi}{1 + \pi} m, \qquad (3.10)$$

as long as there is no uncertainty beyond date t.

Notice that since π and m are determined by the central bank's peg of the nominal interest rate, the price level is determined by the present value of the stream of future primary surpluses—plus seigniorage, relative to the quantity of government debt in circulation. The money supply can then be obtained by multiplying P_t by m.

The Fiscal Theory and Policy Messages

Does the fiscal theory lead to different policy messages? The short answer to this question is "no." The fiscal theory still sends the message that a government's deficits are inflationary if the government does not explicitly default on its debt obligations. The only distinction between the fiscal theory and the literature discussed earlier in this chapter is that inflation can happen in one of two ways.

First, consistent with the discussion where debt was real, inflation could result from the central bank using a money supply rule that preserves the real value of the government's debt at the time it was issued. Second, inflation could result from the government issuing nominal debt without attempting to preserve the real value of that debt. In the face of a fiscal shock that reduces the present value of the government's future primary surpluses, the price level might jump to ensure that (1.9) holds.

4   Uncertainty

In the theory outlined in section 1 of this chapter, the analysis abstracted from the possibility that the government might default on its debt. This was explicit in the statement of the government's flow budget constraint.

Subject to the assumption that default does not occur, and that the condition (1.8) is satisfied, the government's lifetime budget constraint as stated in (1.9) will hold. This must be true, not only in expectation at time t, but also along every possible realization of the paths for $\{x_s\}_{s=t}^{\infty}$ and $\{\sigma_s\}_{s=t}^{\infty}$.

However, the discussion of fiscal and monetary policy in section 2 worked within a simple framework in which the future paths for $\{x_s\}_{s=t}^{\infty}$ and $\{\sigma_s\}_{s=t}^{\infty}$ were deterministic. This allows the statement of some simple propositions about the relationship between inflation and fiscal policy, and yields some lessons about policy coordination.

Of course, deterministic processes for the government's primary balance and the money supply do not allow one to address the issue of uncertainty. In a setting where all debt is real, and default is ruled out, exogenous shocks to x_t or M_t have implications for the conduct of future fiscal and monetary policy. In a setting with nominal debt, exogenous shocks to x_t or M_t can have one of two consequences. And which consequence arises depends on whether policy is Ricardian or non-Ricardian, distinctions referred to by Woodford (1995). A Ricardian policy refers to a situation where, in the event of a shock, the government adjusts future fiscal and monetary policy to satisfy the lifetime budget constraint without any jump in the price level, making the analysis of the budget constraint identical to the case where debt is real. If the government follows a non-Ricardian policy, the price level is allowed to jump in response to the shock so that the lifetime budget constraint holds; but how much it jumps depends on the precise policies followed by the government.

No matter which case is considered, once there are stochastic shocks to a government's budget flows, an enormous number of issues can emerge. Some interesting positive questions arise: If the government followed policy x in response to shock y, what would the consequences be for goods prices, interest rates, and the real economy? How does the volatility of government revenue and expenditure affect the government's ability to borrow? Interesting normative questions also arise: What is the best policy response to shock y, according to some welfare criterion? How might default arise, and what might the consequences be?[12] The scope of these issues, however, is enormous, requires additional theorizing, and is, for the most part, beyond the scope of this volume. In chapters 8 and 9, default continues to be ruled out, but models of currency crises in which the consequences of a one-time-only fiscal shock for inflation and depreciation are considered. In the end, however, the analysis here will only scratch the surface of the issues that arise with regard to uncertainty.[13]

5   Conclusion

In chapter 2 the government's lifetime budget constraint was derived under some simple assumptions about government debt: time is discrete; debt is issued for one period, is real, and bears a constant real interest rate. It was shown that under these assumptions, fiscal sustainability revolves around whether the fiscal and monetary authorities set the paths of the primary surplus, x_t, and the supply of base money, M_t, consistent with (1.9). It was argued that there are many combinations of fiscal and monetary policy consistent with (1.9). However, it was also argued that the inevitable consequence of loose fiscal policy, $\sum_{t=0}^{\infty}(1+r)^{-(t+1)}x_t \ll b_{-1}$, is inflation. The monetary authority cannot fight inflation indefinitely without the cooperation of the fiscal authority. Thus, the goal of low inflation, combined with fiscal sustainability, can be achieved only if monetary and fiscal policies are coordinated. This message does not change when alternative interpretations of the government's lifetime budget constraint are considered, such as those provided by the fiscal theory of the price level.

Notes

1. The government might also issue new debt in order to finance the repurchase of old debt. In this case, one would still be concerned with the net proceeds raised.
2. The assumptions that debt is real and has a maturity of one year are immaterial if one works, as in most of this text, within a framework of perfect foresight. Here these assumptions are used to simplify notation.
3. The correspondence between (1.2) and (1.3) can be verified if one assumes that interest payments, I_t, include the indexation adjustment for both the interest and the principal on the loan:

$$I_t = [(P_t/P_{t-1})(1+r) - 1]B_{t-1}.$$

   Given the one-period maturity assumption, one can abstract from changes in the market valuation of longer-term debt.
4. In deriving (1.9), the condition (1.8) was imposed without stating its origin. Absent a theoretical model, of course, there is no reason for

imposing this condition, as it is not obvious (without a theory) why the stock of debt should evolve in a way that satisfies (1.8). Section 3 of this chapter discusses the appropriate interpretation of (1.8).

5. See Sims (1994), Woodford (1995), and Cochrane (2001, 2005), which discuss the fiscal theory in a closed economy context. Dupor (2000), Daniel (2001), and Corsetti and Mackowiak (forthcoming) analyze the implications of the fiscal theory for open economies.

6. For the Cagan money demand function, this point corresponds to $\mu = \ln(1 + 1/\eta)$. For higher values of μ, the fact that the demand for real money balances is decreasing in the nominal interest rate overwhelms the fact that the money supply is increasing, and the net change in real seigniorage is negative.

7. Here, the strategic interaction of the fiscal and monetary policy authorities is not considered. See Tabellini (1986) for one example of a model in which strategic considerations are important. Persson and Tabellini (2000) provide an excellent review of the literature.

8. The results in this section, regarding the qualitative properties of the path of inflation, hold true for more general money demand specifications.

9. The reader should note that the expressions in (2.8) and (2.9) are slightly different because in the latter case, real balances (m) are assumed to be invariant to the interest rate and in the former case, the money growth rate is expressed in logarithmic form.

10. Note that, since $x < rb_{-1}$, for small values of μ, the term in square brackets will be negative, indicating that there is insufficient seigniorage revenue to prevent the government from accumulating debt over time.

11. As shown with the Cagan money demand examples, the current price level depends on current and expected future money supplies. Hence, even if the government eliminates its use of monetary financing today, it must convince other agents that it will avoid monetary financing in the future.

12. See Uribe (2002) for an extension of the fiscal theory of the price level that allows for default.

13. The literature on uncertainty and fiscal sustainability is still in its infancy. See Burnside (2004) for a discussion of recent theoretical and practical developments.

References

Burnside, Craig. 2004. "Assessing New Approaches to Fiscal Sustainability Analysis." Duke University. http://www.duke.edu/acb8/res/fs_assmnt2.pdf.

Cagan, Phillip. 1956. "Monetary Dynamics of Hyperinflation." In Milton Friedman, ed. *Studies in the Quantity Theory of Money*. Chicago: University of Chicago Press.

Christiano, Lawrence J., and Terry J. Fitzgerald. 2000. "Understanding the Fiscal Theory of the Price Level." *Federal Reserve Bank of Cleveland Economic Review* 36 (2): 1–37.

Cochrane, John H. 2001. "Long-Term Debt and Optimal Policy in the Fiscal Theory of the Price Level." *Econometrica* 69 (1): 69–116.

———. 2005. "Money as Stock." *Journal of Monetary Economics* 52 (3): 501–28.

Corsetti, Giancarlo, and Bartosz Mackowiak. Forthcoming. "Fiscal Imbalances and the Dynamics of Currency Crises." *European Economic Review*.

Daniel, Betty. 2001. "A Fiscal Theory of Currency Crises." *International Economic Review* 42 (4): 969–88.

Dupor, William. 2000. "Exchange Rates and the Fiscal Theory of the Price Level." *Journal of Monetary Economics* 45 (3): 613–30.

Hamilton, James D., and Marjorie A. Flavin. 1986. "On the Limitations of Government Borrowing: A Framework for Empirical Testing." *American Economic Review* 76 (4): 808–19.

McCallum, Bennett T. 1984. "Are Bond-Financed Deficits Inflationary? A Ricardian Analysis." *Journal of Political Economy* 92 (1): 123–35.

Persson, Torsten, and Guido Tabellini. 2000. *Political Economics: Explaining Economic Policy*. Cambridge, MA: MIT Press.

Sargent, Thomas. 1983. "The Ends of Four Big Inflations." In Robert E. Hall, ed. *Inflation: Causes and Effects*. Chicago: University of Chicago Press for the National Bureau of Economic Research.

———. 1985. "Reaganomics and Credibility." In Albert Ando, Hidekazu Eguchi, Roger Farmer, and Yoshio Suzuki, eds. *Monetary Policy in Our Times*. Cambridge, MA: MIT Press.

Sargent, Thomas, and Neil Wallace. 1981. "Some Unpleasant Monetarist Arithmetic." *Federal Reserve Bank of Minneapolis Quarterly Review* 5 (3): 1–17.

Sims, Christopher. 1994. "A Simple Model for the Determination of the Price Level and the Interaction of Monetary and Fiscal Policy." *Economic Theory* 4 (3): 381–99.

Tabellini, Guido. 1986. "Money, Debt, and Deficits in a Dynamic Game." *Journal of Economic Dynamics and Control* 10 (4): 427–42.

Uribe, Martin. 2002. "A Fiscal Theory of Sovereign Risk." NBER Working Paper 9221, National Bureau of Economic Research, Cambridge, MA.

Woodford, Michael. 1995. "Price Level Determinacy without Control of a Monetary Aggregate." *Carnegie-Rochester Conference Series on Public Policy* 43 (December): 1–46.

2

Chapter 3

35-79

3

Some Tools for Fiscal Sustainability Analysis

Craig Burnside

H 61 H63

(Turkey Bulgaria) E62 O23

P35

In chapter 2 the concept of the government budget constraint was introduced. Two versions of the constraint were then derived: the flow version and the lifetime version. In this chapter both of these versions are used as tools for fiscal sustainability analysis.

Section 1 of this chapter considers a simple tool based on the lifetime budget constraint: a long-run version of this constraint that *assumes* constant values of (1) the flow variables in the constraint relative to some measure of real output, say, GDP; and (2) the real interest rate and the growth rate of real output. This tool determines the stock of initial debt (relative to output) that a government can sustain given particular values of the flow variables. It turns out that—given the assumptions on which this tool is based—the debt-to-GDP ratio will remain constant at its initial level, if that initial level is consistent with the lifetime budget constraint being satisfied. In this sense, the first tool for analyzing fiscal sustainability can be interpreted as follows: Given the initial level of debt, this tool determines the size of the primary balance the government would need to run in order to keep its debt stock constant as a fraction of GDP.

Section 2 considers a simple variant of the first tool. This variant is designed to capture the fact that some governments set stronger fiscal targets for themselves than mere solvency. In some cases, a government might have a legal obligation to attempt to achieve a particular debt target in

3

steady state. Another example, of particular relevance in recent years, is the set of fiscal rules imposed by the European Union (EU) on countries seeking EU accession. These rules require that a particular debt-to-GDP ratio must be achieved for a country to be accepted into the union. The second tool considered here for the analysis of fiscal sustainability modifies the first tool by calculating the size of the primary balance needed to achieve a particular debt-to-GDP target by a specified date.

Section 3 explains how the lifetime budget constraint can be used to form the basis of formal statistical tests of fiscal sustainability.

Section 4 introduces the concept of debt dynamics. Simply stated, the term debt dynamics is used for analysis that attempts to relate changes in measured debt-to-GDP ratios to the flows that appear in the government budget constraint. As shown in section 4, understanding changes in the debt-to-GDP ratio requires the introduction of a number of new features to the budget constraint—in order to deal with such issues as the currency denomination of debt, the effects of recessions, and the effects of inflation on the real value of nominal debt.

Section 5 shows how some of the complications described in the section on debt dynamics could be used to modify the simple tools described in the first two sections. Forward-looking fiscal sustainability analysis that considers currency risk, time-varying interest rates, and the effects of recessions is a particular focus.

Finally, section 6 explores more thoroughly a variety of issues related to the measurement of debt and interest payments that arise early in this chapter and in chapter 2.

1   The Long-Run Fiscal Sustainability Condition

The analysis in chapter 2 assumed that time is discrete, that all debt has a maturity of one period, that debt is real—in the sense that its face value is indexed to the price level and pays a constant real rate of interest, r. In this case, the government's flow budget constraint can be written as

$$b_t = (1 + r)b_{t-1} - x_t - \sigma_t, \tag{1.1}$$

where b_t is the end-of-period t stock of real debt, x_t is the real primary surplus, and σ_t is the real value of seigniorage revenue.

It was shown that forward iteration on this equation combined with the condition

$$\lim_{j \to \infty} (1 + r)^{-(j+1)} b_{t+j} = 0 \tag{1.2}$$

implies

$$b_{t-1} = \sum_{i=0}^{\infty} (1 + r)^{-(i+1)} (x_{t+i} + \sigma_{t+i}). \tag{1.3}$$

This equation, designated as the government's lifetime budget constraint, states that the government finances its debt at the end of period $t - 1$ by (from date t forward) raising seigniorage revenue and running primary surpluses with an equal present value.

The most basic tool for fiscal sustainability analysis uses a steady-state version of the lifetime budget constraint, (1.3). To begin, consistent with the presentation in most World Bank and International Monetary Fund (IMF) documents, it is useful to rewrite (1.3) in terms of stocks and flows expressed as fractions of GDP. Letting y_t represent real GDP, define $\bar{b}_t = b_t/y_t$, $\bar{x}_t = x_t/y_t$, and $\bar{\sigma}_t = \sigma_t/y_t$. Given this notation, (1.3) can be rewritten as

$$\bar{b}_{t-1} y_{t-1} = \sum_{i=0}^{\infty} (1 + r)^{-(i+1)} (\bar{x}_{t+i} + \bar{\sigma}_{t+i}) y_{t+i}$$

or

$$\bar{b}_{t-1} = \sum_{i=0}^{\infty} (1 + r)^{-(i+1)} (\bar{x}_{t+i} + \bar{\sigma}_{t+i}) \frac{y_{t+i}}{y_{t-1}}. \tag{1.4}$$

Imagine a steady state in which (1) real GDP grows at a constant rate g, so that $y_t/y_{t-1} = 1 + g$; (2) the primary surplus as a fraction of GDP is a constant $\bar{x}$; and (3) seigniorage as a fraction of GDP is a constant $\bar{\sigma}$. In this case, (1.4) reduces to

$$\bar{b}_{t-1} = \sum_{i=0}^{\infty} \left(\frac{1 + g}{1 + r}\right)^{i+1} (\bar{x} + \bar{\sigma}). \tag{1.5}$$

Assuming that $r > g$, (1.5) reduces to

$$\bar{b}_{t-1} = \bar{b} \equiv (\bar{x} + \bar{\sigma})/\bar{r}, \tag{1.6}$$

where $\bar{r} = (r - g)/(1 + g)$.[1]

Here are two ways in which one might consider using (1.6) to assess fiscal sustainability. First, one could imagine making assumptions about "reasonable" values of $\bar{x}$, $\bar{\sigma}$, r, and g. These assumptions might be based on historical trends in the country's fiscal accounts, as well as typical historical values of seigniorage revenue, the real interest rate, and the real growth rate. Together these assumptions could be mapped into an estimate of $\bar{b}$ using (1.6). If the government's actual stock of debt exceeded this estimate, then the government's finances could be argued to be unsustainable.

Alternatively, (1.6) could be rearranged as

$$\bar{x} = \bar{r}\bar{b}_{t-1} - \bar{\sigma}. \tag{1.7}$$

Given estimates of $\bar{r}$ and $\bar{\sigma}$ and data on the size of the government's actual debt stock, $\bar{b}_{t-1}$, (1.7) could be used to determine the necessary size of the primary balance to ensure fiscal sustainability. That is, rather than setting $\bar{x}$ equal to some historical average, one could determine the value that $\bar{x}$ would need to take in the future in order to maintain sustainable finances.

A final interpretation of (1.7) is obtained by noting that if $\bar{x}$ were set consistent with it, then the debt-to-GDP ratio would remain constant in the steady state described earlier. In other words, when $\bar{x}$, $\bar{\sigma}$, r, and g are constant, and $\bar{x}$ is given by (1.7), not only will the government's finances be sustainable, but it will also be true that $\bar{b}_t$ will be constant and equal to $\bar{b}$. This follows trivially from (1.1) and the definition of $\bar{b}_t$.

An Example

To put the tools discussed in this section into practice, consider Bulgaria, which, at the end of 2001, had a debt stock estimated to be about 72 percent of GDP. So one could think of period t as 2002, and set $\bar{b}_{t-1} = 0.72$. Equation (1.7) can be used to determine the primary balance Bulgaria would have needed to run from that date forward in order to achieve fiscal sustainability. To do this, benchmark values are needed for the parameters that determine the right-hand side of (1.7): the real interest rate, r, and the real growth rate, g, that determine $\bar{r}$, and the flow of seigniorage relative to GDP, $\bar{\sigma}$. The analysis will be conducted from the perspective of an economist working with data that were available in early 2002.

Interest rates. To determine a benchmark value of the real interest rate, first consider the nominal interest rate, R, and the inflation rate, π, and compute the real interest rate from the equation $r = (R - \pi)/(1 + \pi)$. In 2001, Bulgaria was fortunate in that the cost of servicing its debt was relatively modest: The public sector interest bill was well below 10 percent of the public sector debt stock between 1998 and 2001. In 2001, total interest payments were projected to be about 4.1 percent of GDP, which represented about 5 percent of the debt stock at the end of 2000. This might suggest that R should be set equal to 0.05, but given the structure of Bulgaria's debt at the end of 2001, one must be more careful.

Most of Bulgaria's public debt at the end of 2001 was external debt owed to official creditors or was in the form of Brady bonds, with only a small fraction of the debt denominated in *leva*, the local currency. Much of this external debt paid interest at rates that should be regarded as somewhat concessional. In the longer run, as Bulgaria made the transition toward integration with the EU, and being a more fully developed market economy, two important factors were likely to influence interest rates. First, less and less of Bulgaria's debt would be concessional, especially once the Brady bonds were retired. Since this older debt was likely to be rolled into newer debt at higher interest rates, this would tend to raise Bulgaria's interest costs. But Bulgaria's credit rating in private markets was likely to improve, so yields on its privately held debt were likely to come down.

This discussion implies that benchmarking an interest rate for Bulgaria that would apply to a long-run steady state could be quite difficult. In late 2001, secondary market yields on Bulgarian Bradys were at or near 12 percent. However, because of its substantial concessional debt, Bulgaria's average interest cost was much lower. Here, assume that $R = 0.085$, an assumption that lies above Bulgaria's effective interest cost in 2001, but well below its marginal borrowing cost in private markets.

Inflation. The inflation rate in Bulgaria was 7 percent in 1999, 11 percent in 2000, and about 4.5 percent in 2001. Bulgaria had (and has) a fixed exchange rate with respect to the euro, so some further convergence toward the European inflation rate might have been expected.[2] In early 2002, inflation projections for Bulgaria for the coming two years ran at about 3.5 percent. Although some further modest decline might have been expected beyond that horizon, a working assumption is that the inflation rate, π, would be 0.035 in perpetuity. Together with the assumption about the nominal interest rate, this implies a real interest rate, $r \approx 0.048$.

Growth. In the period 1998–2000, Bulgaria averaged real GDP growth of 3.9 percent, despite the poor external environment it faced during this period resulting from the Russian, Kosovo, and Turkish crises. Thus, it would have been reasonable, in 2002, to assume an average real GDP growth rate of at least 4 percent. So consider $g = 0.04$.[3] These assumptions about the real interest rate and growth imply that $\bar{r} \approx 0.008$.

Seigniorage. Seigniorage is the change in reserve money.[4] In Bulgaria, in 1998, 1999, and 2000, the change in reserve money represented about 1.0, 1.5, and 1.2 percent of GDP, respectively. In 2001, reserve money grew much faster (from 3.0 to 4.0 billion leva), meaning that seigniorage was well over 3 percent of GDP. An economist looking forward from 2001 would have considered it unlikely that seigniorage would be collected at the pace seen in 2001, especially in a long-run steady state. The argument is simple: Suppose base money remained constant as a fraction of GDP; that is, $M_t = \bar{m} P_t y_t$, where P_t is the price level and y_t is real GDP. If inflation and growth were constant and equal to π and g, respectively, then seigniorage revenue would be a constant fraction of GDP:[5]

$$\bar{\sigma} = \frac{\pi + g + \pi g}{(1 + \pi)(1 + g)} \bar{m}. \tag{1.8}$$

In early 2002, base money was about 14 percent of GDP. If one were to assume that $\bar{m} = 0.14$ and, as above, that $\pi = 0.035$ and $g = 0.04$, then seigniorage would be about 1 percent of GDP, that is, $\bar{\sigma} \approx 0.01$.

Summary assessment. Combining the assumptions that $R = 0.085$, $\pi = 0.035$, $g = 0.04$, and $\bar{m} = 0.14$, along with the fact that $\bar{b}_{t-1} = 0.72$, implies, from (1.7) and (1.8), that $\bar{x} \approx -0.0042$. This would mean that Bulgaria could achieve fiscal sustainability, along with a constant debt-to-GDP ratio of 72 percent, by running a primary balance of –0.42 percent of GDP.

A summary assessment such as this provides a useful benchmark, but is obviously very dependent on the assumptions of the analysis. In reality, one would want to be cautious and examine the sensitivity of $\bar{x}$ to the assumptions being made. What if growth were slower? What if the nominal interest rate on debt were greater? These questions would need to be addressed. Furthermore, as shown in section 2, simple analysis like this may well miss important policy goals of the government. In Bulgaria's case, the government wished to achieve a much more ambitious goal than simple constancy of the debt-to-GDP ratio: It set the European Union's 60 percent debt limit as its target to be achieved within four years. Achieving this goal would require a much tighter primary balance.

2 Achieving a Target Debt Level

Suppose that a country has a debt-to-GDP ratio at the end of period t equal to $\bar{b}_t$ and wishes to achieve some specified debt target, $\bar{b}^*$, within J periods. To determine the restriction this imposes on fiscal policy, begin by dividing both sides of (1.1) by real GDP to describe the evolution of the debt-to-GDP ratio:

$$\bar{b}_t = (1 + r)\bar{b}_{t-1} y_{t-1}/y_t - \bar{x}_t - \bar{\sigma}_t.$$

Under the assumption of constant real growth at the rate g, one has

$$\bar{b}_t = (1 + \bar{r})\bar{b}_{t-1} - \bar{x}_t - \bar{\sigma}_t, \tag{2.1}$$

where, as above, $\bar{r} = (r - g)/(1 + g)$.

If one iterates on (2.1) from time t to time $t + J$, one obtains the equation

$$\bar{b}_t = (1 + \bar{r})^{-1}\bar{b}_{t+1} + (1 + \bar{r})^{-1}(\bar{x}_{t+1} + \bar{\sigma}_{t+1})$$

$$= (1 + \bar{r})^{-2}\bar{b}_{t+2} + (1 + \bar{r})^{-1}(\bar{x}_{t+1} + \bar{\sigma}_{t+1}) + (1 + \bar{r})^{-2}(\bar{x}_{t+2} + \bar{\sigma}_{t+2})$$

$$= \cdots = (1 + \bar{r})^{-J}\bar{b}_{t+J} + \sum_{i=1}^{J}(1 + \bar{r})^{-i}(\bar{x}_{t+i} + \bar{\sigma}_{t+i}). \tag{2.2}$$

Assume that the government runs a constant primary balance, $\bar{x}$, and obtains constant seigniorage revenue, $\bar{\sigma}$, between period $t + 1$ and period $t + J$. If the government is to achieve the debt target $\bar{b}^*$ by period $t + J$, then it is clear from (2.2) that its primary balance must be at least as large as

$$\bar{x} = \bar{r}\frac{(1 + \bar{r})^J\bar{b}_t - \bar{b}^*}{(1 + \bar{r})^J - 1} - \bar{\sigma}. \tag{2.3}$$

If $\bar{r} = 0$, (2.3) must be replaced with the equation $\bar{x} = (\bar{b}_t - \bar{b}^*)/J - \bar{\sigma}$.

A Modified Example

Suppose one reconsiders the example of Bulgaria from section 1. There the value of $\bar{x}$ was solved for, consistent with fiscal sustainability in a steady state. This was equivalent to solving for the value of $\bar{x}$ consistent with maintaining a constant debt-to-GDP ratio at 72 percent of GDP.

In 2002, the Bulgarian government set a goal of achieving the EU's debt ceiling (60 percent of GDP) prior to 2007, the date at which it

3

hoped to achieve EU accession. In fact, the date it set as its target for achieving this target was 2005. Thus, one might think of using (2.3) to solve for $\bar{x}$, while maintaining some of the other assumptions of the first section.

If time t is treated as 2001, and time $t + J$ as 2005, then $\bar{b}_t = 0.72$ and $\bar{b}^* = 0.6$. Consistent with the example in section 1, one can set $\bar{\sigma} = 0.01$ and $\bar{r} \approx 0.008$. Solving for $\bar{x}$ using (2.3), one obtains $\bar{x} \approx 0.0255$. Thus, to achieve its goal, the government would need to run a primary surplus of about 2.55 percent of GDP.[6] This result stands in marked contrast to the one for the previous example, because here the government has a goal of reducing its debt stock by 12 percentage points of GDP in four years. In the previous example, the government wanted only to hold its debt stock constant as a percentage of GDP.

At this stage, it makes some sense to consider how sensitive the estimated value of $\bar{x}$ is to the assumptions underlying it. One might expect that the most important of these assumptions are the ones that matter for $\bar{r}$: the assumptions about the real interest rate, r, and the economy's real growth rate, g. In the baseline example, it was assumed that these were 4.8 and 4 percent, respectively. Table 3.1 provides some idea of how sensitive the results are to various assumptions about real interest rates and real growth. It computes $\bar{x}$ for a variety of combinations of r and g.

Table 3.1 shows that the estimated primary surplus is very sensitive to the assumptions about growth and interest rates. Roughly speaking, for each additional percentage point of growth, the government has room to run a smaller primary surplus by about 0.8 percent of GDP. For each additional percentage point on the interest rate, the required primary surplus rises by about 0.65 percent of GDP. This indicates that if a country in Bulgaria's position

Table 3.1: Size of the Primary Surplus Needed for Bulgaria to Achieve a 60 Percent Debt Target between 2001 and 2005
(percentage of GDP)

Real growth rate (percent)	Real interest rate (percent)					
	1	3	5	7	9	11
3	0.82	2.13	3.44	4.76	6.08	7.40
4	0.06	1.36	2.66	3.96	5.26	6.57
5	−0.68	0.60	1.88	3.17	4.46	5.75

Source: Author's calculations (as described in chapter 3).

were to suffer a sustained rise in interest rates or a sustained decline in its growth, it would need to run a substantially larger primary surplus to meet its debt target.

There are a number of other dimensions along which one could be critical of the model used here to assess sustainability to this point. First, despite Bulgaria's changing debt profile, it was assumed that the real interest rate is constant: Perhaps the interest rate should have been modeled as increasing over time. Second, the fact that Bulgaria does not have real debt was ignored: Bulgaria has debt denominated in leva, euros, and, for the most part, U.S. dollars. Yet the analysis here did not allow for currency risk or for the effects of unexpected inflation on debt. Third, issues related to the maturity and revaluation of debt were not examined. Some of these issues will be dealt with later in this chapter. However, formal statistical tests of fiscal sustainability are now considered.

3   Formal Statistical Tests

Nearly all formal statistical tests of fiscal sustainability stem from Hamilton and Flavin's (1986) analysis, which was applied to the United States government's debt.[7] To understand their approach, return to the government's flow budget constraint described in chapter 2. There this simple accounting identity was presented:

$$B_t - B_{t-1} = I_t - X_t - (M_t - M_{t-1}), \qquad (3.1)$$

where B_t is the end-of-period stock of debt measured in local currency, I_t is interest payments, X_t is the primary balance, and $M_t - M_{t-1}$ is seigniorage revenue. The analysis in chapter 2 did not carefully define what was meant by "the stock of debt." Later, when $b_t = B_t/P_t$ was defined and the real flow budget constraint was derived, assumptions about government debt were made (ones that Hamilton and Flavin avoid)—that time is discrete, and that bonds have a constant maturity of one year and bear a constant real interest rate.

If one were to put (3.1) in real terms by defining $i_t = I_t/P_t$, $x_t = X_t/P_t$ and $\sigma_t = (M_t - M_{t-1})/P_t$, then one would get

$$b_t - \frac{1}{1 + \pi_t} b_{t-1} = i_t - x_t - \sigma_t, \qquad (3.2)$$

where $\pi_t = P_t/P_{t-1} - 1$. Suppose, rather than assuming there is a constant real interest rate, that r is defined as the *average ex post* real interest rate on government debt over a one-year horizon. Then (3.2) could be rewritten as

$$b_t = (1 + r)b_{t-1} - x_t - \sigma_t + i_t - \left(\frac{r + \pi_t + r\pi_t}{1 + \pi_t}\right)b_{t-1}. \quad (3.3)$$

Notice that in (3.3), because the ex post real interest rate is not assumed to be constant, there is an error term, $i_t - (r + \pi_t + r\pi_t)b_{t-1}/(1 + \pi_t)$, that does not appear in (1.1). Hamilton and Flavin (1986) further point out that, if one is careful to define b_t as the real *market value* of government debt held by the public at the end of period t, then one may need an additional term on the right-hand side that measures the capital loss (if positive), or gain (if negative), from any changes in the market value of existing government debt.[8] One also needs a term to deal with any asymmetry of timing, within the year, between the issuance of debt and the flows that are debt creating or reducing. In conclusion, Hamilton and Flavin argue that, regardless of the structure of the debt and the behavior of interest rates,

$$b_t = (1 + r)b_{t-1} - x_t - \sigma_t + v_t, \quad (3.4)$$

where v_t is an error term. Given the discussion above, it is arguable that this error term should be mean zero.

Forward iteration on (3.4) implies that

$$b_t = (1 + r)^{-j}b_{t+j} + \sum_{i=1}^{j}(1 + r)^{-i}(x_{t+i} + \sigma_{t+i} - v_{t+i}). \quad (3.5)$$

Hamilton and Flavin point out that the hypothesis that the government is subject to a present-value borrowing constraint implies that

$$b_t = E_t \sum_{i=1}^{\infty}(1 + r)^{-i}(x_{t+i} + \sigma_{t+i} - v_{t+i}), \quad (3.6)$$

where E_t is the expectations operator conditional on information available at time t. This is equivalent to the hypothesis that

$$\lim_{j \to \infty}(1 + r)^{-j}E_t\,b_{t+j} = 0. \quad (3.7)$$

The condition in (3.6) is similar to the lifetime budget constraint derived in chapter 2, yet it is expressed in expectational form. Of course, (3.6) is also the pricing equation for government debt according to the fiscal theory of the price level, once one recognizes that in the fiscal theory $b_t = B_t/P_t$.

Hamilton and Flavin propose a test of the null hypothesis that (3.6) holds. One could interpret such a test as a test of fiscal sustainability. Formally, Hamilton and Flavin test the equivalent null hypothesis, that (3.7) holds against an alternative:

$$\lim_{j \to \infty} (1 + r)^{-j} E_t b_{t+j} = a(1 + r)^t,$$

with $a \neq 0$. So their test boils down to whether $a = 0$ or $a \neq 0$. Notice that if the alternative hypothesis is correct, one can write

$$b_t = E_t \sum_{i=1}^{\infty} (1 + r)^{-i} (x_{t+i} + \sigma_{t+i} - v_{t+i}) + a(1 + r)^t. \tag{3.8}$$

Defining $\eta_t = -E_t \sum_{i=1}^{\infty} (1 + r)^{-i} v_{t+i}$ and $z_t = x_t + \sigma_t$, (3.8) can be written as:

$$b_t = E_t \sum_{i=1}^{\infty} (1 + r)^{-j} z_{t+i} + a(1 + r)^t + \eta_t. \tag{3.9}$$

In related work, Flood and Garber (1980) propose a test for bubbles in prices. They consider the Cagan (1956) model of money demand, in which the fundamentals-based solution for the price level is the conditional expectation of a forward-looking discounted sum of future money supplies.[9] Their fundamentals-based solution for prices is analogous to the expression for debt in our equation (3.6). They also consider a nonfundamental solution for prices in which the fundamental solution is augmented with a bubble term like the $a(1 + r)^t$ term that appears on the right-hand side of (3.9). Thus, Hamilton and Flavin's tests for fiscal sustainability are similar to tests for bubbles in prices.

The first test that Hamilton and Flavin perform is based on Diba and Grossman (1984) and Hamilton and Whiteman's (1985) critique of Flood and Garber's tests. Hamilton and Whiteman propose a test for bubbles based on tests for nonstationarity. In our context, these tests can be summarized as follows. Suppose that $E_t \sum_{i=1}^{\infty} (1 + r)^{-j} z_{t+i}$ and η_t are stationary processes. Then b_t will be stationary if, and only if, $a \neq 0$. So Hamilton and Flavin propose a simple test of fiscal sustainability requiring the following steps:

1. Assume that η_t is stationary (this seems like a reasonable assumption given its definition) and test for a unit root in z_t, using a Dickey and

Fuller type (1979) test statistic. If the presence of a unit root in z_t can be rejected, then z_t is apparently stationary, and one can assume that $E_t \sum_{i=1}^{\infty} (1+r)^{-j} z_{t+i}$ is also stationary and proceed to the second step.

2. Test for a unit root in b_t. If the presence of a unit root cannot be rejected, then (3.6) is rejected in favor of (3.9), with $a \neq 0$. If the presence of a unit root can be rejected, then (3.6) apparently holds.

Of course, this simple test suffers from all the well-known drawbacks of unit root tests, in particular, that they are generally weak against alternatives close to a unit root. The second test proposed by Hamilton and Flavin is based on a regression. Here, they assume that time t expectations of v_{t+i} and z_{t+i} are rationally formed by projecting them on current and lagged values of z_t and lagged values of b_t. In this case, (3.9) can be rewritten as:

$$b_t = \beta_0 + \sum_{i=1}^{k_b} \gamma_i b_{t-i} + \sum_{i=0}^{k_z} \kappa_i z_{t-i} + a(1+r)^t + \varepsilon_t,$$

where ε_t is a white noise error term. The constants k_b and k_z and the parameters γ_i, $i = 1, \dots, k_b$ and κ_i, $i = 1, \dots, k_z$ are determined as functions of r and the coefficients in the rules for rationally forecasting v_t and z_t. A test for fiscal sustainability, in this case, is simply a test of whether or not $a = 0$.

Obviously, the formal statistical tests described here are much more complex than the simple methods proposed in sections 1 and 2. The question is whether they are more useful. The main advantage of statistical tests is that they do not involve the arbitrary assumptions made in previous sections: There is no need to assume the economy is in a long-run steady state, or that growth and the real interest rate are constant.

However, statistical methods have a number of drawbacks:

1. Since these methods are based on testing for unit roots or explosive trends in the data, they suffer from the inherent weakness of tests for these phenomena against alternative hypotheses, where the data are nearly (but not) explosive.
2. The tests are based on historical data and are therefore fundamentally backward-looking. They identify, in a sense, violations of fiscal sustainability in the past, but say little, in a forward-looking way, about the state of the government's finances. They also require substantial amounts of historical data, which are frequently lacking for developing and industrializing countries.

3. Ultimately, these tests are narrowly focused on the question of whether (3.6) holds. Suppose one looks at the historical data for a country and finds no evidence against (3.6). Does this mean that fiscal sustainability is not an issue? Surely the answer to this question is "no." In the end, the question of fiscal sustainability comes down to whether *future* surpluses will be sufficient to service the most recently observed debt level. As argued in chapter 2, fiscal sustainability analysis is also meant to deal with broader issues than whether or not the government will satisfy its lifetime budget constraint. So, in the end, one must step beyond the statistical tests presented in this section in order to provide useful policy analysis.

To conduct policy analysis in developing countries, the simple approaches in sections 1 and 2 are perhaps more useful than statistical tests. But perhaps they are too simple. Section 5 will explore extensions of these methods that abstract from a number of the simplifying assumptions made to this point.

4   Debt Dynamics

The term *debt dynamics* refers to the study of the evolution of the measured debt-to-GDP ratio. Often it is useful to describe how debt levels have evolved in the past, as this provides a useful perspective on the future. Debt dynamics can be helpful in describing why a country that has found itself with a debt problem got into that situation in the first place. It also helps identify what steps a country might have to take in order to resolve its debt problem. Debt dynamics are also useful in illustrating sources of risk to a government's finances.

Theoretical Background

The analysis in chapter 2 began from the simple budget identity, expressed in local currency units:

$$\text{net debt issued} = I_t - X_t - (M_t - M_{t-1}). \qquad (4.1)$$

Here I_t represents interest payments, X_t is the primary surplus, and $M_t - M_{t-1}$ represents seigniorage revenue.

A Baseline Case

Begin by making the following assumptions: (1) debt is issued for one period only and (2) all debt is issued in local currency units at nominal interest rates, which may vary from period to period. The second assumption is different than in the analysis in chapter 2, and in sections 1 and 2 of this chapter, where debt was assumed to be real (or indexed to the price level) and issued at constant real interest rates.

As section 6 shows, if B_t is defined as the market value of the government's stock of debt at the end of period t, then the market value and book value of the government's debt are the same, and net debt issued equals $B_t - B_{t-1}$. In this case, one can write

$$B_t - B_{t-1} = I_t - X_t - (M_t - M_{t-1}). \qquad (4.2)$$

Typically, one does not want to describe the evolution of the nominal stock of government debt. Instead, one wants to describe the evolution of its ratio to GDP. So, as in chapter 2, let P_t and y_t represent the GDP deflator and real GDP, and define $\bar{b}_t = B_t/(P_t y_t)$, $\bar{\imath}_t = I_t/(P_t y_t)$, $\bar{x}_t = X_t/(P_t y_t)$, and $\bar{\sigma}_t = (M_t - M_{t-1})/(P_t y_t)$. If both sides of (4.2) are divided by $P_t y_t$, one obtains

$$\bar{b}_t - \frac{P_{t-1} y_{t-1}}{P_t y_t} \bar{b}_{t-1} = \bar{\imath}_t - \bar{x}_t - \bar{\sigma}_t. \qquad (4.3)$$

As in chapter 2, the inflation rate is defined as $\pi_t = P_t/P_{t-1} - 1$, and the growth rate of real GDP, $g_t = y_t/y_{t-1} - 1$. Suppose, for the moment, that these are both zero. Then

$$\bar{b}_t - \bar{b}_{t-1} = \bar{\imath}_t - \bar{x}_t - \bar{\sigma}_t. \qquad (4.4)$$

In this case, the change in the debt-to-GDP ratio consists of three components: (1) interest payments, (2) the primary balance, and (3) seigniorage—all expressed as ratios to GDP.

Nonzero inflation. Suppose that $\pi_t \neq 0$, but $g_t = 0$. Then, with some manipulation, (4.3) can be rewritten as

$$\bar{b}_t - \bar{b}_{t-1} = \bar{\imath}_t - \bar{x}_t - \bar{\sigma}_t - \frac{\pi_t}{1 + \pi_t} \bar{b}_{t-1}. \qquad (4.5)$$

In this case, the change in the debt-to-GDP ratio includes a fourth term, which can be referred to as the *inflation effect*. What is the inflation effect? Recall that it was assumed that all debt is issued in local currency and is issued at a fixed interest rate. This means that interest payments at time t are given by $I_t = R_{t-1}B_{t-1}$. Notice that this also means $\bar{\imath}_t = R_{t-1}\bar{b}_{t-1}/(1 + \pi_t)$, given the assumption that $g_t = 0$. The sum of the interest payments term and the inflation effect term is $(R_{t-1} - \pi_t)\bar{b}_{t-1}/(1 + \pi_t)$. In a sense, this sum represents ex post *real* interest payments on the debt issued at time $t - 1$. The inflation effect captures the fact that inflation erodes the real cost to the government of servicing its local currency debt.

Nonzero growth. Now assume that $\pi_t = 0$, but $g_t \neq 0$. Then, with some manipulation, (4.3) can be rewritten as

$$\bar{b}_t - \bar{b}_{t-1} = \bar{\imath}_t - \bar{x}_t - \bar{\sigma}_t - \frac{g_t}{1 + g_t}\bar{b}_{t-1}. \tag{4.6}$$

In this case, the change in the debt-to-GDP ratio includes a term referred to here as the *growth effect*. The growth effect captures the fact that, in and of itself, if GDP gets bigger, then the ratio of any previously accumulated debt to GDP gets smaller.

The general case. Unfortunately, when $\pi_t \neq 0$ and $g_t \neq 0$, it is impossible to perfectly decompose the extra term into inflation and growth effects. This is because the two effects interact with one another. For notational convenience, one can define the growth rate of nominal GDP, $z_t = (1 + \pi_t)(1 + g_t) - 1$. Using this definition, one can manipulate (4.3) to obtain

$$\bar{b}_t - \bar{b}_{t-1} = \bar{\imath}_t - \bar{x}_t - \bar{\sigma}_t - \frac{z_t}{1 + z_t}\bar{b}_{t-1}. \tag{4.7}$$

One can then rewrite (4.7) as

$$\bar{b}_t - \bar{b}_{t-1} = \bar{\imath}_t - \bar{x}_t - \bar{\sigma}_t - \frac{\pi_t}{1 + \pi_t}\bar{b}_{t-1} - \frac{g_t}{1 + z_t}\bar{b}_{t-1}. \tag{4.8}$$

Now the change in the debt-to-GDP ratio is the sum of five components: (1) interest payments, (2) the primary balance, (3) seigniorage, (4) the inflation effect, and (5) the growth effect. Notice, however, that the growth effect has been redefined as $-g_t\bar{b}_{t-1}/(1 + z_t)$, which depends on the rate of inflation as well as the real growth rate.[10]

Indexed Debt

Suppose that some part of the government's debt is indexed to the price level. In particular, suppose that at time t the government issues indexed debt, B_t^I, and this implies that at time $t+1$ the government repays $(1 + r_t)(1 + \pi_{t+1})B_t^I$ to the holders of the debt. If the notation B_t^N is used to represent nonindexed debt, then

$$B_t^N + B_t^I = (1 + R_{t-1})B_{t-1}^N + (1 + r_{t-1})(1 + \pi_t)B_{t-1}^I - X_t - (M_t - M_{t-1}).$$
(4.9)

Hence, with some algebra one can write

$$\bar{b}_t - \bar{b}_{t-1} = \bar{\imath}_t - \bar{x}_t - \bar{\sigma}_t - \frac{z_t}{1 + z_t}\bar{b}_{t-1}$$

$$+ \left[\frac{R_{t-1}}{1 + z_t}\bar{b}_{t-1}^N + \frac{r_{t-1} + \pi_t(1 + r_{t-1})}{1 + z_t}\bar{b}_{t-1}^I - \bar{\imath}_t \right], \quad (4.10)$$

where $\bar{b}_t = \bar{b}_t^N + \bar{b}_t^I$. As in the previous examples, the inflation and growth effects, which add up to $-z_t\bar{b}_{t-1}/(1 + z_t)$, still apply to the entire stock of debt. However, the full breakdown of the change of debt into its components depends on the government's definition of interest payments, $\bar{\imath}_t$. This definition may or may not correspond to

$$\frac{R_{t-1}}{1 + z_t}\bar{b}_{t-1}^N + \frac{r_{t-1} + \pi_t(1 + r_{t-1})}{1 + z_t}\bar{b}_{t-1}^I.$$

If it does, then the analysis is unaffected by the indexation of debt. If it does not, then the last term on the right-hand side of (4.10) will be nonzero.

First accounting rule. If $I_t = R_{t-1}B_{t-1}^N + r_{t-1}B_{t-1}^I$, then $\bar{\imath}_t = (R_{t-1}\bar{b}_{t-1}^N + r_{t-1}\bar{b}_{t-1}^I)/(1 + z_t)$. Hence, one can write

$$\bar{b}_t - \bar{b}_{t-1} = \bar{\imath}_t - \bar{x}_t - \bar{\sigma}_t - \frac{z_t}{1 + z_t}\bar{b}_{t-1} + \frac{\pi_t(1 + r_{t-1})}{1 + z_t}\bar{b}_{t-1}^I. \quad (4.11)$$

Now, in addition to interest payments, the primary balance, seigniorage, the inflation effect, and the growth effect, a term $\pi_t(1 + r_{t-1})\bar{b}_{t-1}^I/(1 + z_t)$ is needed to capture the fact that investors in indexed bonds are compensated for inflation, in both the interest and the principal, and this is not captured in $\bar{\imath}_t$.

Second accounting rule. If $I_t = R_{t-1}B_{t-1}^N + (1 + \pi_t)r_{t-1}B_{t-1}^I$, then $\bar{\imath}_t = [R_{t-1}\bar{b}_{t-1}^N + (1 + \pi_t)r_{t-1}\bar{b}_{t-1}^I]/(1 + z_t)$. This implies that

$$\bar{b}_t - \bar{b}_{t-1} = \bar{\imath}_t - \bar{x}_t - \bar{\sigma}_t - \frac{z_t}{1 + z_t}\bar{b}_{t-1} + \frac{\pi_t}{1 + z_t}\bar{b}_{t-1}^I. \quad (4.12)$$

Now the extra term in the debt dynamics is $\pi_t\bar{b}_{t-1}^I/(1 + z_t)$. It captures the fact that the definition of $\bar{\imath}_t$ includes the interest payment component, but not the amortization component, of the inflation compensation paid to investors in indexed bonds.

Third accounting rule. If $I_t = R_{t-1}B_{t-1}^N + [\pi_t + (1 + \pi_t)r_{t-1}]B_{t-1}^I$, then $\bar{\imath}_t = \{R_{t-1}\bar{b}_{t-1}^N + [\pi_t + (1 + \pi_t)r_{t-1}]\bar{b}_{t-1}^I\}/(1 + z_t)$. This implies that

$$\bar{b}_t - \bar{b}_{t-1} = \bar{\imath}_t - \bar{x}_t - \bar{\sigma}_t - \frac{z_t}{1 + z_t}\bar{b}_{t-1}. \qquad (4.13)$$

Now there is no need for an extra term in the debt dynamics, because the definition of $\bar{\imath}_t$ already captures all inflation compensation paid to investors in indexed bonds.

In summary, indexed debt affects our analysis depending on how the government treats inflation compensation in its accounts. If all such compensation is included in interest payments, then debt dynamics calculations are unaffected. Otherwise, one needs to explicitly account for inflation compensation in the analysis.

Floating Rate Debt

Floating rate debt is debt issued at a flexible interest rate. Typically, floating rate debt is medium- or long-term debt on which the interest payments are somehow linked to shorter-term market interest rates. As was shown for indexed debt, how the accounting is affected depends largely on how the government measures interest payments. Since it is likely that the government's measure of interest payments fully reflects adjustments to the amount of interest actually paid to investors (due to floating rate contracts), there is no need to change the way the debt dynamics are used to account for floating rate debt.

Foreign Currency-Denominated Debt

If governments issue debt in domestic and foreign currency, this affects the calculations. Movements in the exchange rate between local and foreign currency will affect debt valuation much like inflation and growth do.

In this section, ignore indexed and floating rate debt and assume that all debt is issued in nominal currency units, either domestic or foreign, at fixed interest rates. Domestic currency debt will be denoted B_t^D, while foreign currency-denominated debt will be denoted B_t^F. The government's total stock of debt at the end of period t is $B_t = B_t^D + B_t^F S_t$, where S_t is the end-of-period t exchange rate measured in local currency units per foreign currency unit. The end-of-period exchange rate is used to define B_t, because this is the standard method used in debt accounting: Debt is typically measured at the end of a year, and the conversion of foreign to domestic currency is typically done at the same point in time.

The analysis presented here has assumed that all debt is issued for one period. It is convenient to assume that external debt is issued steadily throughout a year, so that the funds raised at time t by issuing external debt, B_t^F, are equivalent to $B_t^F S_{\bar{t}}$ in local currency units, where $S_{\bar{t}}$ is the average exchange rate at time t. The distinction between the average exchange rate and the end-of-period exchange rate is important, in that the funds raised by issuing the debt may be more or less than the value of the debt at the end of the period, depending on how the exchange rate changes within the period. Similarly, this analysis will assume that the stock of previously issued foreign currency debt, B_{t-1}^F, is amortized at a steady pace during period t. So, the local currency value of amortization payments is $B_{t-1}^F S_{\bar{t}}$.

Assume now that the definition of interest payments includes all interest paid on domestic debt, as well as all interest payments made on external debt, valued in local currency at the time the payments were made. For this reason, one can write

$$B_t^D - B_{t-1}^D + \left(B_t^F - B_{t-1}^F\right)S_{\bar{t}} = I_t - X_t - (M_t - M_{t-1}). \quad (4.14)$$

Dividing both sides by $P_t y_t$, and defining $\bar{b}_t^D = B_t^D/(P_t y_t)$ and $\bar{b}_t^F = B_t^F S_t/(P_t y_t)$, one obtains

$$\bar{b}_t^D - \frac{P_{t-1} y_{t-1}}{P_t y_t} \bar{b}_{t-1}^D + \left(\bar{b}_t^F - \frac{S_t}{S_{t-1}} \frac{P_{t-1} y_{t-1}}{P_t y_t} \bar{b}_{t-1}^F\right)\frac{S_{\bar{t}}}{S_t} = i_t - x_t - \sigma_t. \quad (4.15)$$

Thus, the change in the debt-to-GDP ratio is

$$\bar{b}_t - \bar{b}_{t-1} = i_t - x_t - \sigma_t - \frac{z_t}{1 + z_t} \bar{b}_{t-1}^D$$

$$+ \left(1 - \frac{S_{\bar{t}}}{S_t}\right)\bar{b}_t^F + \left(\frac{S_{\bar{t}}}{S_{t-1}} \frac{1}{1 + z_t} - 1\right)\bar{b}_{t-1}^F. \quad (4.16)$$

While (4.16) is useful, the last two terms on the right-hand side of the equation, at first, appear to have little intuitive content. However, some further algebra reveals that (4.16) can be rewritten as

$$\bar{b}_t - \bar{b}_{t-1} = i_t - x_t - \sigma_t - \frac{\pi_t}{1 + \pi_t} \bar{b}_{t-1} - \frac{g_t}{1 + z_t} \bar{b}_{t-1}$$

$$+ \frac{S_t - S_{\bar{t}}}{S_t} \bar{b}_t^F + \frac{S_{\bar{t}} - S_{t-1}}{S_{t-1}} \frac{1}{1 + z_t} \bar{b}_{t-1}^F \quad (4.17)$$

or as the following equation:

$$\bar{b}_t - \bar{b}_{t-1} = \bar{i}_t - \bar{x}_t - \bar{\sigma}_t - \frac{\pi_t}{1 + \pi_t} \bar{b}_{t-1}^D - \frac{g_t}{1 + z_t} \bar{b}_{t-1}$$

$$+ \frac{S_t - S_{\bar{t}}}{S_t} \bar{b}_t^F + \left(\frac{S_{\bar{t}} - S_{t-1}}{S_{t-1}} \frac{1}{1 + z_t} - \frac{\pi_t}{1 + \pi_t} \right) \bar{b}_{t-1}^F. \quad (4.18)$$

Notice that (4.17) and (4.18) agree as to the first, second, third, and fifth components of the change in debt: interest payments, the primary balance, seigniorage, and the growth effect. However, they differ as to their definitions of the fourth and sixth components of the change in the debt-to-GDP ratio. In (4.17) these components are the inflation effect, $-\pi_t \bar{b}_{t-1}/(1 + \pi_t)$, which applies to the entire stock of debt, and a nominal revaluation effect, which is nonzero if, and only if, there are changes in the nominal exchange rate during the period. If local currency depreciates during the period, then the revaluation effect is positive: the depreciation of the currency tends to add to the government's effective indebtedness.

By default, in what follows, the decomposition described by (4.18) is used, where the fourth component is the inflation effect, $-\pi_t \bar{b}_{t-1}^D/(1 + \pi_t)$, which applies only to the stock of domestic debt; and a *real* revaluation effect, which, roughly speaking, is nonzero if the changes in the nominal exchange rate differ from the inflation rate during the period.

Some intuition from the example in continuous time. Readers who are familiar with analysis in continuous time will be aware that (4.17) limits to

$$\partial \bar{b}_t / \partial t = \bar{i}_t - \bar{x}_t - \bar{\sigma}_t - \pi_t \bar{b}_t - g_t \bar{b}_t + \delta_t \bar{b}_t^F \quad (4.19)$$

if one shrinks the time interval between measurements of the stock of debt. Here the flows $\bar{i}_t$, $\bar{x}_t$, and $\bar{\sigma}_t$ represent instantaneous versions of interest payments, the primary balance, and seigniorage revenue, while $\pi_t = (\partial P_t / \partial t)/P_t$, $g_t = (\partial y_t / \partial t)/y_t$, and $\delta_t = (\partial S_t / \partial t)/S_t$ represent the instantaneous inflation, growth, and depreciation rates. There are two reasons why equation (4.19) appears much simpler than (4.17): First, the denominator terms $1 + \pi_t$ and $1 + z_t$ converge to 1, because P_t and y_t become arbitrarily close to P_{t-1} and y_{t-1}; and second, the distinction between end-of-period and period-average exchange rates disappears.

The continuous time equivalent of (4.18) is simply a rearrangement of (4.19):

$$\partial \bar{b}_t / \partial t = \bar{i}_t - \bar{x}_t - \bar{\sigma}_t - \pi_t \bar{b}_t^D - g_t \bar{b}_t + (\delta_t - \pi_t) \bar{b}_t^F. \quad (4.20)$$

If the *real exchange rate* is defined as $E_t = S_t P_t^* / P_t$, where P_t^* is the foreign price level, then the real rate of depreciation is $\varepsilon_t = \delta_t + \pi_t^* - \pi_t$. This allows one to rewrite (4.20) as

$$\partial \bar{b}_t / \partial t = \bar{\imath}_t - \bar{x}_t - \bar{\sigma}_t - \pi_t \bar{b}_t^D - g_t \bar{b}_t + (\varepsilon_t - \pi_t^*) \bar{b}_t^F. \qquad (4.21)$$

Notice that (4.21) can be interpreted as follows. Domestic debt, which is denominated in units of local currency, depreciates in real value at the rate π_t. Foreign currency debt, which is denominated in units of foreign currency, would depreciate in real value at the rate π_t^*, the foreign rate of inflation, if there were no changes in the real exchange rate. To the extent that the real exchange rate depreciates (ε_t is positive), however, the burden of external debt increases.

Debt Dynamics in Practice

There are a number of obstacles to performing the calculations described in the previous paragraphs. First, one must have reasonably accurate fiscal data. As mentioned in chapter 2, one is typically interested in working with some definition of the consolidated nonfinancial public sector, which, importantly, should include the central bank. Often such data are not readily available. Sometimes good data exist for the central government, or perhaps the general government; but an accurate consolidation of the fiscal accounts (especially the debt statistics) across the entire public sector is less prevalent. Sometimes it is difficult to bring the central bank into the consolidated figures for debt. Also, it is important to be aware of the fact that government accounting frequently places extraordinary items below the line; that is, there are items that are not included in standard budget categories and, instead, are placed outside these categories in order to fully explain the government's cash flow.

Not only must measures of stocks and flows correspond in terms of the definition of the public sector, but also the debt data broken down by currency of denomination are needed. Frequently, domestic debt data are hard to come by. Sometimes the currency denomination of foreign debt is not widely published. In addition, as shown in section 6, accurately accounting for all changes in the stock of debt requires analysts to know a lot more than just the currency denomination of debt. The structure of the various payments associated with the government's debt is important as well.

Finally, it should be pointed out that by categorizing the change in the debt-to-GDP ratio into six components, interesting phenomena that may be occurring within these components are hidden. For example, if there are dramatic changes in the primary balance, it is helpful to analyze revenue and expenditure separately.

Some Examples of Debt Dynamics

In this section the use of debt dynamics is illustrated with examples from Turkey and Argentina. In the case of Turkey, debt dynamics are used to help explain how Turkey's debt rose from 45 percent of gross national product (GNP) in 1994 to 93 percent of GNP by 2001. Debt dynamics are then used to assess whether or not Argentina's crisis, at the end of 2001, was fiscally driven. Questions about policy coordination and credibility are also considered.

Turkey 1995–2002

Between the end of 1995 and the end of 2001, Turkey's debt stock more than doubled in terms of the debt-to-GNP ratio. As table 3.2 shows, at the beginning of the period, debt was about 41 percent of GNP, with over two-thirds of the stock being external debt. By the end of the period, debt amounted to 94 percent of GNP. In 2002, the debt stock shrank somewhat (to 79 percent of GNP), but it remained at almost twice its level in 1995, and external debt represented less than half of the stock.

Table 3.2: The Stock of Public Debt in Turkey, 1994–2002
(percentage of GNP)

Type of debt	1994	1995	1996	1997	1998	1999	2000	2001	2002
Domestic	14.0	12.2	20.5	20.4	24.4	40.9	39.3	56.2	47.0
TL-denominated	..	..	..	..	22.7	38.9	36.2	36.0	32.0
FX-denominated	..	..	..	..	1.7	2.0	3.1	20.2	15.0
External	30.7	29.1	26.0	22.5	19.3	20.1	19.0	37.7	32.3
External and FX-denominated	..	..	..	..	21.0	22.1	22.1	57.9	47.3
Total debt	44.7	41.3	46.5	42.9	43.7	61.0	57.4	93.9	79.2

Sources: IMF (1998, 2000–4) and author's calculations.

Note: ".." indicates data are not available or not calculated. TL is the standard abbreviation for Turkish lira; FX, foreign exchange.

As table 3.2 indicates, by 2002 a sizable fraction of Turkey's domestic debt stock was denominated in foreign currency, but this was a relatively new phenomenon. Until 2001, the vast majority of Turkey's domestic debt was denominated in local currency and was issued at fixed interest rates. This changed in 2001, and after the financial crisis a substantial fraction of Turkey's domestic debt was indexed to foreign currency, denominated in foreign currency, or issued at floating interest rates.

From table 3.2, it is clear that Turkey's debt stock was relatively stable from the end of 1995 through the end of 1998. Essentially, it increased in two steps, from 43.7 to 61.0 percent of GNP in 1999 and from 57.4 to 93.9 percent of GNP in 2001. So why was Turkey's debt stable in the earlier period? And why did indebtedness rise so quickly in 1999 and 2001?

Table 3.3 decomposes Turkey's changes in debt into the components just described. In the period 1995–8, on average, Turkey's public sector ran a tiny primary surplus of about 0.1 percent of GNP. Nonetheless, the overall fiscal balance $\bar{i}_t - \bar{x}_t$ was very negative in this period, averaging a deficit of 11.1 percent of GNP. Given these large deficits, it may seem puzzling that Turkey's debt stock stayed roughly constant over the period. Even when seigniorage is accounted for (it averaged 2.7 percent of GNP in this period), one would predict rapid debt accumulation—at an average pace of 8.4 percentage points of GNP per year—if only the standard terms in the debt dynamics were considered.

Of course, a major part of the story is that the three extra terms described earlier played an important role in Turkey. A substantial fraction of Turkey's interest burden was eased by the fact that the real face value of Turkish lira (TL)-denominated debt was being eroded through inflation (the inflation effect averaged −7.5 percent of GNP) and the real value of foreign exchange (FX)-denominated debt was being eroded through real appreciation of the TL (the revaluation effect averaged −2.6 percent of GNP). Turkey was also fortunate to have positive growth throughout the period, at an average rate of 6.8 percent per year, implying an average growth effect of about −1.5 percent of GNP. So, together, these three effects contributed 11.6 percent of GNP per year to the stability of Turkey's debt stock.

But the period 1995–8 is also interesting because it looks like a period in which the government's generally loose fiscal policy was accommodated by loose monetary policy. In chapter 2 it was shown that the central bank can fight inflation in the face of loose fiscal policy—but at the cost of an

Table 3.3: Public Debt Dynamics in Turkey, 1995–2002
(percentage of GNP)

Budget item	1995	1996	1997	1998	1999	2000	2001	2002
Change in debt	−3.4	5.2	−3.6	0.8	17.3	−3.6	36.5	−14.7
(a) Sum of standard terms: $i - \bar{x} - \bar{\sigma}$	1.6	8.8	10.2	12.9	20.9	17.7	19.9	11.1
Interest payments, i	7.3	10.0	11.0	16.2	22.1	21.9	26.6	16.2
Primary balance, $\bar{x}$	2.7	−1.2	−2.1	0.9	−2.0	2.4	5.6	4.1
Seigniorage, $\bar{\sigma}$	3.0	2.4	2.9	2.4	3.2	1.8	1.1	1.0
(b) Sum of extra terms:	−12.6	−8.8	−12.8	−11.8	−4.9	−19.8	4.0	−25.4
Growth effect	−1.7	−1.5	−2.0	−0.9	1.8	−2.4	3.9	−4.8
Inflation effect	−6.5	−5.3	−9.2	−8.8	−8.1	−13.1	−12.9	−11.1
Revaluation effect	−4.3	−1.9	−1.6	−2.1	1.4	−4.3	13.0	−9.5
(c) Net below-the-line terms:	0.0	0.0	−0.1	−0.5	−0.1	0.0	14.4	−0.3
Cost of financial sector bailout	0.0	0.0	0.0	0.0	0.0	0.0	16.3	0.0
Privatization revenue	0.0	0.0	0.1	0.5	0.1	0.0	1.9	0.3
Memo item:								
Standard budget deficit, $i - \bar{x}$	4.6	11.2	13.1	15.3	24.1	19.5	21.0	12.1
Errors and discrepancy	7.5	5.2	−0.9	0.2	1.4	−1.5	−1.8	−0.1
Inflation rate (percent)	87.2	78.0	81.2	75.3	55.8	50.9	55.3	44.4
Real growth rate (percent)	7.9	7.1	8.3	3.9	−6.1	6.3	−9.5	7.9
Depreciation rate (percent)	58.8	71.6	77.7	59.2	64.5	19.9	109.5	22.0

Sources: IMF (1998, 2000–4) and author's calculations.

Notes: The growth effect is computed as $-g_t\bar{b}_{t-1}/(1 + z_t)$, where g_t is the growth rate of real GNP, $\bar{b}_t$ is the end of period t debt-to-GNP ratio, and z_t is the growth rate of nominal GNP. The inflation effect is computed as $-\pi_t\bar{b}^D_{t-1}/(1 + \pi_t)$, where π_t is the inflation rate of the GNP deflator, and $\bar{b}^D_t$ is the end of period t stock of TL-denominated domestic debt. The revaluation effect is computed as $\bar{\delta}_t\bar{b}^F_t + [\delta_t/(1 + z_t) - \pi_t/(1 + \pi_t)]\bar{b}^F_{t-1}$, where $\bar{b}^F_t$ is the end-of-period t stock of external debt plus foreign currency-denominated domestic debt, and $\bar{\delta}_t$ and δ_t are defined as follows. Let S_{it} be the end of period t exchange rate in units of foreign currency i per TL, and let $S_{i\bar{t}}$ be the equivalent period average exchange rate. Then $\bar{\delta}_t = \Sigma^N_{i=1}\theta_i(S_{it} - S_{i\bar{t}})/S_{it}$ and $\delta_t = \Sigma^N_{i=1}\theta_i(S_{\bar{t}} - S_{it-1})/S_{it-1}$, where θ_i represents the average share of currency i in Turkey's external debt in periods $t - 1$ and t. "Errors and discrepancy" equals the difference between the change in debt and the sum of (a), (b), and (c). To compute the depreciation rates, the currency composition of Turkey's external debt was taken into consideration.

increasing stock of debt and higher inflation later. In the period 1995–8, one could argue that the central bank in Turkey did not fight inflation. Money was printed at a rapid pace (as the numbers on seigniorage attest) and inflation was rampant, averaging about 80 percent per year. Had the central bank fought inflation more vigorously, the stock of debt would probably not have been so stable during this period.

In 1999, the various factors that had helped to keep Turkey's debt in check during the period 1995–8 were reversed. The primary balance deteriorated to −2.0 percent of GNP, from an average of 0.1 percent of GNP in 1995–8. This was largely due to two factors: the economy slipping into recession, and the fiscal easing that occurred after the Marmara earthquake in August. The real exchange rate depreciated, implying a revaluation effect of 1.2 percent of GNP, as opposed to an average effect of −2.6 percent of GNP in 1995–8. These two factors raised the financing burden by 5.5 percent of GNP in 1999, compared to the period 1995–8.

Nominal interest rates remained high in 1999, despite a decline in inflation. One interpretation is that this was the result of a monetary policy stance geared at consolidating the disinflation that began in 1998. Another is that real interest rate movements were the result of a loss of confidence in the domestic debt market. Regardless of the explanation, the net impact on the *real* domestic interest burden was substantial—on the order of 9.7 percent of GNP.

The policy mix and other economic events thus created a financing nightmare: The overall balance that needed to be financed deteriorated sharply, but none of the implicit sources of financing (inflation, revaluation, and growth) helped offset this increase to the extent they previously had. With seigniorage revenue already near its natural limit, an enormous increase in net debt was inevitable. The lesson from 1999 appears to be a strong one: A policy geared toward reduced inflation must be coordinated with credible fiscal reform.

There was a slight improvement in Turkey's debt situation in 2000, which coincided with a rebound in the real exchange rate and the resumption of growth. However, after the financial tremor of November 2000, the economy fell into a full-scale financial and economic crisis in February 2001. Much as in 1999, this crisis played havoc with the government's finances.

In 2001, the debt stock rose by 36.5 percent of GNP. One reason for this increase was that the government issued new bonds in order to recapitalize failing banks. These bonds are accounted for below the line; that is, the cost of bailing out the banks is not included as an expenditure item in computing the primary balance. A rough estimate of the quantity of bonds issued for this purpose is about 16.3 percent of GNP.[11] So the direct impact of the financial crisis explains only about half of the increase in the ratio of debt to GNP. In other respects 2001 was similar to 1999, but with some important differences.

Unlike in 1999, the primary fiscal balance did not deteriorate relative to the stance of the mid-1990s. Indeed, the government successfully implemented a sharp fiscal contraction despite the recession, with the primary fiscal balance improving to 5.6 percent of GNP (compared to 0.1 percent of GNP in 1995–8).

In 2001, there was a sharp depreciation of the lira, brought on by the financial and fiscal crisis. Inflation did not bring the price level in line with the exchange rate by the end of the year, so there was a sizable real depreciation and a revaluation effect on the order of 13.0 percent of GNP (compared to –2.6 percent of GNP in 1995–8). The revaluation effect was so large that it completely offset the inflation effect on domestic debt.

As in 1999, the government faced an enormous financing challenge. With seigniorage kept to just 1.1 percent of GNP, and with sharply negative growth, the government was forced to issue a great deal of new debt. Unlike 1999, when the domestic market absorbed most of the government's financing requirement, only about half of the new debt was issued domestically. Furthermore, almost all net financing obtained from the domestic market was raised by issuing debt denominated in or indexed to foreign currency.

In 2002, the debt picture improved, mainly due to the economic rebound. Growth returned and was unusually strong given the depth of the preceding recession. The exchange rate appreciated substantially in real terms after the sharp real depreciation of 2001. Interest rates moderated somewhat. Together these factors implied a sharp reduction in Turkey's public debt, from 93.9 to 79.2 percent of GNP.

While some lessons drawn from Turkey's experience can be related to the theory discussed in chapter 2, it is clear that other important factors come into play. Debt levels can fluctuate wildly depending on the value of the real exchange rate if a country has significant amounts of external or foreign currency-denominated debt. The primary budget, as in 1999, responds to economic conditions. Finally, financial crises, which lie outside our theoretical discussion so far, can have a dramatic impact on the government's finances. Crises will be discussed in greater detail in chapters 8 and 9.

Argentina, 1994–2002

Table 3.4 presents debt data for Argentina, from 1993 through 2002, while table 3.5 illustrates Argentina's debt dynamics from 1994 through 2002. As

Table 3.4: The Stock of Public Debt in Argentina, 1993–2002
(percentage of GNP)

Type of debt	1993	1994	1995	1996	1997	1998	1999	2000	2001	2002
Domestic	2.4	3.3	2.3	3.0	3.2	2.6	2.3	1.6	0.6	5.4
External and FX	27.1	28.1	31.5	32.7	31.3	35.0	40.7	43.5	53.2	143.8
Total debt	29.4	31.3	33.8	35.7	34.5	37.6	43.0	45.0	53.8	149.1

Sources: Argentina, Ministry of Economy and Production (2004) and author's calculations.

Note: FX, foreign exchange.

Table 3.5: Public Debt Dynamics in Argentina, 1994–2002
(percentage of GDP)

Budget item	1994	1995	1996	1997	1998	1999	2000	2001	2002
Change in debt	1.9	2.4	1.9	−1.2	3.1	5.4	2.1	8.7	95.4
(a) Sum of standard terms: $\bar{i} - \bar{x} - \bar{\sigma}$	−0.1	2.2	1.8	0.8	1.3	2.5	2.9	4.4	−4.0
Interest payments, $\bar{i}$	1.2	1.6	1.7	2.0	2.2	2.9	3.4	3.8	2.2
Primary balance, $\bar{x}$	0.9	0.6	−0.5	0.5	0.8	0.3	1.0	0.5	0.7
Seigniorage, $\bar{\sigma}$	0.4	−1.2	0.4	0.7	0.1	0.0	−0.5	−1.2	5.5
(b) Sum of extra terms:	−2.4	−0.1	−1.8	−2.5	−0.7	2.0	−0.1	2.6	97.7
Growth effect	−1.6	0.9	−1.8	−2.7	−1.3	1.3	0.3	2.1	5.0
Inflation effect	−0.1	−0.1	0.0	0.0	0.1	0.0	0.0	0.0	−0.1
Revaluation effect	−0.8	−0.9	0.0	0.2	0.5	0.7	−0.4	0.5	92.8
(c) Privatization revenue	0.3	0.5	0.1	0.0	0.0	0.9	0.1	0.0	0.0
Memo item:									
Standard budget deficit, $\bar{i} - \bar{x}$	0.3	1.0	2.1	1.6	1.4	2.6	2.4	3.3	1.5
Errors and discrepancy	4.7	0.8	2.0	0.6	2.5	1.7	−0.7	1.7	1.7
Inflation rate (percent)	2.8	3.2	−0.1	−0.5	−1.7	−1.8	1.0	−1.1	30.8
Real growth rate (percent)	5.8	−2.8	5.5	8.1	3.9	−3.4	−0.8	−4.4	−10.9
Depreciation rate (percent)	0	0	0	0	0	0	0	0	206.3

Sources: Argentina Ministry of Economy and Production (2004), Central Bank of the Argentine Republic (2004), and author's calculations.

Notes: The growth and inflation effects are computed as for Turkey (see table 3.3), except that GDP is the income concept. The revaluation effect is computed as $\bar{\delta}_t \bar{b}_t^F + [\underline{\delta}_t/(1 + z_t) - \pi_t/(1 + \pi_t)]\bar{b}_{t-1}^F$, where $\bar{b}_t^F$ is the end of period t stock of external debt plus foreign currency-denominated domestic debt, and $\bar{\delta}_t$ and $\underline{\delta}_t$ are defined as follows. Let S_t be the end of period t exchange rate in U.S. dollars per peso, and let $S_{\bar{t}}$ be the equivalent period average exchange rate. Then $\bar{\delta}_t = (S_t - S_{\bar{t}})/S_t$ and $\underline{\delta}_t = (S_{\bar{t}} - S_{t-1})/S_{t-1}$. "Errors and discrepancy" equals the difference between the change in debt and (a) + (b) − (c).

table 3.4 shows, Argentina gradually accumulated debt, beginning from a stock of just under 30 percent of GDP in 1993. By 1998, the stock of debt had grown to 37.6 percent of GDP. But the process accelerated in 1999 (as the economy entered recession) and again in 2001 (as the recession deepened), and by the end of that year the stock of debt had grown to 53.8 percent of GDP.

Many observers of the Argentine economy during the 1990s argued that Argentina did not have a fiscal problem, because it was generally running a primary surplus. This fact is confirmed by table 3.5. But, as shown earlier, running a primary surplus is not a sufficient criterion for achieving fiscal sustainability. Indeed, the long-run condition stating that a government must run a primary balance $\bar{x} = \bar{r}\bar{b} - \bar{\sigma}$ is needed to achieve fiscal sustainability.

From the end of 1993 to the end of 2001, Argentina's debt stock, as a percentage of GDP, grew in every year except 1997. A country can accumulate debt and continue to have sustainable finances; but to do so it must eventually implement a fiscal adjustment, loosen monetary policy, or be lucky enough to begin growing faster.[12] As shown in table 3.5, Argentina made no fiscal adjustment significant enough to raise its primary surplus over this period. Under the currency board, loosening monetary policy was not an option: The size of the monetary base was dictated by the current account. To make matters worse, after 1998 the economy began to shrink rather than grow faster. Thus, rather than reversing the trend of a growing debt stock and interest burden, Argentina's government found itself in a situation where the trend worsened.

It is difficult to argue that by the end of 2001, Argentina had achieved some magic number for debt that meant it was bound to suffer a crisis. However, it is not surprising that in the context of a growing fiscal problem and a stagnant economy, investors lost confidence in the government's ability to sustain its finances.

One aspect of table 3.5 that deserves mention is the large residuals observed in the period 1994–8. The large positive residuals imply that important factors which contributed to the accumulation of debt do not appear in the debt dynamics detailed in table 3.5. This suggests that the primary balance was probably overstated—and omitted off-balance sheet items.[13]

It is also worth noting how well the debt dynamics explain changes in Argentina's indebtedness during 2002. The accounting residual is only 1.7 percent of GDP, despite the enormous revaluation effect that took place in the period.

In summary, Argentina looks like a country that in the early 1990s had public finances which were close to sustainable. The government might have been able to correct the situation via a small fiscal adjustment. However, it did not do so, and its debt stock began to grow. This, combined with the deep recession entered in 1999, led to an acceleration of Argentina's fiscal problem.

5   Using Debt Dynamics in Forward-Looking Analysis

Sections 1 and 2 presented simple tools that can be used to assess fiscal sustainability in a forward-looking way. Section 4 explained how debt dynamics can be used as a tool for analyzing historical debt data. This section considers how some of the details of section 4 can be adapted for use in the type of forward-looking analysis presented in sections 1 and 2.

First, reconsider the basic accounting identity

$$\text{net debt issued} = I_t - X_t - (M_t - M_{t-1}).$$

In chapter 2 and in sections 1 and 2 of this chapter, these assumptions were adopted: that all debt has a maturity of one period, and that debt is real and pays a constant real rate of interest, r. In this case, the budget constraint can be rewritten in real terms, as $b_t = (1 + r)b_{t-1} - x_t - \sigma_t$. But rather than proceed in this fashion, one can instead adopt the budget constraint (measured in units of local currency) that was derived in the section on debt dynamics:

$$B_t^D - B_{t-1}^D + \left(B_t^F - B_{t-1}^F\right)S_{\bar{t}} = I_t - X_t - (M_t - M_{t-1}).$$

Now maintain the assumption that all debt has a maturity of one period, but allow the interest rates on domestic and external debt, R_t^D and R_t^F, to be time varying.

In the section on debt dynamics, it was assumed that amortization, the issuance of new debt, and interest payments took place at a steady pace within the year, so that the period average exchange rate, $S_{\bar{t}}$, was the appropriate one to use in valuing foreign currency transactions. For simplicity, in this section it will be assumed that the period average exchange rate is the same as the end-of-period exchange rate, so that $S_{\bar{t}} = S_t$. One can then rewrite the budget constraint as

$$B_t^D - B_{t-1}^D + S_t\left(B_t^F - B_{t-1}^F\right) = R_{t-1}^D B_{t-1}^D + S_t R_{t-1}^F B_{t-1}^F - X_t - (M_t - M_{t-1}).$$

Dividing both sides by nominal GDP, $P_t y_t$, one obtains

$$\bar{b}_t^D + \bar{b}_t^F = \left(\frac{1 + R_{t-1}^D}{1 + z_t}\right)\bar{b}_{t-1}^D + \frac{S_t}{S_{t-1}}\frac{1 + R_{t-1}^F}{1 + z_t}\bar{b}_{t-1}^F - \bar{x}_t - \bar{\sigma}_t. \quad (5.1)$$

Using assumptions about nominal interest rates, inflation, real growth, the primary balance, the monetary base, and the exchange rate, (5.1) can be used to simulate the path of debt for an economy. If, in the simulation, the debt-to-GDP ratio continues to grow faster than the effective nominal interest rate net of the inflation and growth rates—that is, an appropriate weighted average of $(1 + R_{t-1}^D)/(1 + z_t)$ and $(1 + R_{t-1}^F)/(1 + z_t)$—then debt will not be sustainable. This is the analog to verifying whether the long-run sustainability condition of section 1 holds. Alternatively, one could simulate the path of debt using (5.1), to see whether a debt target like the one illustrated in section 2 could be achieved. But (5.1) is especially useful because one can simulate many paths of debt using random paths for specific variables, in order to assess risk factors. The possibilities will be illustrated here using two extensions of the Bulgaria example from section 2.

Time-Varying Interest Rates

The case study of Bulgaria presented in section 2 included a calculation of the primary balance that the government would need in order to achieve a debt target of 60 percent of GDP by 2005. To calculate an estimate of the necessary primary balance, it was assumed that the nominal interest rate would be $R = 0.085$ in perpetuity, while the inflation rate would be $\pi = 0.035$. This implied a real interest rate, $r = 0.048$. The real growth rate was assumed to be $g = 0.04$. Finally, it was assumed that the monetary base would stay constant as a percentage of GDP at $\bar{m} = 0.14$, so that $\bar{\sigma} = z\bar{m}/(1 + z) \approx 0.01$ where $z = \pi + g + \pi g$. This analysis found that, in order for Bulgaria to reduce its debt stock from 72 percent of GDP at the end of 2001 to 60 percent of GDP at the end of 2005, it would require a primary balance $\bar{x} = 0.0255$, or 2.55 percent of GDP.

Table 3.1 measures the sensitivity of this result to assumptions made about the real interest rate and growth. Recall, however, that concern about the interest rate assumption was based on the fact that Bulgaria's debt profile is changing. In 2001, Bulgaria was fortunate in that it was servicing its debt, which was largely concessional, at an effective nominal interest rate of about 5 percent. But when borrowing in private markets, it was borrowing

Table 3.6: Bulgaria's Debt Dynamics with Time-Varying Interest Rates, 2001–7
(percentage of GDP)

	Date/interest rate						
	2001	*2002*	*2003*	*2004*	*2005*	*2006*	*2007*
Budget item	*5*	*6*	*7*	*8*	*9*	*10*	*11*
(a) Public debt (assuming $\bar{x} = 0.0255$)	72.0	66.7	62.1	58.2	54.9	52.0	49.6
(b) Public debt (assuming $\bar{x} = 0.0127$)	72.0	68.0	64.7	62.0	60.0	58.5	57.5

Source: Author's calculations.

at rates closer to 12 percent. Since Bulgaria is expected to retire a great deal of its concessional debt by 2007, it might be desirable to assume that Bulgaria's effective borrowing cost will rise over time.

Rather than choose a constant interest rate between 5 and 12 percent, it might be interesting to assume that the effective nominal interest rate would start out at 5 percent in 2002, but gradually rise to, say, 10 percent, by 2006. After that the rate might be assumed to be constant at 10 percent.

Making this small change in the assumptions of section 2, and ignoring the issues raised by external debt, (5.1) can be rewritten as

$$\bar{b}_t = \left(\frac{1 + R_{t-1}}{1 + z}\right)\bar{b}_{t-1} - \bar{x} - \frac{z}{1 + z}\bar{m}. \qquad (5.2)$$

The assumptions here are that $\pi = 0.035$, $g = 0.04$, and $\bar{m} = 0.14$, so $z = 0.0764$ and $\bar{\sigma} \approx 0.01$. It turns out that if the primary surplus is set to $\bar{x} = 0.0255$ (as before), then Bulgaria would more than meet the goal of the 60 percent debt rule by 2005. In fact, it would achieve a 54.9 percent debt-to-GDP ratio, as shown in table 3.6. Bulgaria could even run a primary balance of just 1.27 percent of GDP and achieve the debt target by that date. Of course, this result is due to the new assumption that the nominal interest rate, though growing, would lie below 8.5 percent through 2004. In section 2, a constant nominal interest rate of 8.5 percent was assumed, so not surprisingly, this implied a much larger primary surplus.

Exchange Rate Risk

At the end of 2000, 65 percent of Bulgaria's external public sector debt was denominated in U.S. dollars. But Bulgaria's currency board maintains a peg between the lev and the euro. Hence, the government faces considerable exchange rate risk due to movements in the euro-dollar exchange rate, even if it maintains the peg.

To gauge the risk that movements in the euro-dollar exchange rate pose to the sustainability of Bulgaria's debt, one could consider a simple simulation exercise that uses (5.1) to allow for the varied currency composition of the debt.

Suppose that one maintains the assumption that inflation, growth, the primary balance, and the monetary base (as a percentage of GDP) are constant, so that $\pi_t = \pi$, $g_t = g$, $z_t = z = \pi + g + \pi g$, $\bar{x}_t = \bar{x}$, and $\bar{\sigma}_t = \bar{\sigma} = \bar{m}z/(1+z)$. Further, suppose that there are no expected exchange rate movements, and there is no risk premium to borrowing in either currency, so that $R_t^D = R_t^F = R_t$ for all t. Lev or euro borrowing can be treated as borrowing in domestic currency, while U.S. dollars are treated as foreign currency. One can rewrite (5.1) as

$$\bar{b}_t^D + \bar{b}_t^F = \left(\frac{1 + R_{t-1}}{1 + z}\right)\bar{b}_{t-1}^D + \frac{S_t}{S_{t-1}}\frac{1 + R_{t-1}}{1 + z}\bar{b}_{t-1}^F - \bar{x} - \bar{\sigma}. \quad (5.3)$$

Notice that if θ_t represents the fraction of the debt that is denominated in U.S. dollars at the end of time t, then (5.3) can be rewritten as

$$\bar{b}_t = (1 + \delta_t\theta_{t-1})\left(\frac{1 + R_{t-1}}{1 + z}\right)\bar{b}_{t-1} - \bar{x} - \frac{z}{1+z}\bar{m}, \quad (5.4)$$

where δ_t is the rate of depreciation of the euro against the dollar.

Table 3.7 illustrates the result of using (5.4) to simulate 1,000 debt paths that assume an initial 65 percent dollar composition of debt, while maintaining the assumptions used in making the projections in table 3.6: $\pi = 0.035$, $g = 0.04$, $\bar{m} = 0.14$, $\bar{x} = 0.0255$. The two tables use identical time-varying interest rate assumptions. The simulated paths for debt depend on simulated values of the dollar-euro exchange rate drawn from a random number generator. These simulations assume that the draws of δ_t are independent and identically distributed, and normal, with mean zero and standard deviation equal to 0.128.[14] The simulations also assume that in each period, the government acts to ensure that 65 percent of the debt is dollar denominated.

The simulations in table 3.7 show that exchange rate risk could have been a serious issue for Bulgaria. In 5 percent of the simulations, debt rises to almost 76 percent of GDP by the year 2007. In just over 8 percent of the

Table 3.7: Bulgaria's Debt Dynamics with Exchange Rate Risk, 2001–7

	Date/interest rate						
	2001	*2002*	*2003*	*2004*	*2005*	*2006*	*2007*
Budget item	*5*	*6*	*7*	*8*	*9*	*10*	*11*
Public debt (% of GDP)							
Mean	72.0	67.2	62.9	59.3	56.1	53.6	51.5
Median	72.0	67.0	62.7	58.5	55.0	51.9	49.8
5th percentile	72.0	58.3	50.9	45.1	40.3	36.3	32.7
95th percentile	72.0	77.7	77.3	75.6	75.2	75.6	75.8
Percentage of observations in which							
debt is greater than 60% of GDP	100.0	89.8	61.9	42.9	32.7	28.7	23.9

Source: Author's calculations.

simulations, debt remains above its 2001 level in 2007. In addition, in about 33 percent of the cases the EU accession target is not reached by 2005, although the target is reached 76 percent of the time by 2007.[15]

Simulations based on (5.4) do not, of course, take into account the possibility that the primary surplus, growth, or seigniorage could be affected by dollar-euro exchange rate movements. This may or may not be a reasonable assumption depending on the structure of government spending and government revenue. However, it seems reasonable to assume that Bulgaria is more tightly integrated into the European economy, and that growth and government finance are more likely to be affected by real exchange rate movements between the lev and the euro rather than by changes in the dollar-euro nominal exchange rate.

In the end, these simulations could have been used to argue that the government should consider hedging some of the exchange rate risk it faced. One could conduct similar simulations to account for the effects of recessions. This would imply making assumptions about the stochastic process governing g_t, and, perhaps, making assumptions about the interaction between growth and the primary balance.

It is important to keep in mind that, in computing these simulated debt paths for Bulgaria, this analysis has assumed that the government uses an arbitrary rule for allocating its debt across the two currencies—and that the interest rate Bulgaria pays on dollar or euro debt is determined in world markets without any particular country premium tied to it. Another important point is that, along the various paths, markets do not charge a higher or lower premium to Bulgaria as its dollar-denominated debt rises or falls. So the simulations are probably useful only for benchmarking the risk level of the government's debt. It is also very important to note that similar exercises would be even less appropriate if a country was issuing debt in its own currency and foreign currency, and the exercises treated the local-foreign currency exchange rate as an exogenous variable. As is shown in chapters 8 and 9, the exchange rate is endogenous and depends on a government's finances. In the Bulgarian example shown here, the exchange rate in question is, arguably, exogenous to the Bulgarian economy.

3

6   Measuring Debt

We now highlight issues in the measurement of debt. In particular, this section shows how the structure of a government's debt creates problems in defining the stock of debt that is relevant in our analysis. The main issue is that, when interest rates change, the market value of previously issued long-term debt changes. So should one use market value or book value as our measure of debt? To keep things simple, this section focuses on examples where the government issues only nonindexed debt that is denominated in local currency units. It would be straightforward to extend the analysis to more complex debt structures.

Baseline Example: Single-Period Debt

Suppose that the government issues all of its debt in the form of single-period bonds denominated in local currency units, which, for convenience, are called *pesos*. The government issues two types of bonds: zero coupon bonds and coupon bonds.

The government uses the following accounting rules. If, at time t, the government issues a zero coupon bond with a face value of one peso, with an effective yield to maturity given by R_t, then this bond contributes first: $1/(1 + R_t)$ to the book value of government debt at time t; second: $1/(1 + R_t)$ to time $t + 1$ amortization payments; and third: $R_t/(1 + R_t)$ to time $t + 1$ interest payments. If, however, the government issues a coupon bond with a face value of one peso, and coupon rate c_t, with an effective yield to maturity given by R_t, then this bond contributes first: $(1 + c_t)/(1 + R_t)$ to the book value of government debt at time t; second: $(1 + c_t)/(1 + R_t)$ to time $t + 1$ amortization payments; and third: $(1 + c_t)R_t/(1 + R_t)$ to time $t + 1$ interest payments. These accounting rules imply that coupon bonds and zero coupon bonds receive symmetric treatment in the government's books. They also imply that the book value of any debt is the same as its market value at the time of issuance.

Here, repeat the accounting identity (4.1) as

$$\text{net debt issued} = I_t - X_t - (M_t - M_{t-1}). \tag{6.1}$$

Net debt issued is proceeds raised from the sale of debt at time t, which can be denoted with B_t, minus any amortization payments at time t, denoted as A_t. So one can write

$$B_t - A_t = I_t - X_t - (M_t - M_{t-1}). \tag{6.2}$$

Notice, given the description used in the baseline example, that $A_t = B_{t-1}$, so that

$$B_t - B_{t-1} = I_t - X_t - (M_t - M_{t-1}). \tag{6.3}$$

Also, notice that if one assumes that all debt issued by the government at time t is issued at the same effective yield, R_t, then $I_t = R_{t-1}B_{t-1}$. Hence,

$$B_t - B_{t-1} = R_{t-1}B_{t-1} - X_t - (M_t - M_{t-1}). \tag{6.4}$$

In the baseline example, (6.4) holds, regardless of whether B_t represents gross proceeds from issuing debt, the book value of the government's debt, or the market value of the government's debt. The simplicity of the example with only single-period debt is precisely why the single-period debt assumption was adopted throughout chapters 2 and 3.

Two-Period Debt

Once two-period debt is introduced, the accounting becomes more complicated. Earlier it was shown that as long as the accounting was done carefully, there was no distinction between a one-period zero coupon bond and a one-period coupon bond. Both are promises to pay a lump-sum one period ahead, and that lump-sum can be divided between interest and amortization in a way that blurs the distinction between the two types of bonds. This is no longer the case with two-period bonds. A zero coupon bond issued for two periods postpones the entire cash flow for two periods, whereas a coupon bond does not. Hence, these types of bonds are fundamentally different.

Nonetheless, it is still possible to summarize all debt by how much it promises to pay in what period. In general, the notation $D_{s,j}$ will be used to represent debt contracted at date s, with maturity j. When debt can be issued for at most two periods, then at the end of period t, the government will have commitments to pay the nominal amounts $D_{t-1,2}$ and $D_{t,1}$ in period $t+1$, as well as $D_{t,2}$ in period $t+2$. The market value of the government's debt at the end of period t is

$$B_t^m = \frac{D_{t-1,2} + D_{t,1}}{1 + R_{t,1}} + \frac{D_{t,2}}{(1 + R_{t,2})^2},$$
(6.5)

where $R_{t,j}$ is the yield to maturity of a j-period zero coupon bond issued at date t. The book value of the government's debt is

$$B_t^b = \frac{D_{t-1,2}}{(1 + R_{t-1,2})^2} + \frac{D_{t,1}}{1 + R_{t,1}} + \frac{D_{t,2}}{(1 + R_{t,2})^2}.$$
(6.6)

The government's gross proceeds from issuing debt at time t are

$$G_t = \frac{D_{t,1}}{1 + R_{t,1}} + \frac{D_{t,2}}{(1 + R_{t,2})^2},$$
(6.7)

while amortization plus interest at time t is

$$A_t + I_t = D_{t-1,1} + D_{t-2,2}.$$
(6.8)

Here, assume that, in all cases, the net issuance of debt is defined as $G_t - A_t$ (the gross issuance of debt net of amortization), so that

$$G_t - A_t = I_t - X_t - (M_t - M_{t-1}).$$
(6.9)

At this stage one can demonstrate the circumstances under which the net issuance of debt corresponds to the change in the stock of debt, measured either as B_t^m or B_t^b. Notice that

$$B_t^m - B_{t-1}^m = G_t - A_t \Leftrightarrow B_t^m = G_t + B_{t-1}^m - A_t.$$

If these statements are true then, given (6.5), (6.7), and (6.8), one has

$$\frac{D_{t-1,2} + D_{t,1}}{1 + R_{t,1}} + \frac{D_{t,2}}{(1 + R_{t,2})^2}$$
$$= \frac{D_{t,1}}{1 + R_{t,1}} + \frac{D_{t,2}}{(1 + R_{t,2})^2} + B_{t-1}^m + I_t - (D_{t-1,1} + D_{t-2,2})$$

or, equivalently,

$$D_{t-1,1} + D_{t-2,2} + \frac{D_{t-1,2}}{1 + R_{t,1}} = B_{t-1}^m + I_t.$$
(6.10)

From (6.5) one can see that

$$D_{t-1,1} + D_{t-2,2} + \frac{D_{t-1,2}}{1 + R_{t,1}} = (1 + R_{t-1,1})B^m_{t-1}$$

$$+ \left[\frac{1}{1 + R_{t,1}} - \frac{1 + R_{t-1,1}}{(1 + R_{t-1,2})^2} \right] D_{t-1,2}.$$

Hence, (6.10) can be rewritten as

$$I_t = R_{t-1,1}B^m_{t-1} + \left[\frac{1}{1 + R_{t,1}} - \frac{1 + R_{t-1,1}}{(1 + R_{t-1,2})^2} \right] D_{t-1,2}. \qquad \textbf{(6.11)}$$

So, $B^m_t - B^m_{t-1} = I_t - X_t - (M_t - M_{t-1})$ if, and only if, the government's measure of interest payments corresponds to (6.11). Notice that this measure of interest payments is the one-period interest rate at time $t - 1$, $R_{t-1,1}$, times the market value of the debt at the end of period $t - 1$, B^m_{t-1}, *plus* a capital loss term that results from any change in the holding period yield that applies to the interval between period t and period $t + 1$. Notice that $(1 + R_{t-1,2})^2/ (1 + R_{t-1,1})$ represents the portion of the gross return on a two-period zero coupon bond, purchased at time $t - 1$, that accrues between periods t and $t + 1$. The gross return on a one-period zero coupon bond held between t and $t + 1$ is $1 + R_{t,1}$. Notice that if the latter is less than the former, the second term on the right-hand side of (6.11) is positive. This is because the government takes a capital loss resulting from the decline in the cost of borrowing money between periods t and $t + 1$. The total loss is proportional to the amount of money that was tied down for two periods at time $t - 1$.

However, when one considers the book value of debt,

$$B^b_t - B^b_{t-1} = G_t - A_t \Leftrightarrow B^b_t = G_t + B^b_{t-1} - A_t.$$

If these statements are true, then

$$\frac{D_{t-1,2}}{(1 + R_{t-1,2})^2} + \frac{D_{t,1}}{1 + R_{t,1}} + \frac{D_{t,2}}{(1 + R_{t,2})^2} = \frac{D_{t,1}}{1 + R_{t,1}} + \frac{D_{t,2}}{(1 + R_{t,2})^2}$$

$$+ B^b_{t-1} + I_t - (D_{t-1,1} + D_{t-2,2})$$

or

$$D_{t-1,1} + D_{t-2,2} + \frac{D_{t-1,2}}{(1 + R_{t-1,2})^2} = B^b_{t-1} + I_t.$$

Using (6.6), one can substitute out B_{t-1}^d and solve for I_t:

$$I_t = R_{t-1,1}\frac{D_{t-1,1}}{1 + R_{t-1,1}} + [(1 + R_{t-2,2})^2 - 1]\frac{D_{t-2,2}}{(1 + R_{t-2,2})^2}. \qquad (6.12)$$

So,

$$B_t^b - B_{t-1}^b = I_t - X_t - (M_t - M_{t-1})$$

if, and only if, the government's measure of interest payments corresponds to (6.12). Notice that this measure of interest payments takes the book value of the payments being made at time t—that is, $D_{t-1,1}/(1 + R_{t-1,1})$ and $D_{t-2,2}/(1 + R_{t-2,2})^2$—and computes the accumulated book interest on these amounts, given the periods over which the funds were borrowed.

Multi-period Debt

When debt is issued for at most K periods, then at the end of period t, the government will have commitments to pay the nominal amounts $(D_{t-K+1,K}, D_{t-K+2,K-1},\ldots, D_{t-1,2}, D_{t,1})$, $(D_{t-K+2,K},\ldots, D_{t-1,3}, D_{t,2}),\ldots,$ $(D_{t-1,K}, D_{t,K-1})$, $D_{t,K}$ in periods $t + 1, t + 2,\ldots, t + K - 1, t + K$, respectively. The market value of the government's debt is

$$B_t^m = \sum_{j=1}^{K}(1 + R_{t,j})^{-j}\sum_{i=j}^{K}D_{t+j-i,i}. \qquad (6.13)$$

The book value of the government's debt is

$$B_t^b = \sum_{j=1}^{K}\sum_{i=j}^{K}(1 + R_{t+j-i,i})^{-i}D_{t+j-i,i}. \qquad (6.14)$$

The government's gross proceeds from issuing debt at time t are

$$G_t = \sum_{j=1}^{K}(1 + R_{t,j})^{-j}D_{t,j}, \qquad (6.15)$$

while amortization plus interest at time t is

$$A_t + I_t = \sum_{j=1}^{K}D_{t-j,j}. \qquad (6.16)$$

As before, the net issuance of debt is $G_t - A_t$, and is given by (6.9).

As in the previous section, $B_t^m - B_{t-1}^m = G_t - A_t$ if $B_t^m = G_t + B_{t-1}^m - A_t$, or

$$\sum_{j=1}^{K}(1 + R_{t,j})^{-j}\sum_{i=j}^{K}D_{t+j-i,i} = \sum_{j=1}^{K}(1 + R_{t,j})^{-j}D_{t,j} + B_{t-1}^m + I_t - \sum_{j=1}^{K}D_{t-j,j}.$$

(6.17)

Notice that

$$B_{t-1}^m = \sum_{j=1}^{K}(1 + R_{t-1,j})^{-j}\sum_{i=j}^{K}D_{t-1+j-i,i}$$

so that

$$(1 + R_{t-1,1})B_{t-1}^m = \sum_{j=1}^{K}\frac{1 + R_{t-1,1}}{(1 + R_{t-1,j})^j}\sum_{i=j}^{K}D_{t-1+j-i,i}.$$

Hence, (6.17) can be rewritten as

$$I_t = R_{t-1,1}B_{t-1}^m + \sum_{j=1}^{K}\left\{(1 + R_{t,j})^{-j}\left[\sum_{i=j}^{K}D_{t+j-i,i} - D_{t,j}\right]\right.$$

$$\left. - \frac{1 + R_{t-1,1}}{(1 + R_{t-1,j})^j}\sum_{i=j}^{K}D_{t-1+j-i,i} + D_{t-j,j}\right\}.$$

(6.18)

Considerable algebra shows that (6.18) can be rewritten as

$$I_t = R_{t-1,1}B_{t-1}^m + \sum_{j=1}^{K-1}\left[(1 + R_{t,j})^{-j} - \frac{1 + R_{t-1,1}}{(1 + R_{t-1,j+1})^{j+1}}\right]\sum_{i=j}^{K-1}D_{t-i,i+j}.$$

(6.19)

So, $B_t^m - B_{t-1}^m = I_t - X_t - (M_t - M_{t-1})$ if, and only if, the government's measure of interest payments corresponds to (6.19). This measure of interest payments is the one-period interest rate at time $t - 1$, $R_{t-1,1}$, times the market value of the debt at the end of period $t - 1$, B_{t-1}^m, *plus* a capital loss term that results from any change in the market holding period yields that are relevant in valuing preexisting debt that matures at date $t + 1$ or later.

As before, $B_t^b - B_{t-1}^b = G_t - A_t$ if $B_t^b = G_t + B_{t-1}^b - A_t$, or

$$\sum_{j=1}^{K}\sum_{i=j}^{K}(1 + R_{t+j-i,i})^{-i}D_{t+j-i,i} = \sum_{j=1}^{K}(1 + R_{t,j})^{-j}D_{t,j} + B_{t-1}^b + I_t - \sum_{j=1}^{K}D_{t-j,j}.$$

Using (6.14), one can substitute out B_{t-1}^d and solve for I_t:

$$I_t = \sum_{j=1}^{K} \left[\sum_{i=j}^{K} (1 + R_{t+j-i,i})^{-i} D_{t+j-i,i} - (1 + R_{t,j})^{-j} D_{t,j} \right.$$

$$\left. + D_{t-j,j} - \sum_{i=j}^{K} (1 + R_{t-1+j-i,i})^{-i} D_{t-1+j-i,i} \right].$$

Considerable algebra shows that this can be simplified considerably:

$$I_t = \sum_{j=1}^{K} [(1 + R_{t-j,j})^j - 1] \frac{D_{t-j,j}}{(1 + R_{t-j,j})^j}. \tag{6.20}$$

So, $B_t^b - B_{t-1}^b = I_t - X_t - (M_t - M_{t-1})$ if, and only if, the government's measure of interest payments corresponds to (6.20). As in the case of two-period debt, this measure of interest payments takes the book value of the payments being made at time t—that is, $D_{t-j,j}/(1 + R_{t-j,j})^j$—and computes the accumulated book interest on these amounts given the periods over which the funds were borrowed.

Relevance of Debt and Interest Measures

From the point of view of computing debt dynamics, it is likely that B_t^b is the relevant measure. Why? Largely because it is likely that government accounting methods are consistent with the definition of B_t^b in (6.14) and the definition of I_t given in (6.20). Thus, as long as these definitions are used consistently, the identity (6.3) will hold, at least up to any measurement error.

However, to calculate B_t^m using the definition in (6.13) requires that a sophisticated and active market for government debt exists, thus enabling the evaluation of the interest rate components of the formula. Frequently such markets do not exist, and governments rarely publish up-to-date revaluations of their own debt stocks, consistent with (6.13). Furthermore, it is unlikely that the government will use a definition of interest payments, such as (6.19), which includes a capital loss term that marks the government's future debt payments to market.

Nonetheless, from the point of view of theory, the market-value-based measure of debt is the most relevant one. It is straightforward to demonstrate this in a finite horizon example. Suppose that the final period in which the government exists is period T. In this case, because the government cannot issue new debt in period T, its time T budget constraint is

$$\sum_{j=1}^{K} D_{T-j,j} = X_T + M_T - M_{T-1}.$$

The government must retire its debt obligations by running a sufficiently large primary balance inclusive of seigniorage revenue. The market value of the government's debt at time $T-1$ is

$$B^m_{T-1} = \frac{\sum_{j=1}^{K} D_{T-j,j}}{1 + R_{T-1,1}}.$$

Hence,

$$B^m_{T-1} = \frac{X_T + M_T - M_{T-1}}{1 + R_{T-1,1}},$$

so that a simple version of the present value budget constraint holds for the market-value-based measure of debt.

However, the book value of debt is

$$B^b_{T-1} = \sum_{j=1}^{K} \frac{D_{T-j,j}}{(1 + R_{T-j,j})^j}.$$

Quite clearly, a simple version of the present-value budget constraint does not hold for the book value of debt. There is a discount factor $\bar{R}$ for which

$$B^b_{T-1} = \frac{X_T + M_T - M_{T-1}}{1 + \bar{R}}.$$

But $\bar{R}$ is a nonlinear average of the book yields on the government's debt:

$$1 + \bar{R} = \frac{\sum_{j=1}^{K} D_{T-j,j}}{\sum_{j=1}^{K}(1 + R_{T-j,j})^{-j} D_{T-j,j}}.$$

7   Conclusion

This chapter introduced several tools used in fiscal sustainability analysis. The simplest tool was explained first: the long-run version of the government's lifetime budget constraint. This tool links the size of the primary balance the government must run to maintain fiscal sustainability to the size of its debt, the flow of seigniorage it raises, the real interest rate, and the real growth rate. After modifying this tool to account for the fact that governments often set fiscal goals that go beyond mere sustainability, examples showed that the first tool can be used to calculate the primary balance needed to achieve a specific, quantitative, debt target.

Section 3 explored related statistical tests for fiscal sustainability, and argued that these tests are more useful for examining historical data than for projecting the future.

Section 4 introduced the concept of debt dynamics and showed how these can be used to analyze historical changes in a country's public debt. Section 5 showed how debt dynamics can be adapted to assess the future sustainability of a government's finances.

Finally, section 6 addressed a number of complex issues related to the measurement of debt. It was argued that if one is working with historical data, then it is most likely that the debt and interest payment series are based on book values. As long as this is true, the budget constraints used in the analysis presented here should be valid for both multi-period and single-period debt. However, it was also argued that market-value-based measures of debt are the most relevant ones when working with theoretical models of the government's lifetime budget constraint.

Notes

1. If, contrary to this assumption, $r < g$, the economy is dynamically inefficient. For a discussion of dynamic inefficiency and its implications for fiscal sustainability, see Blanchard and Weil (2001).

   An alternative interpretation of (1.6) when assumptions 1 through 3 do not hold is as follows: Defining $\bar{r}$ as the average future value of $(r - g_t)/(1 + g_t)$, notice that $\bar{x} + \bar{\sigma}$ can be interpreted as the annuity value of the right-hand side of (1.4), using $\bar{r}$ as the annuity rate.

   Readers should also note that the asymmetry with which r and g enter the expression for $\bar{r}$ is an artifact of the use of discrete time in this analysis. In continuous-time models, $\bar{r} = r - g$.

2. At the time, euro-area inflation rates had been in the low single-digit range: In 2000–1 inflation in the euro area was about 3 percent and was expected to average about 2 percent in 2002–3.

3. At the time, the government targeted a higher growth rate on the order of 5 to 6 percent.

4. Some readers will be familiar with the fact that Bulgaria's fixed exchange rate is supported by a currency board arrangement. Under a currency board, reserve money is backed with foreign assets. This does not have any direct implications for the government budget constraint; equation (1.1) still holds, but the budget constraint does have implications for the government's debt composition. In particular, more reserve money implies greater holdings of liquid foreign assets by the consolidated public sector. In this sense, seigniorage is a revenue source that is tied to a particular use—the acquisition of foreign assets. This issue aside, seigniorage is still a revenue source for the public sector.

5. This expression simplifies considerably in a continuous-time framework, reducing to $\bar{\sigma} = (\pi + g)\bar{m}$.

6. In 2002 and 2003, Bulgaria's primary balance ended up averaging 2.15 percent of GDP, yet Bulgaria achieved the 60 percent debt target by the end of 2002. This was due to the fortuitous depreciation of the U.S. dollar against the euro. With the lev pegged to the euro, and the depreciation of the dollar, Bulgaria benefited from significant revaluation effects. Revaluation effects are discussed in sections 4 and 5.

7. Extensions of Hamilton and Flavin's approach, and other variations on statistical tests of the lifetime budget constraint, include Trehan and Walsh (1988, 1991), Wilcox (1989), Hakkio and Rush (1991), Haug (1991), Ahmed and Rogers (1995), Bohn (1995), Quintos (1995), and Martin (2000). For statistical work related to the fiscal theory of the price level, see Bohn (1998) and Canzoneri, Cumby, and Diba (2001).

8. Section 6 shows that if the market value of the government's debt is used in defining B_t, then (3.1) only holds exactly if I_t is defined using an accounting procedure that takes into account capital gains or losses on debt. Since this procedure is unlikely to be used in practice, an error term must be added to (3.3).

9. Their model is the same one considered in chapter 2 of this volume, with the additional feature of uncertainty with regard to future money supplies.

10. Alternatively, one could decompose $-z_t\bar{b}_{t-1}/(1 + z_t)$ into three terms: $-\pi_t\bar{b}_{t-1}/(1 + \pi_t)$, $-g_t\bar{b}_{t-1}/(1 + g_t)$, and $-\pi_t g_t\bar{b}_{t-1}/(1 + z_t)$, and call the last term the interaction term.

11. See World Bank (2003).

12. If the economy began to grow faster, the $\bar{r}$ term in the fiscal sustainability condition would become smaller.

13. Another possibility is a conceptual mismatch between table 3.5, which presents the fiscal accounts of the nonfinancial public sector, and table 3.4, where the measure of debt includes government-backed debt taken on by public sector banks.

14. From 1973 to 2000, the average depreciation of the deutsche mark/euro against the U.S. dollar was close to zero, while the standard deviation of the rate of depreciation was about 12.8 percent, with a moderate degree of serial correlation (0.28).

15. As it happens, Bulgaria's debt position benefited from the euro's 16 percent appreciation against the dollar in 2002, and more rapid economic growth than assumed in the baseline projection—so that the 60 percent debt target was met in one year. This occurred only in 10 percent of the simulations used to generate table 3.7.

References

Ahmed, Shaghil, and John Rogers. 1995. "Government Budget Deficits and Trade Deficits: Are Present Value Constraints Satisfied in Long-Term Data?" *Journal of Monetary Economics* 36 (2): 351–74.

Argentina Ministry of Economy and Production (Republica Argentina, Ministerio de Economía y Producción). 2004. Macroeconomic Statistics Database. http://www.mecon.gov.ar/peconomica/basehome/infoecoing.html.

Blanchard, Olivier, and Philippe Weil. 2001. "Dynamic Efficiency, the Riskless Rate, and Debt Ponzi Games under Uncertainty." *Advances in Macroeconomics* 1 (2): Article 3.

Bohn, Henning. 1995. "The Sustainability of Budget Deficits in a Stochastic Economy." *Journal of Money, Credit, and Banking* 27 (1): 257–71.

———. 1998. "The Behavior of U.S. Public Debt and Deficits." *Quarterly Journal of Economics* 113 (3): 949–63.

Cagan, Phillip. 1956. "Monetary Dynamics of Hyperinflation." In Milton Friedman, ed. *Studies in the Quantity Theory of Money*. Chicago: University of Chicago Press.

Canzoneri, Matthew, Robert Cumby, and Bezhad Diba. 2001. "Is the Price Level Determined by the Needs of Fiscal Solvency?" *American Economic Review* 91 (5): 1221–38.

Central Bank of the Argentine Republic (Banco Central de la Republica Argentina). 2004. Statistics Database. http://www.bcra.gov.ar.

3

Diba, Behzad T., and Herschel I. Grossman. 1984. "Rational Bubbles in the Price of Gold." NBER Working Paper 1300, National Bureau of Economic Research, Cambridge, MA.

Dickey, David A., and Wayne A. Fuller. 1979. "Distribution of the Estimators for Autoregressive Time Series with a Unit Root." *Journal of the American Statistical Association* 74 (366): 427–31.

Flood, Robert P., and Peter M. Garber. 1980. "Market Fundamentals versus Price Level Bubbles: The First Tests." *Journal of Political Economy* 88 (4): 745–70.

Hakkio, Craig S., and Mark Rush. 1991. "Is the Budget Deficit Too Large?" *Economic Inquiry* 29 (3): 429–45.

Hamilton, James D., and Marjorie A. Flavin. 1986. "On the Limitations of Government Borrowing: A Framework for Empirical Testing." *American Economic Review* 76 (4): 808–19.

Hamilton, James D., and Charles H. Whiteman. 1985. "The Observable Implications of Self-Fulfilling Expectations." *Journal of Monetary Economics* 16 (3): 353–73.

Haug, Alfred A. 1991. "Cointegration and Government Borrowing Constraints: Evidence for the United States." *Journal of Business and Economic Statistics* 9 (1): 97–101.

IMF (International Monetary Fund). 1998. "Turkey: Recent Economic Developments and Selected Issues." IMF Staff Country Report 98/104, IMF, Washington, DC.

———. 2000. "Turkey: Selected Issues and Statistical Appendix." IMF Staff Country Report 00/14, IMF, Washington, DC.

———. 2001. "Turkey: Sixth and Seventh Reviews under the Stand-By Arrangement— Staff Supplement; and Press Release on the Executive Board Discussion." IMF Country Report 01/89, IMF, Washington, DC.

———. 2002. "Turkey: Tenth Review under the Stand-By Arrangement— Staff Report; and News Brief on the Executive Board Discussion." IMF Country Report 02/21, IMF, Washington, DC.

———. 2003. "Turkey: Fifth Review under the Stand-By Arrangement, Request for Waiver of Performance Criteria and Extension of Repurchase Expectations—Staff Supplement; and Press Release on the Executive Board Discussion." IMF Country Report 03/324, IMF, Washington, DC.

———. 2004. "Turkey: Seventh Review under the Stand-By Arrangement, Requests for Waiver of Applicability and Nonobservance of Performance

3

Criteria, Rephasing of Purchases, and Extension of Arrangement—Staff Report; and Press Release on the Executive Board Discussion." IMF Country Report 04/227, IMF, Washington, DC.

Martin, Gael M. 2000. "U.S. Deficit Sustainability: A New Approach Based on Multiple Endogenous Breaks." *Journal of Applied Econometrics* 15 (1): 83–105.

Quintos, Carmela E. 1995. "Sustainability of the Deficit Process with Structural Shifts." *Journal of Business and Economic Statistics* 13 (4): 409–17.

Trehan, Bharat, and Carl E. Walsh. 1988. "Common Trends, the Government Budget Constraint, and Revenue Smoothing." *Journal of Economic Dynamics and Control* 12 (2–3): 425–44.

———. 1991. "Testing Intertemporal Budget Constraints: Theory and Applications to U.S. Federal Budget and Current Account Deficits." *Journal of Money, Credit, and Banking* 23 (2): 206–23.

Wilcox, David W. 1989. "The Sustainability of Government Deficits: Implications of the Present-Value Borrowing Constraint." *Journal of Money, Credit, and Banking* 21 (3): 291–306.

World Bank. 2003. "Turkey Country Economic Memorandum: Toward Macroeconomic Stability and Sustained Growth." Report No. 26301-TU, World Bank, Washington, DC.

3

Chapter 4

81- 112

(LDC, CEEC)

Debt and Debt Indicators in the Measurement of Vulnerability

Punam Chuhan

H63

F34 P35

4

The debt crises of the 1980s and 1990s, as well as more recent crises, suggest that the origins of repayment problems vary greatly across countries. While causal links are not unambiguously established in theory, it is clear that certain macroeconomic indicators should be associated with the underlying causes. Thus, most empirical studies of debt problems look for statistical characterizations of payment difficulties. The idea is to identify standard economic indicators that provide insights to crises or that can predict ex ante payment difficulties and even defaults. The objective of this chapter is to present debt concepts and issues in the measurement of debt, review standard debt indicators that are used in measuring external vulnerability to shocks, and discuss the salient aspects of a framework for assessing external debt sustainability in a comprehensive way.

1   Definition and Measurement of Debt

Debt allows for the intertemporal smoothing of consumption over time. At any one point in time, some economic agents in an economy will have income in excess of their current consumption and investment needs, while other economic agents will have inadequate income. Through lending and borrowing activities, both sets of economic agents can smooth out their consumption over time. Thus, the creation of debt helps to improve welfare.

Debt in a Closed Economy

Government (or public) and household (or private) saving and debt in a closed economy can be illustrated by the budget constraints facing these entities. As shown in chapter 2, in a simplified model of the closed economy, the government flow budget constraint is

$$B_t - B_{t-1} = i_t B_{t-1} - (T_t - G_t) - (M_t - M_{t-1}),$$

where B is government debt stock, T is tax revenue, G is government noninterest expenditure, M is monetary base (or high powered money), i is the nominal interest rate, and t is time. This equation is an accounting identity and simply states that the government finances any gap between its revenues and expenditures and its obligations through debt financing $(B_t - B_{t-1})$ or seigniorage revenues $(M_t - M_{t-1})$. For presentation purposes, one can assume that tax and nontax revenues such as seigniorage are included in T, so that the above equation can be rewritten as

$$B_t - B_{t-1} = i_t B_{t-1} - (T_t - G_t). \tag{1.1}$$

Rearranging (1.1) one obtains

$$B_{t-1} = (1 + i_t)^{-1} B_t + (1 + i_t)^{-1}(T_t - G_t). \tag{1.2}$$

The flow budget constraint can be used to derive the government's lifetime budget constraint by iterating forward on (1.2) and imposing the transversality condition that in the limit the discounted value of government debt is zero. Thus, the budget constraint expressed in real terms is

$$b_{t-1} = \sum_{i=0}^{\infty} (1 + r)^{-(i+1)} ps_{t+i}. \tag{1.3}$$

The variable b is real debt, r is the real interest rate (assumed to be constant), and ps is the real primary surplus. The lifetime budget constraint simply states that the government finances any initial debt obligation through running primary surpluses, and that the present value of these surpluses is equal to the initial debt outstanding. The implication of the lifetime budget constraint is that if the government runs primary deficits today, in the future it will have to run primary surpluses that are larger than today's deficits.[1]

The household budget constraint in this simple closed-economy model is

$$A_t - A_{t-1} = i_t A_{t-1} + (Y_t - C_{pt} - T_t), \qquad (1.4)$$

where A represents financial assets of households, Y is income, and C_p is private consumption. The change in assets represents household savings.[2] Rearranging (1.4), one obtains

$$A_{t-1} = (1 + i_t)^{-1}A_t - (1 + i_t)^{-1}(Y_t - C_{pt} - T_t). \qquad (1.5)$$

The household's lifetime budget constraint can be derived in an analogous way to that of the government

$$a_{t-1} = -\sum_{i=0}^{\infty}(1 + r)^{-(i+1)}s_{t+i}. \qquad (1.6)$$

In (1.6), s is the real value of income less consumption and taxes or real savings net of interest receipts. The lifetime budget constraint simply states that the household's present value of dissavings equals the initial amount of its outstanding assets. The implication of the lifetime budget constraint is that if the household saves today, it will dissave in the future.

Debt in an Open Economy

In an open economy, residents of a country can borrow resources from or lend resources to the rest of the world. Through international borrowing and lending, an economy can smooth consumption over time—and the economy's current consumption need not be tied to its current output. When an economy borrows, it accumulates external debt; that is, it incurs a contractual obligation to make future payments to the rest of the world. When an economy provides savings to the rest of the world, it accumulates assets.

In an open economy, the country's budget constraint is given by the external accounts, or current account balance (CAB). The external accounts provide the framework for showing the relationship between the investment and spending decisions of the economy and the change in the gross external debt. If a country spends more (or less) than its national income, it will accumulate net debt (or assets). The link between the fiscal deficit and the current account can be illustrated with the basic flow of funds accounts.[3] From the national income and product accounts, gross domestic product (GDP) is

$$GDP = C + I + X - M,$$

where C is the sum of private consumption (C_p) and public consumption (C_g), I is the sum of private investment (I_p) and public investment (I_g), and $X - M$ is the trade balance or balance on goods and nonfactor services. Adding net foreign factor income (Y_f) and net transfers from abroad (Y_{tran}) to GDP gives the country's national income, Y.

$$Y = C + I + X - M + Y_f + Y_{tran}. \tag{1.7}$$

$X - M + Y_f + Y_{tran}$ is the CAB (or the difference between a country's savings and investments); that is, it represents foreign savings. If a country is saving more than it is investing in the domestic economy, then it is net investing overseas and the CAB will be positive; if the country is saving less than it is investing in the domestic economy, then it is receiving net savings from overseas and the CAB will be negative.

Equation (1.7) can be expressed in terms of savings (S) and investment as

$$Y - C - I = S_p + S_g - I = S_p - I + (T - G) = CAB, \tag{1.8}$$

where $S_p = Y - C_g - T$ is private sector saving and $S_g = T - G$ is public sector saving. The accounting identity (1.8) clearly shows the link between the fiscal budget and the current account. The fiscal deficit and the current account deficit are often referred to as "twin deficits," because there are historical periods when these two deficits have tended to move together.[4] It can be seen that if private savings and investment change by the same amount, then the other two terms would move in similar ways.

Since savings and investment decisions are based on intertemporal determinants, it follows that the current account is an "intertemporal phenomenon."[5] The relationships between external debt and the balance of payments on one hand, and between the size of debt and income on the other, are central to debt analysis and its sustainability.[6] The current account is used to derive the debt dynamics and the debt sustainability conditions in section 4.

It is useful to note that a current account deficit can be financed by net foreign borrowing—that is, net debt issuance, nondebt capital flows such as foreign direct investment (FDI) and portfolio equity investment, and by a change in foreign exchange reserves (FXR). The movement of the CAB determines the net financial claims position of the country with respect to the rest of the world. Lane and Milesi-Ferretti (2001) use the balance of payments accounting framework to measure the net foreign asset position of an economy (NFA) as

$$\text{NFA} = \text{FDI(assets)} + \text{Portfolio Equity(assets)} + \text{Debt(assets)}$$
$$+ \text{FXR} - \text{FDI(liabilities)} - \text{Portfolio Equity(Liabilities)}$$
$$- \text{Debt (liabilities)}.$$

Definition of Debt

Simply put then, external debt is the amount of outstanding current financial liabilities that the residents of an economy owe in the aggregate to non-residents and which will require payment of principal and/or interest at some point in the future.[7] One can distinguish between gross external debt and net external debt. Net external debt is debt liabilities less debt assets. The financial instruments that are included in debt liabilities are summarized in box 4.1. These include debt securities (bonds, notes, and money market instruments), loans, trade credits, currency and deposits, and other liabilities, including financial leases and lending between direct investors and related subsidiaries.

Contingent liabilities and derivatives are not debt liabilities, but these instruments have important bearing on the vulnerability of a country to external shocks. By assigning certain rights or obligations that may be exercised in the future, contingent liabilities can have a financial impact on the economic entities involved. Conventional balance sheets do not capture

---

Box 4.1: Debt Instruments

Debt securities
  Bonds and notes
  Money market instruments
Loans
Trade credits
Other capital liabilities to direct investors
Currency and deposits
Other liabilities

Source: IMF (1993).

off-balance sheet items, making it difficult to accurately assess the financial position of a country with regard to nonresidents. Thus, analysis of the macroeconomic vulnerability of an economy to external shocks requires information on both external direct obligations and contingent liabilities. Moreover, there is an increasing realization that the implications of contingent liabilities of the government and the central bank are significant for assessing macroeconomic conditions. For example, fiscal contingent claims can clearly have an impact on budget deficits and financing needs, with implications for economic policy.

Although financial derivatives are financial liabilities, they are not included in debt. Financial derivatives are instruments that are linked to specific financial instruments or indicators and derive their value from the price of the underlying asset. Specific financial risks are traded through derivatives, and these instruments are widely used for hedging financial positions as well as taking open positions (through speculative and arbitrage activities). Derivatives are different from debt instruments in that, when the derivative is created, no principal amount is advanced that need be repaid and no interest is earned over time. However, these instruments can add to the liabilities of an economy; and if derivatives are not managed appropriately, they can exacerbate the external vulnerability of an economy.[8]

Measurement of Debt

Valuation and accounting methodology are important issues in the measurement of debt. Debt liabilities can be valued at nominal or market value. And as is so often the case when there are different measurements, the right measurement depends on the particular question being addressed. The nominal value of a debt claim is the amount that is owed to the creditor by the debtor. For practical purposes, this is the amount that the debtor would at this instant have to pay the creditor to cancel the debt contract. This amount is measured as the initial value of the debt instrument when it is contracted and the effect of subsequent transactions (payments) and treatments (restructurings, debt reduction) to the debt. This measure incorporates valuation changes other than market price movements in the debt instrument. The common practice is to measure debt at nominal value, especially for nontraded financial instruments. Nominal valuation principles also underlie the standard debt indicators that are used in the analysis of debt sustainability. The market value of a debt instrument, however, represents the value that economic agents assign to the liability and reflects market conditions and expectations at that point in time. The concept of market valuation is more relevant for traded instruments as opposed to non-traded instruments. One point to bear in mind in using market valuation is that this approach will underreport the amount of contractual obligations of a country when a country's debt is impaired.

Another issue that arises in the measurement of debt has to do with the accounting methodology used for the treatment of accrued interest. In an accrual method of measuring debt, interest that is accrued in a period but is not yet payable or due adds to the value of debt. This approach presents the amount of liabilities from an economic instead of a payment perspective: Interest is the cost of capital, and it accrues continuously, adding to the amount of debt. There is a corresponding reduction in the value of debt when the interest is paid off. In a cash-based approach to measuring debt, only actual cash flows affect debt stock.[9]

Table 4.1 presents the valuation, accounting, and residency principles that underlie the debt (assets for the IMF's International Investment Position, or IIP) statistics that are in common use and are produced by the Bank for International Settlements (BIS), International Monetary Fund (IMF), Organisation for Economic Co-operation and Development (OECD), and the World Bank. Variations in valuation and accounting methodology explain some of the observed differences in statistics from these sources.

Data problems may complicate the accurate measurement of a country's net asset position, including its net debt position. For example, it is well

Table 4.1: Core Principles in the Measurement of Debt

Measurement principle	BIS	IMF-IIP	OECD	WB-DRS
Valuation				
Nominal	X		X	X
Market		X		
Accounting				
Cash basis	X		X	X
Accrual basis		X		
Residency	X	X	X	X
Currency				
Foreign and local	X	X	X	
Foreign				X

Source: Author's compilation.

Notes: "X" indicates the principle that applies to the measurement of debt. WB-DRS, World Bank's Debtor Reporting System.

4

known that developing country debt assets are underestimated because of capital flight. Although IMF efforts to strengthen the reporting of asset positions through the International Investment Position database should help to improve the availability and quality of statistics on a country's external balance sheet (its financial assets and liabilities), problems remain in compiling data on private sector investment positions. Moreover, not all countries participate in the IIP. Researchers have attempted to improve statistics on assets and liabilities by using balance of payments data. Thus, one way to correct for the underestimation of debt assets is to count errors and omissions as representing additions to debt assets. Lane and Milesi-Ferretti (2001) measure the net asset position and its various components by cumulating the current account balances over a long period and adjusting for unrecorded capital flight, exchange rate fluctuations, debt reduction schemes, and other valuation changes.[10]

2   Debt Analysis and Standard Indicators of Indebtedness

When economic entities borrow, they incur contractual obligations to pay in the future. If a debtor has insufficient income or assets to meet its contractual obligations, then debt problems occur. The debt problems of an economic entity such as a firm can be assessed by examining its ability to pay based on its balance sheet (assets and liabilities) and current and prospective cash flows. While debt problems of firms can be assessed merely from an ability to pay aspect, the debt problems of an economy cannot. The solvency of an economy (or government) depends on both a willingness to pay and the ability to pay. Thus, the debt problems of an economy need to be considered from the standpoints of liquidity, solvency, and willingness to pay.

Debt Payment Problems: Liquidity and Solvency

Because an economy is different from a firm, analysis of its debt problems requires different considerations. An economy faces a liquidity problem when its debt liabilities coming due in a given period exceed its liquid foreign currency assets, including funds that it has borrowed from overseas. That is, an economy may face a cash flow problem, even though it may be solvent in the long run. Liquidity problems generally emerge when there is a sudden change in investor sentiment that results either in a sharp stop or reversal of capital flows from nonresidents or in intensified capital flight by residents. Consequently, the economy is unable to meet its immediate external obligations. An economy's vulnerability to an external liquidity crisis is affected by the maturity structure, interest, and currency composition of its debt. A solvency problem, by contrast, is when the economy may never be able to service its debt out of its own resources. Thus, the discounted sum of current and future trade balances is generally considered to be less than its current outstanding debt.[11] A solvency problem implies that the balance of payments is unsustainable over the medium- to long-term horizon. While a solvency problem will generally be associated with a liquidity problem, it is possible for a liquidity problem to arise independently of a solvency problem. And although it is possible to draw a distinction between illiquidity and solvency in theory, it may be difficult to distinguish between these two phenomena on the basis of observable consequences.

A country may decide to stop servicing its debt well before it is insolvent. Since debt service payments reduce current income and reduce welfare, a country may be able to improve welfare by repudiating its debt—or by not meeting its current obligations. In fact, it is the size of the net welfare loss from defaulting that determines the threshold of payments before countries default. If a sovereign could default without consequences, it presumably would. Since, in practice, sovereigns typically try to avoid defaults, there must be penalties for default.[12] Economic models of default include penalties such as restricted access to credit or market closure, seizure of overseas assets, and trade interruptions that can result in loss of output. Indeed, private foreign lending relies on the threat of output losses as an incentive for repayment (or a deterrent to default).[13]

Debt Ratios as Measures of External Vulnerability

From the debt crises of the 1980s and 1990s, it is clear that the origins of repayment problems vary greatly across countries. Emerging market debt crises can be categorized into old-style and new-style crises. Krugman (1979) labeled the old-style-type crises as "first-generation" crises. These crises are the result of inconsistent fiscal policies that give rise to excessive domestic debt creation, widening trade imbalances, run down of reserves, and large devaluations. The 1990s crises, including the Mexican crisis of 1994 and the East Asian crisis of 1997, represented different types of phenomena. Economists developed second- and third-generation crisis models to explain these events. Second-generation models suggest that for a given set of fundamentals, multiple equilibria are possible. Thus, it is possible for a country with strong macroeconomic policies to be affected by crisis and move into a bad equilibrium. Third-generation models argue that problems in the structure of a country's financial system or balance sheet can lead to severe crises.

Although the origins of payments problems vary, there is a common factor observed in these crises, and that is insufficient foreign exchange inflows to finance current account deficits.[14] Since payment difficulties are manifested in the balance of payments, systematic relations between macroeconomic variables and payment difficulties might be expected. Indeed, the empirical literature on creditworthiness shows some evidence of this. Studies covering earlier periods of debt crisis—such as those by Frank and Cline (1971), Grinols (1976), and Sargen (1977) using discriminant analyses; and by Cline (1983), Feder and Just (1977), Feder, Just, and Ross (1981), and Mayo and Barrett (1978) using logit analyses—find macroeconomic indicators that are correlated with payment problems. The idea is to identify standard economic indicators that are associated with crises so they can be used to predict ex ante payments difficulties and even defaults. While the results of these studies are consistent with what macroeconomic theory might suggest (certain factors should be important in predicting debt defaults), one must be cautious in interpreting these as causal or even leading (rather than coincident) indicators of payment difficulties (see table 4.2)

More recent studies of currency and financial crises find that a broad set of indicators can be useful in anticipating crises.[15] Kaminsky, Lizondo, and Reinhart (1998) find that out of 17 empirical studies that quantitatively tested for the most useful indicators in predicting a crisis, international reserve movements and real exchange changes were among the most useful. Other important indicators included export behavior, output performance, and the fiscal deficit. Some of their results are summarized in table 4.3.

The indicators identified by earlier studies and, more recently, by the literature on currency and financial crises, are widely used in assessing an economy's debt situation and the exposure to debt-related risks (liquidity and solvency risk). The indicators are used in both a static (point-in-time)

Table 4.2: Significant Macroeconomic Correlates of Repayment Crises in Developing Countries

Variable	Frank-Cline (1971)	Grinols (1976)	Feder-Just-Ross (1981)	Sargen (1977)	Saini-Bates (1978)	Cline (1983)
Debt service/exports	+		+	+		+
Principal service/debt	−					−
Imports/reserves	+		+			+
Debt/GDP		+				
Debt/exports		+		+		+
Debt service/reserves		+				
GNP per capita			−			
Foreign exchange inflows/debt service			−			
Current account/exports						−
Exports/GNP			−			
Rate of domestic inflation				+		
Growth rate of money supply					+	
Growth rate of reserves					−	−
Growth rate of GNP per capita						−
Total borrowing/imports						−

Source: McFadden and others (1985).

Notes: "+" indicates a positive correlation between an indicator and a payment crisis; "−" indicates a negative correlation.

and dynamic (intertemporal) context. Although these indicators can give useful information about ability to pay, no one indicator provides information on all the dimensions of a payment problem. Moreover, critical debt levels are likely to vary from country to country, as well as over time. So indicators must be accompanied by comprehensive economic evaluation. For example, Reinhart, Rogoff, and Savastano (2003) find that the "safe" debt to GNP threshold for countries that have experienced a series of defaults is much lower than that for industrial countries. Clearly, this type of debt intolerance has implications for the analysis of debt sustainability, as countries with serial defaults are likely to experience market closure at much lower levels of debt to GNP than other countries. Similarly, the debt-burden thresholds that have been established under the heavily indebted poor countries (HIPC) framework to determine sustainability may have less applicability for non-HIPCs.[16]

Table 4.3: Performance of Selected Economic Indicators in 17 Empirical Studies of Currency Crises

Indicator	Number of studies in which the economic variable was considered	Statistically significant results
Capital account variables		
International reserves	12	11
Short-term capital flows	2	1
Foreign direct investment	2	2
Capital account balance	1	
Domestic-foreign interest differential	2	1
Debt profile		
External debt	2	
Public debt	1	
Share of commercial bank loans	1	2
Share of concessional loans	2	2
Share of variable rate debt	2	
Share of short-term debt	2	
Share of multilateral development bank debt	1	
Current account		
Real exchange rate	14	12
Current account balance	7	2
Trade balance	3	2
Exports	3	2
Imports	2	1
International		
Foreign interest rates	4	2
Real sector		
Inflation	5	5
Real GDP growth or level	9	5
Fiscal		
Fiscal deficit	5	3

Source: Adapted from Kaminsky, Lizondo, and Reinhart (1998).

Note: Based on 17 empirical studies that tested the usefulness of indicators in predicting a crisis.

Standard indicators that help to identify debt-related risks fall into two broad categories: flow indicators and stock indicators. Flow indicators are scaled on flow variables, typically gross domestic income or exports (and sometimes government revenue). From an intertemporal perspective, these variables represent the resources that are available to meet debt obligations. Flow indicators, especially GDP-based ones, may thus be useful in assessing solvency problems, since a solvency problem implies that an economy may never be able to service its debt out of its own resources. Stock indicators are based on stock variables (like reserves) and tend to reflect availability of liquidity.[17]

Solvency and Debt-Service Indicators

One type of widely used flow indicator relates debt service to resources that are available to meet these obligations, namely, gross domestic product (GDP) and exports. This type of indicator is useful for evaluating both solvency and liquidity risk. While debt service technically includes amortization and interest payments on all debt, in practice only amortization payments on long-term debt are included. The assumption is that short-term debt is normally rolled over. Recent episodes of financial crises have shown that countries subjected to sudden downgrades in investor sentiment have had difficulty rolling over short-term debt as well. Moreover, the larger the share of short-term claims in total claims, the weaker is this variable as a measure of vulnerability. Therefore, a more comprehensive measure of debt service should include all amortizations.

Another limitation of the standard practice of measuring debt service is that it uses the concept of debt service paid (cash basis) instead of debt service due. If a country is current in its obligations, the two concepts are the same. But if a country is in arrears on its debt payments, the debt service paid concept undercounts the true obligation. Thus, debt service due is a better measure than debt service paid. Estimating debt service due is complicated, however, by debt instruments with put options. For example, if a bond has a put option, it is difficult to know whether or not the option will be exercised.[18] Since this is not known with certainty, one way to value the option is at full nominal value. Admittedly, this is a simplistic approach, and alternative methods of valuing the option may be available from finance theory. For example, consider a put on a bond with a nominal value of F, and let the underlying value of the asset (bond) on which the put is based be V. If the value of the asset is less than the nominal value ($V - F < 0$), then the put option is exercised and the lender receives the exercise price of F. The value of the put option is $F - V$. When $V > F$, the option is not exercised.

The debt service-to-GDP indicator is a common measure of vulnerability. Since GDP is the total value added by all the economic units in an economy, it provides a measure of the resources of the economy. Some analysts prefer to use gross national income (GNI) instead of GDP, because the GNI includes net income from abroad and, therefore, is presumably a better measure of the resources that are available to residents for meeting their obligations. Using GDP or GNI as the deflator in this indicator has some limitations. Most important among these is the impact of "excessively" large, yet temporary, exchange rate movements on the nominal values of these variables. One way to overcome this valuation problem is to use a three-year average of GDP or GNI.[19]

Debt service to exports is another common indicator for external vulnerability. Using an export-based indicator as a measure of external vulnerability may have some disadvantages. For example, with more open economies, higher exports are often accompanied by higher imports. Moreover, the import content of exports is also higher. If exports are unadjusted for import intensity, the debt service-to-exports indicator will be more favorable and underestimate the extent of vulnerability of the economy. Again, with the growing importance of regional trading blocks and free trade agreements, the vulnerability of a country's exports to common shocks to the trading block and country-specific shocks to members of the trading arrangement are likely to be more pronounced.[20] One possibility is to exclude the component of exports that is highly sensitive to such shocks.

Solvency and Debt-Level Indicators

Another type of widely used flow indicator relates the level of external debt to GDP and to exports. This type of indicator is closely related to the repayment capacity of a country and is used for evaluating solvency risk. For example, a rising debt-to-GDP ratio signals that the rate of growth of debt exceeds the growth rate of the economy, and if this continues the country might then have difficulty in meeting its future debt obligations. Again, a higher debt-to-exports ratio indicates a larger amount of resources needed to service obligations. This, in turn, implies increased vulnerability to the balance of payments and larger repudiation risk.

The debt-level indicators use either gross nominal debt or the present value of debt. In countries with high foreign assets, net debt (gross debt minus assets) may be a more appropriate variable to use instead of gross debt. When assets are used to offset debt in this way, the quality of assets is a central factor. Most important, assets should be liquid so that they can be sold at low transactions costs when needed; and they should be able to generate income.[21] International reserve assets, which are controlled by the monetary authorities, are usually the most liquid foreign assets available to an economy. Bank foreign-exchange holdings are likely to be liquid as well (although the government may not have a legal basis for borrowing the foreign-exchange holdings for repaying public debt). Also, portfolio assets like bonds and equities, which are tradable, are likely to be fairly liquid. Loans, by contrast, are often nontradable and quite illiquid (unless packaged and resold). Likewise, direct investment is rather illiquid in the short term. If private sector assets are large, then net debt by sector might be a more meaningful way to present net debt information used for assessing vulnerability.

In countries with substantial amounts of concessional debt, the present value of debt is the more appropriate variable. The present value of debt is the sum of the discounted value of all future debt service. The present value of debt is sensitive to the interest rate used to discount future debt service. The higher is this discount rate relative to the contractual interest rate on the debt, the lower the present value of the debt. Debt on highly concessional terms is likely to have a present value of debt much smaller than the nominal value.

Indicators with total debt have many limitations, the most important being that the size of debt to GDP or to exports is likely to be influenced by the stage of development of a country. From economic theory it is known that, in the early stages of development, countries have small stocks of capital. The rates of return on capital in countries at this stage are likely to be higher than returns in other countries. Countries can improve their growth by borrowing funds from overseas for productive investment.[22] Therefore, the debt-level-based indicators are expected to be higher in the early stages of development. Thus, using a debt-level-based indicator without an intertemporal or dynamic context can be misleading. It follows that the trends of the debt-to-GDP and debt-to-exports indicators contain useful information on external vulnerability.

Another drawback of aggregate debt-level indicators is that they do not provide any information on debt structure in terms of maturity, borrower (public or private), creditor, currency, or interest rate composition. All these aspects of debt structure have important implications for vulnerability to external shocks, especially liquidity shocks. Poorly structured debt can heighten or even trigger a financial crisis. In the Asian crisis of 1997, the heavy concentration of debt maturing in the short term was a primary factor in propagating the crisis; and in the debt crisis of the 1980s, the large

4

4

share of debt at variable interest rates in a rising interest rate environment was the most important factor in precipitating the crisis. Thus, measures using the total debt stock (instead of the characteristics of debt) ignore the fact that some debt is more vulnerable to an external shock than others.[23]

Using the present value (PV) of debt resolves only some of the problems of using the total stock of debt. For example, it accounts for concessionality of debt. Since low-income countries are likely to attract concessional financing, using the present value of debt instead of the nominal value is more appropriate for measuring debt burden. However, the computation of present value is sensitive to the interest rate used for discounting the future stream of amortization and interest payments. Since PV-based indicators are sensitive to movements in the discount rate, the value of these indicators can change with interest rate movements—even when the contractual terms of the underlying debt do not. In addition, PV-based indicators are also dependent on forward projections of debt service payments, and data on projected payments are not commonly available.

Liquidity Indicators

Among indicators of liquidity, the ratio of international reserves to short-term debt is perhaps the most useful. It relates the size of international reserves of the monetary authority to the amount of debt coming due within a year, and is an important indicator of liquidity risk. This indicator shows whether the economy has enough foreign exchange reserves to cover the amount of debt that is coming due in the short term.[24] For countries that rely heavily on global capital markets and which tend to be subject to temporary market closures, this reserve adequacy indicator is important in assessing the vulnerability to rollover risk. The risk associated with a relatively large concentration of maturities in the near term relative to reserves can be high, as was evident in the East Asian financial crisis of 1997. The reserve adequacy indicator was low in all the East Asian crisis countries, and liabilities maturing in the short term far exceeded usable foreign exchange reserves.[25]

While clearly useful for countries that rely heavily on global markets, the reserves-to-short-term-debt indicator may not be particularly useful for open economies that have a relatively large amount of short-term trade credits. This is because trade credits are less likely to be withdrawn during a crisis. Another limitation of this indicator is that it does not provide any information on the quality of international reserves. If international reserves are illiquid, then they cannot be used to meet immediate external obligations.

An overview of solvency and liquidity indicators is presented in table 4.4.

Table 4.4: Overview of Debt Indicators

Solvency indicators	
External debt/exports	Useful as a trend indicator, closely related to the repayment capacity of an economy.
External debt/GDP	Relates debt to resource base (including the potential to shift production to exports).
Present value of debt/exports	Key sustainability indicator for HIPC analysis.
Present value of debt/GDP	Key sustainability indicator for HIPC analysis.
Interest service ratio	Indicates terms of external indebtedness and debt burden.
Debt service/exports	Hybrid indicator of solvency and liquidity.
Debt service/GDP	Hybrid indicator of solvency and liquidity.
Liquidity indicators	
Reserves/debt maturing in the short term	Single most important indicator of reserve adequacy in countries with significant but uncertain access to capital markets. Ratio can be predicted forward to assess future vulnerability to liquidity crises.
Short-term debt/total debt	Indicates relative reliance on short-term financing. Together with indicators of maturity structure, allows monitoring of future repayment risk.
Public sector indicators	
Public sector debt service/exports	Useful indicator of willingness to pay and transfer risk.
Public debt/fiscal revenue	Solvency indicator of public sector.
Public sector foreign currency debt/ public debt	Includes foreign currency indexed debt. Indicator of the impact of a change in the exchange rate of debt.
Financial sector indicators	
Open foreign exchange position	Foreign currency assets minus liabilities plus net long positions in foreign currency stemming from off-balance sheet items. Indicator of foreign exchange risk.
Foreign currency maturity mismatch	Foreign currency liabilities minus foreign currency assets as % of these foreign currency assets at given maturities. Indicator for pressure on central bank reserves in case of a cut-off of financial sector from foreign currency funding.
Gross foreign currency liabilities	Useful indicator to the extent assets are not usable to offset withdrawals in liquidity.

Source: Adapted from BIS and others 2003.

Note: HIPC, heavily indebted poor country.

3 Assessing Debt Sustainability

When an economy borrows, it takes on an obligation to make payments in the future. So an issue that arises is whether the economy can meet its contractual obligations, that is, whether it can generate sufficiently large future surpluses in its trade balance to pay off its debt without a significant adjustment in its policy stance. The external budget constraint for a country can be used to derive the external debt dynamics and the sustainability of external debt. Thus,

$$D_{ft} = (1 + i_{ft})\, D_{ft-1} + CA_t, \tag{3.1}$$

where D_f is external debt (both public and private sector) in dollars (foreign currency), i_f is the foreign interest rate on debt, and CA is the noninterest current account, also expressed in dollars. Scaling debt in terms of GDP measured in dollars yields

$$d_{ft} = \frac{(1 + i_{ft})(1 + \delta_t)}{(1 + g_t)(1 + \pi_t)} d_{ft-1} - ca_t, \tag{3.2}$$

where d_f is external debt to GDP, g is the real growth rate of output, π is the inflation rate, δ is the rate of exchange rate depreciation of the local currency, and ca is the noninterest current account over GDP. By rearranging (3.2) and subtracting d_{ft-1} from both sides, one obtains

$$d_{ft} - d_{ft-1} = \frac{(1 + i_{ft})(1 + e_t) - (1 + g_t)}{1 + g_t} d_{ft-1} - ca_t, \tag{3.3}$$

where e_t is the real revaluation effect of the exchange rate, defined as $e_t = (\delta_t - \pi_t)/(1 + \pi_t)$.

Simplifying further,

$$d_{ft} - d_{ft-1} = \frac{r_{ft} - g_t}{1 + g_t} d_{ft-1} - ca_t, \tag{3.4}$$

where $r_{ft} = i_{ft} + e_t + i_{ft}\, e_t$. In (3.4) the larger the differential between the foreign interest rate term and growth rate of the economy (other things constant), the larger the current account surplus needed to stabilize the external debt-to-GDP ratio.

Definition of Debt Sustainability

A country's debt is said to be sustainable if the present value of resource transfers to nonresidents is equal to the value of the initial debt owed to them; that is, the intertemporal budget constraint holds. A country's debt is said to be unsustainable if the discounted sum of current and future trade balances is less than its current outstanding debt with the current policy stance. An alternative way of stating insolvency is that the present value of the sum of future income net of expenditure is less than the initial level of indebtedness. Since government debt often dominates external debt, an external debt problem is frequently one of government debt.

Because an economy may decide to stop servicing its debt well before it is insolvent, assessing the sustainability of its debt can be complex. Debt service payments reduce current account income and reduce welfare, so an economy may be able to improve welfare by repudiating (not servicing) its debt. Thus, there may be limits to the share of output that an economy is politically or socially willing to use toward repaying external debt. Because of potential limits to the adjustment that countries are willing to undertake, a country's debt is said to be sustainable if it can meet its debt obligations without an "excessively" large adjustment in either its balance of income and expenditure or a restructuring of its debt obligations.[26] This concept of sustainability is comparable to the one used for fiscal sustainability in chapters 2 and 3.

The sustainability of an economy's debt and its vulnerability to exogenous shocks should be of keen interest to policymakers and international financial market participants alike. Policymakers' interest in assessing external vulnerabilities is obvious, namely, to enhance macroeconomic management through better anticipation and prevention or minimization of crises. Foreign investors' interest in assessing an economy's creditworthiness is critical to their decisions regarding cross-border flows—investment flows or lending—to the economy. If investors believe that a country's problem is one of liquidity, then they will assume that additional financing is likely to tide the country over its short-term problem. If the problem is viewed as one of insolvency, then debt reduction is likely to be the more appropriate solution (and investors will be reluctant to provide additional financing). Since the early 1980s, groups of emerging market economies have experienced many episodes of international capital market closure; that is, investors were unwilling to roll over amounts coming due or to provide additional financing. Such closures can have potentially large costs to the economy in terms of output and welfare loss.[27]

Evidence from the 1970s to the present indicates that debt payment problems are far from uncommon in emerging market economies. Standard & Poor's September 2002 survey of default episodes finds 84 events of sovereign default on private-source debt between 1975 and 2002 (see annex table A4.1). A default episode is defined as any interruption of contractual debt payments. Therefore, it includes events of nonpayment of interest or principal, or both, along with outright debt repudiation. Over the survey period, episodes of default on external debt outstrip those on domestic debt; and both rated and nonrated sovereign issuers have experienced defaults on private debt (annex table A4.2). The origins of defaults vary greatly across countries, but the evidence strongly points to the importance of appropriately analyzing a country's debt dynamics.

The Core Elements of Traditional Debt Sustainability Analysis

Debt sustainability analysis (DSA) assesses the sustainability of an economy's debt over time. It provides a forward-looking perspective on whether an economy can meet its contractual obligations—and is an important tool for debt and macroeconomic management. Traditional debt sustainability analysis has the following three dimensions: (1) debt and debt-service indicators, (2) medium-term balance of payments projections, and (3) sensitivity analysis.[28] Section 2 discussed the debt and debt-service indicators that are widely used in assessing an economy's debt situation and the exposure to debt-related risks of liquidity and solvency. Appropriate DSA should scrutinize debt and debt-service ratios in both a static (point-in-time) and a dynamic (intertemporal) context. Although these indicators can provide useful information about the ability to pay, no one indicator is relevant to all the dimensions of a payment problem. Moreover, critical debt levels are likely to vary from country to country, as well as over time. So the indicators must be accompanied by comprehensive economic evaluation.

Medium-term balance of payment projections are key in determining the intertemporal paths of debt and debt-service indicators and the sustainability of debt. Two broad types of models have been commonly used to derive balance of payment projections: flow-of-funds models (consistency models) and other macroeconomic models.

Flow-of-funds models are perhaps the most common type of models used to project a country's balance of payments and key macroeconomic variables. A central feature of these models is the reliance on flow-of-funds accounting. So a source of funds for one economic sector is a use of funds for another economic sector. For example, direct taxes are a source of funds for the public sector and a use of funds for the private sector. Also, each sector's total sources of funds must equal its total uses of funds. Flow-of-funds models rely on standard national accounting identities, especially the fundamental accounting identity of gross domestic output or income equal (ex post) to total expenditure

$$GDP = C + I + X - M,$$

where Y is GDP, C is consumption, I is investment, X is exports, and M is imports. These models identify gaps, usually a domestic savings gap given by the investment-savings identity

$$S_{dom} = GDP - C = I + X - M$$

so that

$$S_{dom} - I = X - M$$

and a foreign exchange or trade gap given by the resource balance $(X - M)$. For the dynamics of the two-gap model to be stable, the savings and trade gaps as percentages of GDP have to decline over time, implying that the marginal rate of saving has to rise above the marginal rate of investment. Typically, these models have four economic sectors—the government, monetary, private, and foreign (balance of payments) sectors. These models incorporate very simple behavior on the part of economic agents, based on simple historical relationships of variables. For example, the relationship between investment and income may be specified through the historical ICOR (incremental capital output ratio), or the Harrod-Domar growth model.[29] Again, imports may be related to income through the income elasticity of imports.

Flow-of-funds models are different from general equilibrium models in that they do not describe economic processes. For example, a flow-of-funds model will not be useful for determining the effect of an exchange rate change on output growth. It will, however, be useful in determining the foreign financing that is consistent with a given configuration of output growth and exchange rate.[30]

Despite numerous shortcomings, flow-of-funds models are commonly used to project the balance of payments and assess a country's external debt sustainability. The main reasons for their use are that (1) these models are not complex (in that their principles are relatively simple), (2) the data requirements are not onerous (the data are available through the national accounts), and (3) these models provide a consistent macroeconomic framework for assessing debt dynamics.

Other macroeconomic models that represent the underlying structure of the economy might be more analytically robust than flow-of-funds models. Structural models attempt to show how economies move toward equilibrium through price and quantity adjustments. For example, these types of models might determine the real output growth rate resulting from a terms of trade shock. As with flow-of-funds models, the parameters of these models are based on historical time-series data and are backward-looking. Structural models, however, are likely to have more predictive accuracy than flow-of-funds models.

Although the importance of using the appropriate model for generating macroeconomic projections is crucial, a comprehensive discussion of the pros and cons of the different types of models is not presented here. Moreover, the particular situation of a country is relevant to determining the macroeconomic model that should be used. The purpose here is to alert readers to some of the methods that are commonly used, and to present the various dimensions of performing a debt sustainability analysis.

The next step in a DSA is to develop a baseline run showing the debt dynamics under the most likely outcome for key macroeconomic variables such as output growth, exchange rate, and interest rate. These variables are determined by domestic economic policies, macroeconomic developments overseas, and international financial market developments. Thus building a baseline scenario requires in-depth knowledge of the structure of the country and the domestic policy environment, as well as an understanding of how relevant external factors are likely to evolve. Once the baseline has been generated, stress testing can begin.

Stress testing is increasingly viewed as a critical element of DSA, and in the context of DSA examines the expected outcomes (or vulnerability) of debt and debt service indicators under various conditions, especially extreme ones.[31] A report by the Bank for International Settlements (BIS 2001) distinguishes between a "sensitivity stress test" and a "stress test scenario." A sensitivity stress test measures the impact on economic outcomes of changing the value of one or more exogenous variables that are uncertain. Typically, one uncertain variable is shocked symmetrically (up and down), while holding others constant. Simulating the effect of shocks of two standard deviations is commonly recommended (IMF 2002). Some studies recognize that shocks of this magnitude are not sufficient, and that stress testing should:[32]

- simulate large shocks that have a historical precedent but are not common;
- simulate shocks that reflect a structural break in economic relationships; and
- simulate shocks that might never have occurred but are plausible.

A "sensitivity stress test" should be used to yield a range of possible outcomes associated with a range of values of an exogenous variable. Clearly, this type of sensitivity analysis provides a simple technique for measuring vulnerability to uncertain events and for answering "what if" questions. The one major drawback of a sensitivity stress test is that there are no probabilities attached to the values of the uncertain variables and, therefore, to the outcomes.

"Stress test scenario" analysis constitutes developing a range of scenarios of possible states of the world: those that are highly negative for the economy (such as low oil prices for oil exporters or high oil prices for oil importers), internally consistent, plausible, highly unlikely to occur, and so forth. It is important to remember that there are no widely accepted standards or criteria for stress testing the baseline results of the DSA model. However, limiting stress testing to simulating shocks of two standard deviations is clearly not enough, and scenarios of highly unlikely shocks should be developed. A problem in developing alternative stress scenarios is how to shock risk factors in an internally consistent way. Another problem in using stress scenarios is that they typically do not have probabilities attached to them, so the relevance of the stress results may be difficult to interpret. One way to provide a probabilistic structure is to subjectively assign probabilities to various events.

4   Conclusion

The historical evidence on the occurrence of debt payment problems in some countries, and the subsequent high costs to these economies in terms of output losses, points to the importance of appropriately analyzing an economy's debt situation. Such an analysis involves assessing the sustainability of an economy's debt and its vulnerability to exogenous shocks. This chapter has presented the standard debt indicators that are used to measure external vulnerability to shocks. It has also highlighted the salient aspects of a framework for assessing external debt sustainability in a comprehensive way. A special focus has been on the importance of "stress testing" the debt dynamics of an economy, even though there are no widely accepted standards for stress testing.

5 Annex

Table A4.1: Sovereign Defaults on Debt to Private Creditors, Rated Issuers, 1975–2002

Issuer	Local currency debt	Foreign currency bond debt	Foreign currency bank debt
Argentina	1982, 1989–90, 2002	1989, 2001–2	1982–93
Bolivia		1989–97	1980–4, 1986–93
Brazil	1986–87, 1990		1983–94
Bulgaria			1990–4
Chile			1983–90
Cook Islands			1995–8
Costa Rica		1984–5	1981–90
Croatia	1993–6		1992–6
Dominican Republic	1981–2001		1982–94
Ecuador	1999	1999–2000	1982–95
Egypt, Arab Republic of			1984
El Salvador	1981–96		
Guatemala		1989	1986
Indonesia			1989–98, 2000, 2002
Jamaica			1978–9, 1981–5, 1987–93
Jordan			1989–93
Kuwait	1990–1		
Mexico			1982–90
Mongolia	1997–2000		
Morocco			1983, 1986–90
Pakistan		1999	1998–9
Panama		1987–94	1983–96
Paraguay			1986–92
Peru			1976, 1978, 1980, 1983–97
Philippines			1983–92

Table A4.1: (*continued*)

Issuer	Local currency debt	Foreign currency bond debt	Foreign currency bank debt
Poland			1981–94
Romania			1981–3, 1986
Russian Federation	1998–9	1998–2000	1991–7
Senegal			1981–5, 1990, 1992–6
Slovenia			1992–6
South Africa			1985–7, 1989, 1993
Trinidad and Tobago			1988–9
Turkey			1978–9, 1982
Ukraine	1998–2000		1998–2000
Uruguay			1983–5, 1987, 1990–1
Venezuela, R. B. de	1995–7, 1998	1995–7	1983–8, 1990
Vietnam	1975		1985–98

Source: Adapted from Standard & Poor's (2002).

Table A4.2: Sovereign Defaults on Debt to Private Creditors, Unrated Issuers, 1975–2002

Issuer	Local currency debt	Foreign currency bond debt	Foreign currency bank debt
Albania			1991–5
Algeria			1991–6
Angola	1992–2002		1985–2002
Antigua and Barbuda			1996–2002
Bosnia and Herzegovina			1992–7
Burkina Faso			1983–96
Cameroon			1985–2002
Cape Verde			1981–96
Central African Republic			1981, 1983–2002
Congo, Rep. of			1983–2002
Congo, Dem. Rep. of			1976–2002
Côte d'Ivoire		2000-2	1983–98
Cuba			1982–2002
Ethiopia			1991–9
Gabon			1986–94, 1999, 2002
Gambia, The			1986–90
Ghana	1979		1987
Guinea			1986–8, 1991–8
Guinea-Bissau			1983–96

(Continued on the next page)

Table A4.2: (*continued*)

Issuer	Local currency debt	Foreign currency bond debt	Foreign currency bank debt
Guyana			1976, 1982–99
Haiti			1982–94
Honduras			1981–2002
Iran, Islamic Republic of			1978–95
Iraq			1987–2002
Kenya			1994–2002
Korea, Democratic People's Republic of			1975–2002
Liberia			1987–2002
Macedonia, FYR			1992–7
Madagascar	2002		1981–4, 1986–2002
Malawi			1982, 1988
Mauritania			1992–96
Moldova		1998, 2002	
Mozambique			1983–92
Myanmar (Burma)	1984		1998–2002
Nauru			2002
Nicaragua			1979–2002
Niger			1983–91
Nigeria		1986–8, 1992	1982–92
São Tomé and Principe			1987–94
Serbia and Montenegro			1992–2002
Seychelles			2000–2
Sierra Leone	1997–8		1983–4, 1986–95
Solomon Islands	1995–2002		
Sri Lanka	1996		
Sudan			1979–2002
Tanzania			1984–2002
Togo			1979–80, 1982–4, 1988, 1991–7
Uganda			1980–93
Yemen, Republic of			1985–2001
Former Yugoslavia		1992–2002	1983–91
Zambia			1983–94
Zimbabwe		1975–80[a]	2000–2

Source: Adapted from Standard & Poor's (2002).

a. Bonds initially defaulted in 1965. Debt initially defaulted on in 1974.

Notes

1. See chapter 3 for a description of government debt dynamics.
2. In this simple, closed-economy model, Ricardian equivalence implies that household savings rise by the amount that public savings fall. According to Ricardian equivalence, a tax cut that is financed by issuing debt will not affect total consumption and saving, because consumers would realize that lower taxes today imply higher taxes in the future. Consumers will save today to offset the increase in tax liabilities in the future. See Barro (1974) for more on Ricardian equivalence.
3. See Ley (2004) and IIE (2000).
4. For a recent review of the behavior of private saving-investment balance, public saving-investment balance, and the current account in the United States, see Obstfeld and Rogoff (2004).
5. Obstfeld and Rogoff (1996).
6. See Dornbusch (1985) and Obstfeld and Rogoff (1996).
7. For a comprehensive review of the definition of debt, see BIS and others (2003).
8. Because price movements in the underlying instruments can cause derivative positions to change, it is useful to monitor both the market and notional value of derivative positions.
9. Interest that is accrued and not paid when due adds to the amount of debt under the cash-based approach.
10. Lane and Milesi-Ferretti use this methodology to estimate the net asset positions for 66 developed and developing countries.
11. See Cooper and Sachs (1985) for a discussion of optimal borrowing strategies.
12. Because sovereign debt is not backed by collateral, there must be some other reason (or reasons) why sovereigns repay debt. Eaton and Gersovitz (1981) argue that sovereign countries repay their debt so as to avoid the reputation risk of defaulting and the implications of this on their future ability to borrow. Bulow and Rogoff (1989) show that creditors' ability to impose direct costs on debtor countries rather than repayment reputation are the basis for lending activity. Also see Cole and Kehoe (1997).
13. Dooley (2000) argues that efforts to minimize the welfare costs (output losses) for the debtor, following a crisis, might weaken the incentives for private foreign lending.

14. The issue is not whether current account deficits matter. For example, Frankel and Rose (1996) do not find a significant relationship between large current account deficits and financial crisis. Edwards (2001) also does not find that large (arbitrarily defined) deficits always imply a crisis. However, he cautions that because reversals in the current account have a negative impact on GDP, large deficits should be a cause for concern.

15. See Frankel and Rose (1996), Kaminsky, Lizondo, and Reinhart (1998), and Edwards (2001) for empirical indicators associated with crises.

16. The HIPC Initiative (launched in 1996 by the World Bank, IMF, and other creditors) defines sustainable debt to export levels as a ratio of 150 percent (on a net present-value basis). This ratio is lower for HIPCs with more open economies.

17. The discussion on stock and flow indicators in this chapter largely draws upon BIS and others (2003).

18. This is a problem only for amortization that is currently and prospectively due, not for past amortization.

19. The World Bank's Atlas method for measuring per capita income uses a three-year moving average exchange rate to calculate the GNI in dollar terms. (See http://www.worldbank.org/data/aboutdata/working-meth.html.)

20. See Forbes (2002) and Glick and Rose (1999) for trade linkages as a transmission channel for shocks.

21. The currency composition of assets is important as well. Cross-currency movements can affect the debt and asset positions differently if the currency compositions of debt and assets are not comparable.

22. The generally accepted view is that the relationship between debt and growth is nonlinear. While additional borrowing can enhance economic growth at reasonable levels of debt, large amounts of debt can have a perverse impact on growth, that is, the debt overhang effect. See Calvo (1998) and Patillo, Poirson, and Ricci (2002).

23. Comprehensive measures of external debt should contain domestic currency debt held by nonresidents. Some commonly used measures of external debt (such as in the *Global Development Finance* [World Bank 2004]) do not include this debt in a measure of external debt. In several crises, however, in Mexico (1984), Russia (1998), and Brazil (1999), nonresidents had substantial holdings of local currency debt, and their refusal to roll over local-currency debt contributed to a crisis.

24. Debt coming due in the short term includes short-term debt by original maturity and long-term debt that is coming due within a year. This measure of short-term debt is more useful for assessing the amount of resources that will be needed to meet immediate obligations.
25. Indeed, this indicator had been worsening since 1990 in the five East Asian crisis countries. The average value of this indicator fell from 81 percent at the end of 1990 to 47 percent at the end of 1997.
26. See IMF (2002).
27. See Chuhan and Sturzenegger (2004).
28. Traditional DSA does not address the issue of sustainability under uncertainty.
29. The original Harrod-Domar growth model postulated a proportional relationship between investment and GDP in the short run: GDP growth in period t is proportional to the I/GDP ratio in $t-1$. Later uses of this model relied on this relationship to explain long-term growth. William Easterly (1999), however, finds no evidence supporting this proportional relationship in either the short or long term.
30. See Beckerman (2003).
31. Stress testing credit risk models is common practice in financial institutions.
32. See Berkowitz (1999).

References

Barro, Robert J. 1974. "Are Government Bonds Net Wealth?" *Journal of Political Economy* 82 (6): 1095–117.

Beckerman, Paul. 2003. "Medium-Term Macroeconomic Projection Techniques for Developing Economies."

Berkowitz, Jeremy. 1999. "A Coherent Framework for Stress-Testing." Finance and Economics Discussion Series Paper 1999-29 (July), Federal Reserve Board, Washington, DC.

BIS (Bank for International Settlements). 2001. *A Survey of Stress Tests and Current Practices at Major Financial Institutions.* Report prepared by a Task Force established by the Committee on the Global Financial System of the central banks of the Group of 10 countries. Bank for International Settlements, Basle, Switzerland.

BIS, Commonwealth Secretariat, ECB, IMF, OECD, Paris Club, UNCTAD, and World Bank. 2003. *External Debt Statistics: Guide for Compilers and Users*. BIS, Basle, Switzerland. http://www.imf.org/external/pubs/ft/eds/Eng/Guide

Bulow, Jeremy, and Kenneth Rogoff. 1989. "Sovereign Debt Is to Forgive to Forget?" *American Economic Review* 79 (1): 155–78.

Calvo, Guillermo. 1998. "Growth, Debt and Economic Transformation: The Capital Flight Problem." In Fabrizio Coricelli, Massimi di Matteo, and Frank Hahn, eds. *New Theories in Growth and Development*. New York: St Martin's Press.

Chuhan, Punam, and Federico Sturzenegger. 2004. "Default Episodes in the 1980s and 1990s: What Have We Learned?" In Joshua Aizenman and Brian Pinto, eds. *Managing Volatility and Crises*. Washington, DC: World Bank.

Cline, William R. 1983. *International Debt and the Stability of the World Economy*. Washington, DC: Institute for International Economics.

Cole, Harold L., and Patrick J. Kehoe. 1997. "Reviving Reputation Models of International Debt." *Federal Reserve Bank of Minneapolis Quarterly Review* 27 (1): 21–30.

Cooper, Richard N., and Jeffrey D. Sachs. 1985. "Borrowing Abroad: The Debtor's Perspective." In Gordon W. Smith and John T. Cuddington, eds. *International Debt and the Developing Countries*. Washington, DC: World Bank.

Dooley, Michael P. 2000. "Can Output Losses Following International Financial Crises Be Avoided?" NBER Working Paper 7531, National Bureau of Economic Research, Cambridge, MA.

Dornbusch, Rudiger. 1985. "External Debt, Budget Deficits, and Disequilibrium Exchange Rates." In Gordon W. Smith and John T. Cuddington, eds. *International Debt and the Developing Countries*. Washington, DC: World Bank.

Easterly, William. 1999. "The Ghost of Financing Gap: Testing the Growth Model of the International Financial Institutions." *Journal of Development Economics* 60 (2): 423–38.

Eaton, Jonathan, and Mark Gersovitz. 1981. "Debt with Potential Repudiation: Theoretical and Empirical Analysis." *Review of Economic Studies* 48 (2): 289–309.

Edwards, Sebastian. 2001. "Does the Current Account Matter?" NBER Working Paper W8275, National Bureau of Economic Research, Cambridge, MA.

4

Feder, Gershon, and Richard Just. 1977. "A Study of Debt Servicing Capacity Applying Logit Analysis." *Journal of Development Economics* 4 (1): 25–38.

Feder, Gershon, Richard Just, and Knud Ross. 1981. "Projecting Debt-Servicing Capacity of Developing Countries." *Journal of Financial and Quantitative Analysis* 16 (5): 651–69.

Forbes, Kristin. 2002. "Are Trade Linkages Important Determinants of Country Vulnerability to Crises?" In Sebastian Edwards and Jeffrey Frankel, eds. *Preventing Currency Crises in Emerging Markets.* Chicago: University of Chicago Press.

Frank, Charles R., and William R. Cline. 1971. "Measurement of Debt Servicing Capacity: An Application of Discriminant Analysis." *Journal of International Economics* 1 (3): 327–44.

Frankel, Jeffrey A., and Andrew K. Rose. 1996. "Currency Crashes in Emerging Markets: An Empirical Treatment." *Journal of International Economics* 41 (3/4): 351–66.

Glick, Reuven, and Andrew Rose. 1999. "Contagion and Trade: Why Are Currency Crises Regional?" *Journal of International Money and Finance* 18 (4): 603–17.

Grinols, Emmanuel. 1976. "International Debt Rescheduling and Discrimination Using Financial Variables." Manuscript. U.S. Treasury Department, Washington, DC.

IIE (Institute for International Economics). 2000. "Whatever Happened to the Twin Deficits?" http://www.iie.com/publications/chapters_preview/47/2iie2644.pdf.

IMF (International Monetary Fund). 1993. *Balance of Payments Manual* (fifth edition). Washington, DC: International Monetary Fund.

———. 2002. "Assessing Sustainability." Policy Development and Review Department. International Monetary Fund. http://www.imf.org/external/np/pdr/sus/2002/eng/052802.htm

Kaminsky, Graciela, Saul Lizondo, and Carmen M. Reinhart. 1998. "Leading Indicators of Currency Crises." *IMF Staff Papers* 45 (1): 1–48.

Krugman, Paul. 1979. "A Model of Balance of Payments Crises." *Journal of Money, Credit, and Banking* 11 (3): 311–25.

Lane, Philip, and Gian Maria Milesi-Ferretti. 2001. "The External Wealth of Nations: Measures of Foreign Assets and Liabilities for Industrial and Developing Nations." *Journal of International Economics and Statistics* 55 (2): 263–94.

4

Ley, Eduardo. 2004. "Fiscal and External Sustainability." Manuscript. International Monetary Fund, Washington, DC. http://ideas.repec.org/p/wpa/wuwppe/0310007.html

Mayo, Alice L., and Anthony G. Barrett. 1978. "An Early Warning Model for Assessing Developing Country Risk." In Stephen H. Goodman, ed. *Proceedings of a Symposium on Developing Countries' Debt*, sponsored by the Export-Import Bank of the United States, April 1977. New York: Praeger.

McFadden, Daniel, Richard Eckaus, Gershon Feder, Vassilis Hajivassiliou, and Stephen O'Connell. 1985. "Is There Life after Death? An Econometric Analysis of the Creditworthiness of Developing Countries." In Gordon W. Smith and John T. Cuddington, eds. *International Debt and the Developing Countries*. Washington, DC: World Bank.

Moody's. 2002. *Macro Financial Risk Model: An Approach to Modeling Sovereign Contingent Claims and Country Risk*. New York: Moody's Investors Service.

Obstfeld, Maurice, and Kenneth Rogoff. 1996. *Foundations of International Macroeconomics*. Cambridge, MA: MIT Press.

Obstfeld, Maurice, and Kenneth Rogoff. 2004. "The Unsustainable US Current Account Position Revisited." NBER Working Paper 10869, National Bureau of Economic Research, Cambridge, MA.

Patillo, Catherine, Helene Poirson, and Luca Ricci. 2002. "External Debt and Growth." IMF Working Paper 02/96, International Monetary Fund, Washington, DC.

Reinhart, Carmen M., Kenneth S. Rogoff, and Miguel A. Savastano. 2003. "Debt Intolerance," NBER Working Paper 9908, National Bureau of Economic Research, Cambridge, MA.

Saini, Krishnan, and Philip Bates. 1978. "Statistical Techniques for Determining Debt-Servicing Capacity for Developing Countries: An Analytical Review of Literature and Further Empirical Results." Research Paper 7818, Federal Reserve Bank of New York, New York, NY.

Sargen, Nicholas. 1977. "Economic Indicators and Country Risk Appraisal." *Economic Review of the Federal Reserve Bank of San Francisco* (Fall): 19–35.

Standard & Poor's. 2002. *Sovereign Defaults: Moving Higher Again in 2003?* New York: Standard & Poor's, New York, NY.

World Bank. 2004. *Global Development Finance. Vol. II: Summary and Country Tables*. Washington, DC: World Bank.

4

113- 31

Cyclical Adjustment of the Budget Surplus: Concepts and Measurement Issues

Craig Burnside and Yuliya Meshcheryakova

H61
E32

This chapter introduces the concept of the cyclically adjusted budget surplus. Historically, budget surplus measures of this type have reflected an understanding by economists that cyclical movements in output systematically affect the public sector's budget. Cyclically adjusted budget surplus measures therefore attempt to factor out the cyclical effects from conventional measures. Once this is done, the adjusted measures are taken to be indicators of the fiscal policy stance.

Economists have long recognized that budget surplus figures tend to be procyclical. In particular, budget surpluses are procyclical in most Organisation for Economic Co-operation and Development (OECD) countries, for a number of reasons that will be elaborated upon later. In the context of Keynesian macroeconomic theory, when the public sector runs a larger budget surplus than in previous periods, the government is said to have a contractionary fiscal policy stance, because the theory predicts that tighter fiscal policy will have a negative impact on real activity. However, if the budget surplus is larger simply because the economy is going through an expansionary phase of the business cycle, and tax revenue is consequently higher, thinking of fiscal policy as contractionary may be inappropriate. Thus, many economists have proposed that budget surplus figures should somehow be adjusted to allow for the effects of the business cycle on the budget. Presumably this would allow the effects of the budget on the economy to be more accurately assessed.

The literature on adjusted budget surplus measures can be traced back to a 1956 paper by E. Cary Brown, in which he argued that to measure the stance of fiscal policy correctly one must distinguish between "automatic" and "discretionary" policies. Brown did not propose an adjusted measure of the budget surplus, because he explicitly argued in favor of the differential treatment of the various components of revenue and expenditure with reference to an explicit Keynesian model of the economy.

In the half-century since Brown's paper, economists have sought a single indicator of the stance of fiscal policy similar to the budget surplus, expressed as a percentage of GDP, but adjusted for the business cycle. Blanchard (1990) and Buiter (1993) have provided arguments against using single indicators, but a number of government and international agencies produce them, including the OECD, the World Bank, the International Monetary Fund (IMF), the European Union (EU), and their various member governments. This chapter discusses issues in the interpretation and construction of some of these fiscal policy indicators. More thorough discussions of the different indicators can be found in Chouraqui, Hagemann, and Sartor (1990) and Price and Muller (1994).

Cyclical adjustment of the budget usually begins with the decomposition of output into some trend or potential component, and some deviation from trend, usually referred to as the cyclical component. Section 1 describes several methods used to obtain such a decomposition of output fluctuations. Section 2 describes the subsequent steps in cyclical adjustment of the budget surplus, which usually involve measuring the sensitivity of nondiscretionary budget outcomes to the business cycle and adjusting these outcomes accordingly. Section 3 considers whether cyclically adjusted budget data are useful in performing economic analysis; and section 4 offers some concluding remarks.

1   Identifying Trends and Cycles in Aggregate Economic Activity

One way to describe the cyclical properties of fiscal policy would involve comparing the behavior of revenue and expenditure during recessions to their behavior during expansions. However, in general, such an approach would be unsatisfactory, because not all contractions and expansions are alike. Furthermore, whether revenue and expenditure will differ according to whether output is rising or falling (rather than according to whether output is high or low) is not obvious.

The extent to which real output, Y_t, is high or low is typically measured with regard to some benchmark, Y_t^*. That is, the business cycle in output is typically defined as $Y_t^c = Y_t/Y_t^*$ (the cycle is the level of output relative to the benchmark). The literature provides a number of benchmarks that can be the basis of a measure of the business cycle, including:[1]

- The level of potential output
- The trend in output as defined by a linear, possibly piecewise, trend in its logarithm
- The trend in output as defined by the Hodrick and Prescott (1997) filter
- The trend in output residually defined by the band-pass filter, proposed by Baxter and King (1995)
- The permanent component in output, as defined by the Beveridge and Nelson (1981) decomposition
- The trend in output as defined by a peak-to-peak trend line.

Potential Output

The level of potential output is typically defined as the level of output that could be produced if the economy was at full employment or was at the natural rate of employment.[2] The IMF and OECD measures of the cyclically adjusted budget surplus are ultimately based on some measure of potential output. Potential output is usually constructed with reference to some production function that determines GDP as a function of the levels of capital and labor in the economy. Suppose output, Y_t, is written as $Y_t = f(K_t, N_t, A_t)$, where K_t is the level of capital, N_t is the level of labor, and A_t is the level of technology. Then potential output is given by $Y_t^* = f(K_t, N_t^*, A_t^*)$, where N_t^* is the level of full or natural employment and A_t^* is the trend level of technology.

Making the concept of potential output operational is difficult because it requires a measure of capital. Annual series on the capital stock are often available, but ideally, some estimate of capital services that accounts for variable utilization would be used. Furthermore, the parameters of the production function, $f(\cdot)$, must be estimated. Because technology is unobservable, these estimates must be used to decompose fluctuations in output according to their sources: fluctuations in capital, labor, and technology. Finally, the level of full or natural employment and the trend level of technology must be estimated. Generally speaking, practitioners cannot agree on how to define full or natural employment.[3]

Linear Trends

Denote the logarithm of seasonally adjusted real GDP by y_t. A piecewise linear trend in y_t can be found from the following regression equation:

$$y_t = a_0 + b_0t + d_{1t}(a_1 + b_1t) + d_{2t}(a_2 + b_2t) + \cdots + d_{kt}(a_k + b_kt) + \varepsilon_t, \tag{1.1}$$

where $\{d_{1t}, d_{2t}, \ldots, d_{kt}\}$ are dummy variables identifying breakpoints in the data. In particular, if the first break in the trend occurs at some date T_1, then d_{1t} can be defined as follows: $d_{1t} = 1$ for $t > T_1$, and zero otherwise.

If the dates at which breaks occur are treated as known parameters, then estimation—which can be done using ordinary least squares—and inference are standard. The cyclical component of real GDP is constructed as the deviation of real GDP from the piecewise linear trend; that is, it is the residual from the estimated version of (1.1).

A significant problem with piecewise linear trends arises if breakpoint dates are treated as unknown parameters of the model, as in (1.1), which, of course, they should be. In this case, while it is possible to proceed with standard estimation techniques, the rules of inference change. Specifically, as Christiano (1992) argues, if one uses standard t-statistics to determine where the breaks in trend occur, there is a bias toward finding breaks in the data when the true model is one with no breaks. Inference is further complicated if the number of breakpoints is treated as unknown.

Trends and Cycles as Defined by the Hodrick-Prescott Filter

If once again $y_t = \ln(Y_t)$, the trend defined by Hodrick and Prescott (1997), called the HP trend, is the series $\{y_t^*\}_{t=1}^T$ that minimizes the objective function:

$$\sum_{t=1}^T (y_t - y_t^*)^2 + \lambda \sum_{t=2}^{T-1} [(y_{t+1}^* - y_t^*) - (y_t^* - y_{t-1}^*)]^2. \tag{1.2}$$

The parameter λ determines how smooth the trend line will be. It is clear that if $\lambda = 0$, the trend will simply equal the original series for all t. For less extreme but small values of λ, the trend follows the data quite closely. However, if λ is very large, changes in the slope of the trend are avoided, and, in the limit, as $\lambda \to \infty$ the trend will simply be a straight line.[4]

The conventional value of λ for quarterly data is 1,600. This value is arbitrary, although Hodrick and Prescott (1997) provide some motivation for it. They point out that if the cyclical component, $y_t - y_t^*$, and the second difference of the trend component, $\Delta(y_t^* - y_{t-1}^*)$, happened to be independent sequences of independent and identically distributed normal random variables with variances σ_1^2 and σ_2^2, then the series that minimizes (1.2) would correspond to the mathematical expectation of $\{y_t^*\}_{t=1}^T$, given the sample of data $\{y_t\}_{t=1}^T$ if λ were set equal to $(\sigma_1/\sigma_2)^2$. Arguing that the standard deviation of cycles should be roughly 40 times the standard deviation of changes in the trend growth rate, Hodrick and Prescott obtain a value of $\lambda = 1,600$. Burnside (2000) argues that $\lambda = 6.5$ is the roughly equivalent value for annual data, while $\lambda = 129,000$ is the equivalent value for monthly data.

Cycles and Trends as Defined by an Approximate Band-Pass Filter

Baxter and King (1995) propose a method based on band-pass filtering for obtaining the cyclical component, $y_t^c = y_t - y_t^*$, of $y_t = \ln(Y_t)$. A slight digression to describe band-pass filters is necessary to understand the mechanics of their procedure. Typically, these filters are defined in the frequency domain and are designed to remove fluctuations of particular frequencies from the data, while leaving others intact. One might argue, for example, that business cycles are fluctuations of periods between, say, 6 and 32 quarters in length. In this case, the corresponding frequencies would be $\omega_1 = \pi/16$ and $\omega_2 = \pi/3$.[5] A band-pass filter designed to extract the "business cycle component" of output would be one that would completely attenuate the frequencies below ω_1 and those above ω_2, while leaving the frequencies between ω_1 and ω_2 intact. The *gain* of this filter would be 0 for $0 < \omega < \omega_1$, 1 for $\omega_1 < \omega < \omega_2$, and 0 for $\omega_2 < \omega < \pi$.

Baxter and King's method is related to band-pass filtering but is defined in the more familiar time domain. As described in Woitek (1998), their filter defines y_t^c as a symmetric moving average of order K of the original series:

$$y_t^c = a(L)y_t = \sum_{j=-K}^{K} a_j L^j y_t,$$

where L is the lag operator with the property that $Ly_t = y_{t-1}$. A particular choice of the parameters a_j implies the shape of the filter's gain in the frequency domain. Baxter and King choose the a_j's to minimize the squared distance between their filter's gain and the gain of the band-pass filter described above. This leads them to set

$$a_j = b_j + \theta, \quad j = 0, \pm 1, \ldots, \pm K,$$

$$b_j = \begin{cases} (\omega_2 - \omega_1)/\pi & \text{if } j = 0 \\ [\sin(\omega_2 j) - \sin(\omega_1 j)]/\pi j & \text{if } j \neq 0 \end{cases}$$

$$\theta = -\sum_{j=-K}^{K} b_j/(2K + 1),$$

with $K = 12$, $\omega_1 = \pi/16$, and $\omega_2 = \pi/3$.

Beveridge-Nelson Decomposition

Another popular trend concept is the permanent component of a time series as defined by the Beveridge and Nelson (1981) decomposition. This procedure typically involves fitting an ARIMA model (Auto Regressive Integrated Moving Average Model) to the first difference of the logarithm of output, Δy_t. Consider the following model:

$$a(L)(\Delta y_t - \mu) = \theta(L)\varepsilon_t, \qquad (1.3)$$

where μ is the mean of Δy_t, and $a(L)$ and $\theta(L)$ are pth and qth-ordered polynomials in the lag operator. The permanent component of y_t, denoted y_t^*, is defined as the current value of the series plus any predicted stochastic growth in the series:

$$y_t^* = y_t + E_t(\Delta y_{t+1} - \mu + \Delta y_{t+2} - \mu + \cdots). \qquad (1.4)$$

An estimate of the permanent component can be obtained by estimating the model in (1.3) and using it to compute the expectations on the right-hand side of equation (1.4). The model in (1.3) can be estimated by maximum likelihood, while p and q can be chosen according to the Schwarz (1978) criterion.

A simple example, to illustrate the procedure, is the case where output growth is assumed to follow an AR(1) process, obtained by setting $a(L) = 1 - \rho L$, and $\theta(L) = 1$. In this case

$$\Delta y_t - \mu = \rho(\Delta y_{t-1} - \mu) + \varepsilon_t,$$

and so

$$E_t(\Delta y_{t+j} - \mu) = \rho^j(\Delta y_t - \mu).$$

Therefore,

$$y_t^* = y_t + \rho(\Delta y_t - \mu) + \rho^2(\Delta y_t - \mu) + \cdots$$
$$= y_t + \frac{\rho}{1 - \rho}(\Delta y_t - \mu).$$

If $\rho > 0$, then relatively rapid growth today implies higher than normal growth in the future, so the trend level of output is deemed to be above the current value. The more closely output resembles a random walk with drift (the case where $\rho = 0$), the closer the permanent component will be to the series itself.

Peak-to-Peak Trend Lines

Finally, an ad hoc procedure that is sometimes used is to draw peak-to-peak trend lines so that observed output is never above the trend. Obviously, there are problems with any such method, because one must first define where the peaks are in the data. If each data point is a peak, the trend and the original series will be the same by construction. To identify more-meaningful peaks requires either a very complex procedure, such as that used by the National Bureau of Economic Research to choose business cycle dates, or a simple procedure with a greater degree of "ad hockery."

2   Methods for Computing the Cyclically Adjusted Budget Surplus

This section examines the methodological approaches to computing the cyclically adjusted budget surplus measures used by a variety of international organizations and national governments. These methods begin by using the statistical techniques of the previous section to decompose output into "trend" and "cycle." These same techniques can be used to identify trends and cycles in the fiscal accounts of a country. That is, data from the fiscal accounts can be processed so as to remove seasonal components, can be converted into real terms—say, by dividing by the GDP deflator—and can finally be decomposed into trend and cyclical components using one of the methods described earlier.

Once the budget data have been decomposed into trend and cycle, co-movements between the cyclical components of the budget and the cyclical component of output can be deduced. Cyclical adjustment of the budget data involves "correcting" the data for these co-movements between the cycles in output and the budget series.

To compute cyclically adjusted surplus measures, the EU, IMF, and OECD estimate the elasticities of selected components of revenue and expenditure with respect to output. They use the estimated elasticities to make cyclical adjustments to these components of the budget. At this stage an important set of assumptions must be made: One must decide which revenue and expenditure components fall into a category referred to as *automatic,* and which fall into a category referred to as *discretionary.* The underlying assumption is that the business cycle causes the cyclical fluctuations in automatic budget items, while any cyclicality in the fluctuations of discretionary budget items is the result of exogenous policymaking.[6] Thus, if the purpose is to identify exogenous changes in fiscal policy, only those components that fall into the automatic category should be adjusted for the effects of the cycle.

It should be reemphasized that the decision to adjust some revenue and/or expenditure categories and not others is based on strong a priori assumptions about causality rather than on a statistical test. One example is the notion that tax revenues behave cyclically largely because most tax systems rely on statutory tax rates levied on various types of economic activity, and this naturally leads to cyclical movements in tax revenue. Similarly, in many countries transfer programs are structured to respond automatically to business cycle movements. As a result, it seems reasonable, from a theoretical perspective, to treat the cyclical movements of tax revenues and transfers as being determined by the factors that drive the business cycle rather than themselves being the causes of the business cycle. In some countries, expenditure categories such as wages and salaries and capital expenditure are also highly procyclical, but they are typically not adjusted for the cycle; the implicit argument against adjustment is that these expenditure categories are fundamentally more discretionary. Thus, if these expenditures turn out to be procyclical, this is attributed to the choices made by policymakers. Of course, if all revenue and expenditure categories were adjusted for the effects of the business cycle, the adjusted surplus would be uncorrelated, by construction, with the cyclical component of output.

The EU Definition of the Cyclical Component of the Budget

Here, consider the European Union's method of cyclical adjustment, as described by the Directorate-General for Economic and Financial Affairs (European Community 1995).[7] First, a limited number of expenditure and revenue categories are selected for adjustment. To illustrate the method of adjustment, take, as an example, one of the revenue categories that is usually adjusted: personal income tax revenue, denoted for now by R_t. Let its elasticity with respect to output, e, be given by

$$e = \partial \ln (R_t)/\partial \ln(Y_t). \tag{2.1}$$

The elasticity might be estimated using a purely statistical model of the relationship between income tax revenue and GDP. It could also be obtained with reference to statutory tax rates, and a statistical model of the relationship between personal income and GDP, as in the method employed by the Bureau of Economic Analysis (BEA) of the U.S. Department of Commerce, discussed later.

Estimates of the elasticities of various revenue and expenditure categories with respect to the output gap can be obtained using the following statistical model, illustrated by the case of income taxes. Let income tax revenue (expressed in real terms) be R_{yt}, and let R_{yt}^c be the cyclical component of income tax revenue extracted using one of the detrending methods described above. Recall that, in each case, $R_{yt}^c = R_{yt}/R_{yt}^*$, where R_{yt}^* is the trend level of real income tax revenue. Define $r_{yt}^c = \ln R_{yt}^c = \ln R_{yt} - \ln R_{yt}^*$. Similarly, let $y_t^c = \ln Y_t - \ln Y_t^*$, where Y_t^* is the trend level of real GDP. The cyclical elasticity of income tax revenue with respect to output is found by estimating the simple model:

$$r_t^c = e y_t^c + \varepsilon_t. \tag{2.2}$$

Given an estimate of the elasticity, $\hat{e}$, the EU method adjusts income tax revenue by the amount $-R_{yt}[1 - \exp(-\hat{e} y_t^c)]$, so that adjusted income tax revenue is

$$R_{yt}^A = R_{yt}\exp\left(-\hat{e} y_t^c\right) = R_{yt} - R_{yt}\left[1 - \exp\left(-\hat{e} y_t^c\right)\right]. \tag{2.3}$$

If the cyclical component of output is zero, that is, $y_t^c = 0$, then, clearly, no adjustment to tax revenue is made. If the cyclical component is positive and the estimated elasticity, $\hat{e}$, is positive, then the adjustment to revenue will be negative. This makes intuitive sense: During a cyclical upturn, tax revenues rise simply because the economy is expanding. To adjust for this effect, tax revenue is adjusted downward.

In general, with a method such as this the adjusted budget surplus is easy to compute. Any standard budget surplus measure, Δ_t, is defined as the difference between total revenue, R_t, and expenditure, X_t. To adjust the budget surplus for the business cycle and create a new budget surplus measure denoted Δ_t^A, one uses data on the cyclical component of output, y_t^c, along with estimates of the revenue and expenditure elasticities. Suppose there are N revenue categories, $\{R,_{1t}, R_{2t}, \ldots, R_{Nt}\}$, and M expenditure categories, $\{X_{1t}, X_{2t}, \ldots, X_{Mt}\}$, to be adjusted. Suppose the elasticity of R_{jt} with respect to output is given by e_{Rj}, while the elasticity of X_{jt} with respect to output is given by e_{Xj}. The adjusted surplus measure is given by

$$\Delta_t^A = \Delta_t + \text{adjustment}$$

$$= (R_t - X_t) - \left(\sum_{j=1}^{N} R_{jt}\left[1 - \exp\left(-\hat{e}_{Rj}\, y_t^c\right)\right] - \sum_{j=1}^{M} X_{jt}\left[1 - \exp\left(-\hat{e}_{Xj}\, y_t^c\right)\right] \right).$$

$$(2.4)$$

The BEA Method of Cyclical Adjustment

The BEA concept of the budget surplus was originally described as a high-employment budget surplus. It is discussed in numerous papers, including de Leeuw and Holloway (1982, 1983), de Leeuw and others (1980), and Holloway (1984)—and attempts to compute the budget surplus that would prevail if the economy experienced full employment and discretionary policies were unchanged. Later variants make adjustments for the effects of inflation on the budget surplus, via its effects on interest expenditure and indexed transfer programs.

The BEA approach is relatively complicated—and involves going through the budget component by component, to make individual adjustments. For example, to compute adjusted personal income taxes, the adjustment procedure first asks what personal income would be at full employment. It denotes this level of income as Y_P^A and the actual level of personal income as Y_P. To compute Y_P^A, the method proposed involves estimating the elasticity of changes in Y_P with respect to changes in the output gap, which is the difference between actual output and potential output. Roughly speaking, the estimated Y_P^A adds to Y_P that elasticity times the measured output gap. The adjustment process also recognizes that personal taxes are not unit-elastic with respect to personal income. In other words, when personal income rises by 1 percent, personal taxes may rise by some different amount, say, e percent, expressed in decimal form. So adjusted personal tax receipts, T_P^A, will be given by

$$T_P^A = T_P (Y_P^A / Y_P)^e, \qquad (2.5)$$

where T_P represents actual personal tax receipts.

The BEA method presents a number of difficulties in the context of the majority of developing and industrializing countries. First, rather than directly relating each revenue and expenditure category to the output gap, it relates them indirectly. In the example just described, personal taxes are related to personal income, which is then related to the output gap. Measuring the relevant income concepts would add a different layer of complexity to cyclical adjustment and require accurate national income accounts data. In addition, the output gap concept requires the assessment of potential output, which is a difficult task even for the United States. Fellner (1982) has argued that the potential output concept is not useful, because "true" potential output depends on a number of unobservables that are not involved in its estimation. The BEA method sets potential output equal to what is referred to as middle-expansion trend gross national production, or gross national product at the natural rate of unemployment. De Leeuw and Holloway (1983) describe the rather complex methods used to compute these concepts of potential output. Given the degree of complexity, the case study in chapter 6 adopts a simpler trend-fitting method.

The IMF and OECD Methods of Cyclical Adjustment

The IMF and OECD methods resemble each other, and are described in some detail in IMF (1993) and Giorno and others (1995). Like the BEA method, the IMF and OECD methods require obtaining an estimate of potential output. Suppose that output is given by a function of capital, labor, and technology, and suppose further that this function takes the Cobb-Douglas form:

$$Y_t = A_t K_t^\alpha N_t^{1-\alpha}, \qquad (2.6)$$

where the notation is defined as before. Then potential output is given by

$$Y_t^* = A_t^* K_t^\alpha (N_t^*)^{1-\alpha}, \qquad (2.7)$$

where N_t^* is the natural level of employment and A_t^* is the trend level of technology. Generally speaking, the IMF and OECD measures of potential output are derived by first estimating the parameter α in equation (2.6) and then backing out estimates of the level of technology, A_t, using data on output, capital, and labor input. The HP filter-based trend of the series A_t is generally used to define A_t^*. The OECD computes the natural level of employment using a statistical model to determine the unemployment rate consistent with nonaccelerating inflation, while the IMF method uses unemployment rates defined by the HP trend of observed unemployment to define natural employment. Both methods use estimates of the actual capital stock in estimating potential output.

Once the estimate of potential output is obtained, the method for estimating the cyclically adjusted surplus is similar to the ones described earlier. In particular, on the revenue side the OECD, like the EU, makes adjustments to corporate taxes, personal income taxes, social security taxes, and indirect taxes. On the expenditure side, the OECD, like the EU, makes an adjustment that is more complicated, and only adjusts for the effects of the business cycle on unemployment benefits. They both use a model linking the output gap to the unemployment rate, and hence to the level of unemployment benefits. All other expenditure categories are assumed to be discretionary.

3   Usefulness of the Adjusted Surplus Concept

Cyclically adjusted surplus measures have mainly been used as guides to policymakers in the decisionmaking process. Typically, cyclically adjusted budget figures are judged to be useful because there is a sense in which they isolate the component of fiscal policy that is assumed to be exogenous with respect to the business cycle from the part that is determined by the business cycle. One could argue that the cyclically adjusted budget surplus is the component of fiscal policy that reflects discretionary action by the government. Hence, the adjusted surplus provides policymakers with a statistic that summarizes their discretionary actions and their potential impact on economic activity.

Underpinning the various approaches to cyclical adjustment, and their use in policy analysis, is the implicit assumption that a simple Keynesian model can be used to think about the economy. It is this model that allows the effects on output to be identified. Suppose one lets private consumption, C, be given by the standard textbook formula:

$$C = C_a + c(Y + rB - T + V), \tag{3.1}$$

where C_a is autonomous consumption, c is the marginal propensity to consume out of disposable income, Y is GDP, rB is interest paid by the government to the private sector, V is government transfers to the private sector, and T represents taxes. All variables are expressed in real terms. In a closed economy model, output is given by the national income accounting identity

$$Y = C + I + G. \tag{3.2}$$

Substitution of (3.1) into (3.2) implies that

$$Y = \frac{1}{1-c}[C_a + c(rB + V - T) + I + G]. \tag{3.3}$$

Even in this simple model, it is clear that the impact of fiscal policy cannot be assessed with one summary statistic regarding the budget surplus, unless the marginal propensity to consume is close to 1. Since (3.3) can be rewritten as

$$Y = \frac{1}{1-c}(C_a + I - c\Delta) + G, \tag{3.4}$$

where $\Delta = T - rB - V - G$, one can see that both the budget balance, Δ, and government consumption, G, are relevant to the determination of output. Thus, the possible limitations of any single budget balance measure as an indicator of fiscal policy are immediately obvious. Notice that $dY/dT = -c/(1-c)$, whereas $-dY/dG = -1/(1-c)$. If one were to ask, at this stage, what the effects of an improvement in the budget balance, Δ, would be, one would need to ask whether that improvement stemmed from a tax increase or a cut in government purchases.

Cyclically adjusted budget balance indicators are motivated by the fact that T and V are sensitive to the cycle. For example, one might think of tax revenue as being the sum of a lump-sum component, $\overline{T}$, and a component that is proportional to output, so that $T = \overline{T} + \tau Y$. Similarly, one might think that transfer spending is the sum of a discretionary component, $\overline{V}$, and a component that rises during cyclical downturns: $V = \overline{V} - \psi Y$. In this case one would rewrite (3.1) as

$$C = C_a + c[Y + rB + \overline{V} - \overline{T} - (\tau + \psi)Y], \tag{3.5}$$

125

which would lead to the result that

$$Y = \frac{1}{1 - c(1 - \tau - \psi)} [C_a + c(rB + \overline{V} - \overline{T}) + I + G]. \quad (3.6)$$

Notice that (3.6) can be rewritten as

$$Y = \frac{1}{1 - c(1 - \tau - \psi)} (C_a + I - c\overline{\Delta}) + \frac{1 - c}{1 - c(1 - \tau - \psi)} G, \quad (3.7)$$

where $\overline{\Delta} = \overline{T} - rB - \overline{V} - G$. Notice that if a cyclical adjustment procedure were applied to the data generated by this model, it would likely produce cyclically adjusted transfers, $V^A = \overline{V} - \psi Y^*$, and taxes, $T^A = \overline{T} + \tau Y^*$, where Y^* is the "normal" level of output.[8] Notice that this would imply a cyclically adjusted budget balance:

$$\Delta^A = T^A - rB - V^A - G = \overline{\Delta} + (\tau + \psi)Y^*. \quad (3.8)$$

So, Δ^A and $\overline{\Delta}$ would be the same up to a constant. In this example, the government's discretionary policies can be summarized by Δ^A and G, rather than Δ and G. The impact of these policies on output is determined by the parameters c, τ, and ψ.

An alternative fiscal indicator that the IMF uses is the *fiscal impulse*. The discussion here is loosely based on Chand (1993). This indicator compares the stance of fiscal policy in two successive budget years, but it continues to treat government purchases, taxes, and transfers virtually symmetrically. The fiscal impulse measure is based on the so-called cyclical effect of the budget, which is defined as the difference between the actual budget surplus and the budget surplus that would have been achieved in the absence of discretionary policy.

In its simplest form, this approach treats all movements in government expenditure that are not proportional to trend output as discretionary. That is, rB, G, and V are modeled as $rB = \gamma Y^* + \Gamma^D$, $G = gY^* + G^D$, and $V = vY^* + V^D$, where Γ^D, G^D, and V^D are treated as discretionary. Letting $X = rB + G + V$ represent total expenditure, then $X = xY^* + X^D$, where $x = \gamma + g + v$ and $X^D = \Gamma^D + G^D + V^D$. Similarly, all changes in revenue because of changes in the average rate at which revenue is raised are treated as discretionary, that is, $T = tY + T^D$, where T^D is discretionary. Thus, the budget balance, Δ, can be decomposed into two components, the discretionary balance, $T^D - X^D$, and the cyclical component $tY - xY^*$. Thus,

$$\Delta^D = T^D - X^D$$
$$= \Delta - (tY - xY^*) \qquad (3.9)$$

is the discretionary component of the budget surplus. It is typically measured by assuming that t and x are the average ratios of revenue and expenditure to output over some sample period. The discretionary surplus is closely related to the adjusted surplus discussed above. Notice that if $t = \tau$, the adjustments to tax revenue would be the same under the two methods. The treatment of transfers would be different. One method assumes that some components of transfer spending are structurally related to the business cycle, while the other method assumes that any procyclicality is the result of discretionary policy decisions.

The fiscal impulse is defined as the negative of the change in the discretionary budget surplus. So, the fiscal impulse is

$$FI_t = -\left(\Delta_t^D - \Delta_{t-1}^D\right) \qquad (3.10)$$

which, in some sense, measures the change in policy stance. Whenever the fiscal stance is positive, the discretionary surplus is declining, so that policy is moving toward a more expansionary position.

As Chand (1993) acknowledges, the IMF measure of discretionary fiscal policy, like the cyclically adjusted budget surplus measures, is somewhat flawed in that it is a single indicator. Using a single indicator in policy analysis, as shown earlier, ignores the fact that there are potentially different real effects of changes in government purchases, transfers, and taxes—even if they have the same impact on the budget balance. In the simple Keynesian framework outlined above, the multiplier that applies to an increase in government consumption is $1/[1 - c(1 - \tau - \psi)]$ (because G enters into the expression for $\overline{\Delta}$), while the multiplier that applies to an equal increase in transfers (or decrease in taxes) is $c/[1 - c(1 - \tau - \psi)]$.

In more modern dynamic models, of course, the problems with single indicators become more apparent. Dynamic macroeconomic theory suggests that the economy's response to an exogenous increase in government purchases of goods and services depends on the duration of the increase. Furthermore, how greater government spending is financed is also important. The type, duration, and size of tax changes determine the overall response of real activity. In these models, the role of the budget surplus, in and of itself, is limited. Certainly, these models would not suggest the use of the single indicators discussed in this chapter.

4   Conclusion

This chapter described the techniques used and motivations for the cyclical adjustment of budget data. Several methods commonly used to decompose output fluctuations into trends and cycles were described, followed by an explanation of how these methods can be adapted to permit the cyclical adjustment of the budget surplus. Finally, theoretical motivations for the cyclical adjustment of budget data were explored.

The theoretical discussion highlighted that, from the perspective of Keynesian macroeconomic theory, cyclical adjustment of budget data makes sense, although single indicators of the fiscal policy stance can be misleading. From the perspective of modern dynamic macroeconomic theory, however, cyclically adjusted budget data are less useful, because they do not correspond to measures of exogenous fiscal policy shocks; and with a fully dynamic model, one needs to know more than just the current stance of policy to forecast current and future outcomes.

Nonetheless, cyclically adjusted data can be quite useful in discussions of fiscal sustainability. An analyst confronting data for a particular country will want to know if current budget figures are indicative of longer-term trends, or simply the result of cyclical fluctuations in the data. Cyclically adjusting the budget data can help the practitioner determine to what extent the current budget reflects discretionary actions on the part of the government or exogenous shocks to factors that affect the budget other than the current level of GDP.

Furthermore, as shown in chapter 7, a policy of presenting and setting benchmarks in terms of cyclically adjusted data can help discipline national fiscal authorities. By presenting cyclically adjusted figures, and by following policy rules set in those terms, the fiscal authority may find it more politically feasible to avoid procyclical fiscal policy.

Notes

1. To factor out the seasonal component usually present in high-frequency real GDP series, a seasonal adjustment of the series is usually performed before studying its business cycle properties. One example of such a

procedure is the X-11 seasonal adjustment algorithm used by the U.S. Bureau of the Census. Of course, seasonal adjustment is necessary only if the data are sampled quarterly or monthly.

2. Obviously, using such a definition of potential output requires a definition of full employment or the natural rate of employment.

3. For these reasons, the concept of potential output is not used for the empirical work in chapter 6, which explores cyclical adjustment in Mexico.

4. To see these results, consider the first-order conditions for the minimization problem stated earlier:

$$y_1^*: \quad y_1 = y_1^* + \lambda(y_3^* - 2y_2^* + y_1^*)$$

$$y_2^*: \quad y_2 = y_2^* + \lambda(y_4^* - 4y_3^* + 5y_2^* - 2y_1^*)$$

$$y_t^*, t = 3, \ldots, T - 2: \quad y_t = y_t^* + \lambda(y_{t+2}^* - 4y_{t+1}^* + 6y_t^* - 4y_{t-1}^* + y_{t-2}^*)$$

$$y_{T-1}^*: \quad y_{T-1} = y_{T-1}^* + \lambda(-2y_T^* + 5y_{T-1}^* - 4y_{T-2}^* + y_{T-3}^*)$$

$$y_T^*: \quad y_T = y_T^* + \lambda(y_T^* - 2y_{T-1}^* + y_{T-2}^*)$$

Notice that if $\lambda = 0$, these conditions reduce to $y_t = y_t^*$ for all t. Also, as $\lambda \to \infty$, they imply that $y_t^* - y_{t-1}^* = y_2^* - y_1^*$, for all t, which implies a constant linear trend.

5. Frequencies, ω, are related to periodicities, p, according to the formula $\omega = 2\pi/p$.

6. This assumption will be revisited and critically assessed in section 3.

7. This method of adjustment is used in chapter 6 of this volume, in a case study of Mexico.

8. This would be true as long as the cyclical adjustment procedure correctly identifies the elasticity parameters and the data are detrended in an appropriate way.

References

Baxter, Marianne, and Robert G. King. 1995. "Measuring Business Cycles: Approximate Band-Pass Filters for Economic Time Series." NBER Working Paper 5022, National Bureau of Economic Research, Cambridge, MA.

Beveridge, Stephen, and Charles R. Nelson. 1981. "A New Approach to the Decomposition of Economic Time Series into Permanent and Transitory Components with Particular Attention to Measurement of the 'Business Cycle.'" *Journal of Monetary Economics* 7 (2): 151–74.

Blanchard, Olivier. 1990. "Suggestions for a New Set of Fiscal Indicators." Working Paper 79, Department of Economics and Statistics, Organisation for Economic Co-operation and Development, Paris.

Brown, E. Cary. 1956. "Fiscal Policy in the Thirties: A Reappraisal." *American Economic Review* 46 (5): 857–79.

Buiter, Willem H. 1993. "Measurement of the Public Sector Deficit and Its Implications for Policy Evaluation and Design." In Mario I. Blejer and Adrienne Cheasty, eds. *How to Measure the Fiscal Deficit.* Washington, DC: International Monetary Fund.

Burnside, Craig. 2000. "Some Facts about the HP Filter." World Bank Development Research Group. http://www.duke.edu/~acb8/res/hpfilt3.pdf.

Chand, Sheetal K. 1993. "Fiscal Impulse Measures and Their Fiscal Impact." In Mario I. Blejer and Adrienne Cheasty, eds. *How to Measure the Fiscal Deficit.* Washington, DC: International Monetary Fund.

Chouraqui, Jean-Claude, Robert Hagemann, and Nicola Sartor. 1990. "Indicators of Fiscal Policy: A Reexamination." Working Paper 78, Department of Economics and Statistics, Organisation for Economic Co-operation and Development, Paris.

Christiano, Lawrence J. 1992. "Searching for a Break in GNP." *Journal of Business and Economic Statistics* 10 (3): 237–50.

de Leeuw, Frank, and Thomas M. Holloway. 1982. "The High-Employment Budget: Revised and Automatic Inflation Effects." *Survey of Current Business* 62 (4): 21–33.

————. 1983. "Cyclical Adjustment of the Federal Budget and Federal Debt." *Survey of Current Business* 63 (12): 25–40.

de Leeuw, Frank, Thomas M. Holloway, Darwin G. Johnson, David S. McClain, and Charles A. Waite. 1980. "The High Employment Budget: New Estimates, 1955–80." *Survey of Current Business* 60 (11): 13–43.

European Community, Directorate-General for Economic and Financial Affairs. 1995. "Technical Note: The Commission Services' Method for the Cyclical Adjustment of Government Budget Balances." *European Economy* 60: 35–88.

Fellner, William. 1982. "The High-Employment Budget and Potential Output: A Critique." *Survey of Current Business* 62 (11): 25–33.

Giorno, Claude, Pete Richardson, Deborah Roseveare, and Paul van den Noord. 1995. "Estimating Potential Output, Output Gaps, and Structural Budget Balances." Working Paper 152, Department of

5

Economics, Organisation for Economic Co-operation and Development, Paris.

Hodrick, Robert J., and Edward C. Prescott. 1997. "Postwar U.S. Business Cycles: An Empirical Investigation." *Journal of Money, Credit, and Banking* 29 (1): 1–16.

Holloway, Thomas M. 1984. "Cyclical Adjustment of the Federal Budget and Federal Debt: Detailed Methodology and Estimates." Bureau of Economic Analysis Staff Paper 40, U.S. Department of Commerce, Washington, DC.

IMF (International Monetary Fund). 1993. "Structural Budget Indicators for the Major Industrial Countries." *World Economic Outlook* (October): 99–103.

Price, Robert W. R., and Patrice Muller. 1994. "Structural Budget Indicators and the Interpretation of Fiscal Policy Stance in OECD Economies." *OECD Economic Studies* (3): 27–72.

Schwarz, Gideon. 1978. "Estimating the Dimension of a Model." *Annals of Statistics* 6 (2): 461–4.

Woitek, Ulrich. 1998. "A Note on the Baxter-King Filter." University of Glasgow. http://www.gla.ac.uk/Acad/PolEcon/pdf98/9813.pdf.

5

Mexico: A Case Study of Procyclical Fiscal Policy

Craig Burnside and Yuliya Meshcheryakova

023   E62
     E32
     H61
     H50

6

This chapter investigates one aspect of the sustainability of fiscal policy in Mexico. It focuses on the response of fiscal policy to the business cycle and, through the lens of simple Keynesian models, examines the role fiscal policy plays in determining output.[1]

These issues were chosen for a number of reasons. In the post-World War II period, fiscal policy in industrial economies has played the role of cyclical stabilizer. Fiscal policy has been designed to "lean against the wind." That is, the structure of fiscal policy creates a stimulus to output when the economy moves into recession and is contractionary when an expansion broadens. This is usually accomplished in two ways: first, by having components in the budget that respond automatically to the business cycle, such as tax revenues (which respond positively) or unemployment benefits (an expenditure item that responds negatively); and second, by using discretionary components in the budget to provide a stimulus during bad times. A fiscal policy designed in this way leads to a strongly procyclical budget balance.

Generally speaking, Mexico's fiscal policy has not leaned against the wind. The analysis presented here will show that during the period 1980–2003 the budget balance was strongly countercyclical, so that fiscal policy leaned with the wind. The automatic stabilizers in place are weak—and are further weakened by the tendency of another automatic component of the budget, oil-based revenue (which responds sensitively to exogenous world oil prices) to move countercyclically. Furthermore, the discretionary component of the budget surplus also tends to move countercyclically.

If fiscal policy simply did not matter, its leaning with or against the wind would be of little consequence. However, in Mexico, as in many other countries, fiscal policy does matter. The analysis presented here suggests that an increase in the discretionary fiscal balance of 1 percent of GDP causes GDP to decline by 0.6 percent in the following year. It also suggests that when other contractionary shocks hit the economy, the fiscal policy response to these shocks is contractionary as well.

The results imply that Mexico's fiscal policy was not designed in a way that makes it a stabilizing feature of the economy. Furthermore, it was not designed to render itself more sustainable. With *procyclical fiscal policy* (a countercyclical fiscal balance), debt accumulates during economic expansions; and when the economic expansion inevitably ends, this debt suddenly becomes costly to service. To finance this debt, the government must take drastic discretionary fiscal measures, finance the debt by borrowing at high real interest rates, or print money and induce inflation. No matter which action the government takes, the implications are similar: a worsening of the economic downturn.

Section 1 examines the fiscal accounts data. The sample period studied here—1980 through mid-2003—spans several interesting episodes in Mexico's economic history. This choice of time period was largely driven by the availability of data. Quarterly national accounts data for Mexico are available from 1980 onward, while monthly fiscal accounts are available from 1977 onward. Trends and cycles in national accounts measures of real GDP are identified. And similarly, with GDP-based definitions of the business cycle in mind, section 1 describes the trends and cyclical fluctuations observed in various components of the public sector's fiscal accounts.

Section 2 examines a preferred definition of the cyclically adjusted budget surplus for Mexico. The discussion is based on the concepts and methods introduced in chapter 5.

Section 3 presents a more complex analysis of the data. Rather than working with simple indicators of the fiscal policy stance, this section builds a simple vector autoregressive (VAR) model of the Mexican economy that isolates several important features, namely: the nature of the feedback rule that implicitly determines fiscal policy, including the effects of economic activity on the budget; the exogenous shocks to the budget; and the short- and medium-run effects of these shocks on economic activity. The main purpose of such a model is that the summary measures presented in section 2 are typically useful in the context of a narrowly defined economic model. Furthermore, those summary measures are generally used to describe the effects of current policy on current activity. As such, given the lags with which fiscal policy is implemented and its effects are felt, the more forward-looking analysis of section 3 is important.

1   Perspectives on Mexico's Fiscal Accounts, 1980–2003

This analysis begins with an evaluation of quarterly data on Mexico's fiscal accounts from 1980 through mid-2003. Although monthly budget data are available dating back to 1977, high-frequency data on GDP are available only from 1980 onward. The evaluation process defines the business cycle in Mexico with reference to quarterly data on real GDP from the national accounts, divides the fiscal accounts into their revenue and expenditure components, and finally looks at revenue and expenditure trends.

The Business Cycle in Mexico

Figure 6.1 illustrates the behavior of real GDP in Mexico from 1980 through 2003. The raw data show a clear pattern of seasonality. Overlying the general upward trend and cycles is a pattern that indicates relatively low production in the first and third quarters, and relatively high production in the second and fourth quarters. To identify these underlying features in the data, a seasonal adjustment filter was applied.[2]

Figure 6.2 shows the seasonally adjusted data, with shading used to identify recessions. Several episodes are especially worth noting:

- The recession of 1982 through mid-1983 that is associated with the Mexican debt crisis
- The period of slow and erratic growth thereafter, followed by the recession of late 1985 and 1986
- The implementation of the stabilization program in 1988, with an initial slightly recessionary year
- The expansion experienced from 1989–94

Figure 6.1: Real GDP in Mexico, 1980–2003

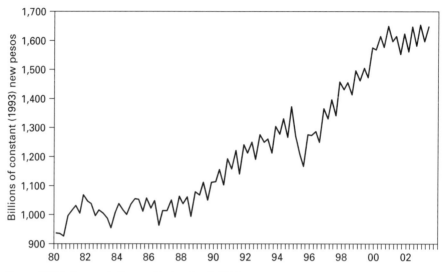

Source: INEGI. Sistema de Cuentas Nacionales de México.

Figure 6.2: Seasonally Adjusted Real GDP in Mexico, 1980–2003

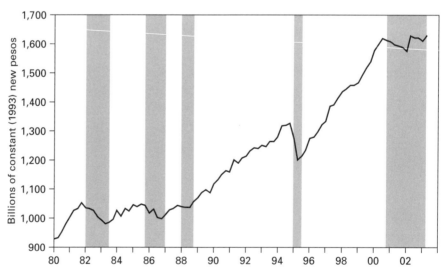

Source: Authors' calculations.

- The short and intense recession of 1995 that was associated with the peso crisis and the subsequent recovery
- A long but shallow recession beginning at the end of 2000 and apparently ending in early 2003.

One can see from figure 6.2 that all expansions and all contractions of the Mexican economy during the period under consideration are not alike. For example, the downturn after the peso crisis of December 1994 was much sharper and deeper than the downturns experienced during the previous and subsequent recessions. This particular contraction involved a cumulative decline in output of 9.7 percent, versus 6.8, 4.7, and 0.8 percent in the previous recessions and 0.4 percent in the most recent recession. It lasted 2 quarters, compared with 6, 5, and 3 quarters in the previous recessions, and 10 quarters for the most recent recession. The economic expansion that followed the 1995 recession was also more rapid than any of the previous expansions.

Chapter 5 describes several methods used in the literature to measure a business cycle. These are the results of those methods when applied to the Mexican GDP series.

Piecewise Linear Trend

Figure 6.3a illustrates a piecewise linear trend fit to real GDP, with a break point at 1989 Q2. This trend represents the fitted values from the regression

$$y_t = a_0 + a_1 d_t^* + b_0 t + b_1 t d_t^* + \varepsilon_t, \tag{1.1}$$

where $y_t = \ln Y_t$, Y_t is real GDP, $d_t^* = 1$ for $t \geq t^*$, and $d_t^* = 0$ for $t < t^*$, and t^* represents 1989 Q2. This date was chosen as the break date because it maximizes the t-statistic for the estimated coefficient, b_1. As cautioned in chapter 5, searching for breaks in this way implies that the small sample distribution of the maximized t-statistic deviates considerably from a standard normal. The estimates of (1.1) are displayed in table 6.1.

A search for further breaks in the pre-1989 and post-1989 period identified only one other possible break in trend, at the beginning of the 2001–3 recession. Until more data are available, it is probably premature to assign this date as a true break in trend.

Figure 6.3: Trends in Real GDP, 1980–2003

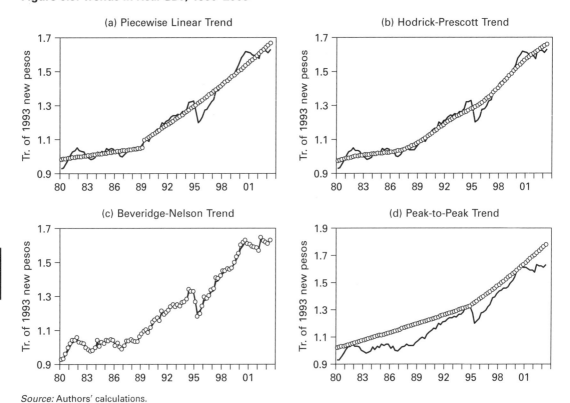

Source: Authors' calculations.

Notes: Trends are indicated by dotted lines

Table 6.1: Estimates of a Piecewise Linear Trend in the Logarithm of Seasonally Adjusted Real GDP, 1980 Q1–2003 Q2

Coefficient	Estimate	Standard error	t-statistic
Constant	20.71	0.045	455
Post-1989 Q2 dummy	−0.173	0.063	−2.76
Trend	0.0018	0.0018	1.03
Trend × post-1989 Q2 dummy	0.0057	0.0019	3.02

Sources: Raw data from INEGI (Instituto Nacional de Estadística Geografia e Informática). Seasonally adjusted data and other statistics based on authors' calculations using quarterly data.

Notes: The estimates were computed using ordinary least squares. The standard errors and t-statistics are robust to heteroskedasticity and serial correlation. A Newey and West (1987) estimator with five lags was used to compute the standard errors. The t-statistics do not have a conventional small sample or asymptotic distribution. See chapter 5.

The deviations from trend implied by the piecewise linear trend are shown in figure 6.4a. The typical pattern is that a peak of GDP relative to trend corresponds to the end of an expansion period. Recessions move GDP from these peaks to below-trend troughs. With each expansion (1980, 1989–94, and 1996–2000), the series slowly rises from a trough and reaches another peak.

The Hodrick-Prescott Filter

Figure 6.3b illustrates the trend defined by the Hodrick-Prescott (HP) filter discussed in chapter 5. As that chapter explains, the trend is the series $\{y_t^*\}_{t=1}^T$ that minimizes the objective function:

$$\sum_{t=1}^{T} (y_t - y_t^*)^2 + \lambda \sum_{t=2}^{T-1} [(y_{t+1}^* - y_t^*) - (y_t^* - y_{t-1}^*)]^2. \qquad (1.2)$$

6

Figure 6.4: Deviations from Trend in Real GDP, 1980–2003

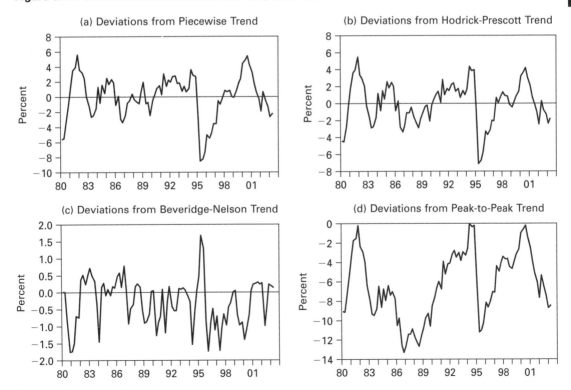

Source: Authors' calculations.

Table 6.2: Correlations among Various Measures of the Cyclical Component of GDP, 1980 Q1–2003 Q2

	Piecewise linear trend	HP trend	Peak-to-peak	BN decomposition
Piecewise linear trend	1			
HP trend	0.955	1		
Peak-to-peak trend	0.707	0.809	1	
BN decomposition	−0.257	−0.324	−0.325	1

Sources: Raw data from INEGI. Seasonally adjusted data and other statistics based on authors' calculations using quarterly data.

Notes: For definitions of the various measures of the cyclical component of GDP, refer to the main text. BN, Beveridge-Nelson decomposition; HP, Hodrick-Prescott filter.

The conventional value for the smoothing parameter for quarterly data is 1,600 and is used here. As figure 6.3 indicates, the HP trend turns out to be similar to the piecewise linear trend. Consequently, the deviations from trend, illustrated in figure 6.4b, are highly correlated with those obtained using the piecewise linear trend (see table 6.2). Note that all of the recessions marked in figure 6.2 correspond to points at which there is a rapid change of sign in the deviations of GDP from the piecewise linear and HP trends.

The Baxter-King Filter

The Baxter-King (BK) approximate band-pass filter discussed in chapter 5 is not discussed here, due to the loss of data it implies. With a somewhat small sample of 94 quarters, one would end up with only 70 observations, since the method uses a symmetric 25-quarter moving average of the raw data to compute the cyclical component. This analysis does, however, show that the correlation between the BK and HP cyclical components is 0.94 over the period 1983 Q1–2000 Q2; and visually, it is difficult to distinguish between the two definitions of the cycle.

Beveridge-Nelson Decomposition

The Beveridge-Nelson (BN) decomposition, also discussed in chapter 5, decomposes a series into permanent and transitory components using an estimated ARIMA model. To compute the BN decomposition, a model of the form

$$\Delta y_t = \mu + a_1(\Delta y_{t-1} - \mu) + \cdots + a_p(\Delta y_{t-p} - \mu)$$
$$+ \varepsilon_t + \theta_1 \varepsilon_{t-1} + \cdots + \theta_q \varepsilon_{t-q} \qquad (1.3)$$

was estimated by maximum likelihood. The orders of the autoregressive terms, p, and the moving average terms, q, were chosen according to the Schwarz criterion, which selected $p = 2$ and $q = 0$. The trend, or permanent component, of the level of the series is its current value plus any predicted stochastic growth:

$$y_t^* = y_t + E_t(\Delta y_{t+1} - \mu + \Delta y_{t+2} - \mu + \cdots), \qquad (1.4)$$

which can, of course, be computed given estimates of the a_is and θ_is in (1.3).

The resulting trend estimates are plotted in figure 6.3c. A notable aspect of the trend, in this case, is that it closely tracks the original series. This is a function of the fact that the growth rate of GDP in Mexico is not very persistent. If Δy_t were a random walk with drift, so that $\Delta y_t = \mu + \varepsilon_t$, the BN trend, or permanent component, would simply be y_t. As it stands, the estimated model for Mexico's GDP growth is $\Delta y_t = 0.0027 + 0.11\Delta y_{t-1} + 0.22\Delta y_{t-2} + \varepsilon_t$, indicating that there is only limited persistence in Mexico's GDP growth rate.

The deviations from trend are plotted in figure 6.4c. These are defined as $y_t^c = y_t - y_t^*$. Notice that these deviations from trend are much smaller and behave differently from those identified using the piecewise linear trend and the HP filter (see also table 6.2). Again, this is a function of the fact that the growth rate of GDP is not very persistent. If Δy_t were a random walk with drift, the BN cyclical component would simply be ε_t.

Peak-to-Peak Trend

In this case, trend lines were used in an ad hoc way to connect the peaks in 1981 Q4, 1994 Q4, and 2000 Q3, as illustrated in figure 6.3d. With the trend specified in this way, output never lies above the trend. The deviations from trend are plotted in figure 6.4d. They are highly correlated with the deviations from trend defined by the HP filter and the piecewise linear trend (see table 6.2).

Given the similarity between the deviations from trend defined by the piecewise linear, HP, and peak-to-peak trend lines, the deviations from trend defined using the HP filter will be examined later.

6

Trends and Cycles in Mexico's Fiscal Accounts

Mexico's fiscal accounts are now examined using an approach similar to the one used in the previous section. As in the analysis of output, the definition of trend and cycle used here to analyze the fiscal accounts is the one implied by the HP filter. Data from the fiscal accounts are treated in the same way as the GDP data; that is, they are converted into real terms by dividing by the GDP deflator. Because many of the resulting series display seasonal patterns, the series are further processed to remove seasonal components.

The public sector accounts used here are those provided by Banco de México (see data sources at the end of this chapter). Included in the definition of the public sector are the federal government and public sector enterprises. State governments are considered only to the extent that federal government transfers to them are included as expenditure items.

Table 6.3 presents summary figures. These show that Mexico moved from a position of large fiscal deficits in the early 1980s to a position of small fiscal deficits in the 1990s and into the new century. The primary deficit was narrowed during the mid-1980s, in response to the debt crisis. This occurred through a drastic reduction in noninterest expenditure, which now represents about 20 percent of GDP, in contrast to between 25 and 30 percent of GDP in the early 1980s. Total expenditure also declined after the 1988 stabilization, with interest expenditure beginning to fall in line with the decline in inflation. Since 1991, interest has represented 5 percent or less of total expenditure, whereas in 1987 it peaked at nearly 19 percent of total expenditure.

Table 6.3: Summary Budget Figures, 1980–2002

	As a percentage of					
	GDP			Revenue		
Budget category	1980–8	1989–2002	Full sample	1980–8	1989–2002	Full sample
Overall surplus	−8.6	−1.3	−5.3	−33.4	−3.6	−15.2
Primary surplus	−4.9	2.5	3.3	7.1	15.8	12.4
Revenue	28.3	23.2	25.2	100.0	100.0	100.0
Expenditure	37.7	24.0	29.3	133.4	103.3	115.1
Interest	11.7	4.6	7.4	40.5	19.4	27.7
Primary expenditure	26.0	19.4	21.9	92.8	83.9	87.4

Sources: Raw fiscal data are from Banco de México. GDP data are from INEGI. Statistics are based on authors' calculations using annual data.

Revenue

It is also interesting to consider a more detailed breakdown of the public sector accounts. On the revenue side, several of the available series are displayed in figure 6.5. Figure 6.5a shows total revenue, in real terms, which displays a very different pattern than GDP. Unlike GDP, public sector revenue grew rapidly through 1985, declined during the 1986 recession, and remained roughly constant in real terms until the mid-1990s. After 1995, real revenue rose rapidly. As tables 6.3 and 6.4 indicate, overall revenue represents a declining share of GDP. In the period 1980–8, revenue averaged 28.3 percent of GDP. After 1988, revenue averaged only 23.2 percent of GDP.

Figure 6.6a displays the deviations of total revenue and GDP from their HP trends. As table 6.5 shows, from 1980 Q1 through 2003 Q2, the cyclical

Table 6.4: Components of Public Sector Revenue and Expenditure, 1980–2002
(percent)

Budget category	GDP			Revenue		
	1980–8	1989–2002	Full sample	1980–8	1989–2002	Full sample
Revenue	28.3	23.2	25.2	100.0	100.0	100.0
Federal tax revenue	10.2	10.7	10.5	36.2	46.5	42.5
Income tax	4.3	4.7	4.6	15.6	20.3	18.5
VAT	2.8	3.1	3.0	10.0	13.6	12.2
Excise tax	2.0	1.7	1.8	6.9	7.5	7.3
Trade taxes	0.7	0.7	0.7	2.7	3.1	2.9
Other taxes	0.3	0.5	0.4	1.0	2.0	1.6
Federal nontax revenue	5.5	4.9	5.1	19.2	20.9	20.3
Oil rights	4.5	3.1	3.7	15.7	13.6	14.4
Other	0.9	1.7	1.4	3.3	7.4	5.8
Revenue of PSEs	12.7	7.6	9.6	44.6	32.6	37.3
PEMEX	5.5	2.5	3.7	19.2	10.7	14.0
Other	7.2	5.1	5.9	25.4	21.9	23.3
Expenditure	37.7	24.0	29.3	133.4	103.3	115.1
Primary expenditure	26.0	19.4	21.9	92.8	83.9	87.4
Wages and salaries	6.0	4.2	4.9	21.5	18.1	19.4
Materials and other	8.1	4.7	6.0	28.3	20.1	23.4
Transfers to states	2.5	3.0	2.8	8.8	12.9	11.3
Transfers to PSEs	2.7	1.2	1.8	9.7	5.3	7.0
Other transfers	4.7	5.2	5.0	17.0	23.0	20.7
Capital expenditure	4.7	2.3	3.2	17.2	9.7	12.6
Interest	11.7	4.6	7.4	40.5	19.4	27.7
Memo item: oil revenue	11.2	6.9	8.6	39.2	29.7	33.4

Sources: Raw fiscal data are from Banco de México. GDP data are from INEGI. Statistics are based on authors' calculations using annual data.

Notes: PEMEX, Petroleos Mexicanos; PSEs, public sector enterprises.

Figure 6.5: Public Sector Revenue in Mexico, 1980–2003

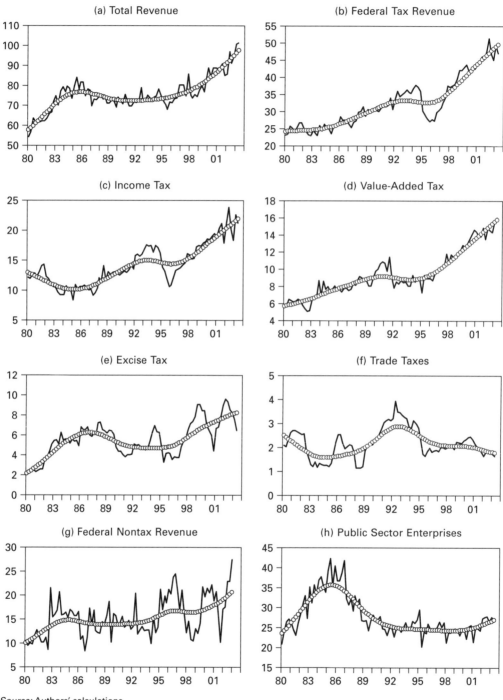

Source: Authors' calculations.

Notes: Each series is measured in billions of 1993 pesos. Dotted lines indicate the HP trend of each series.

Figure 6.6: Cyclical Components of Public Sector Revenue, 1980–2003

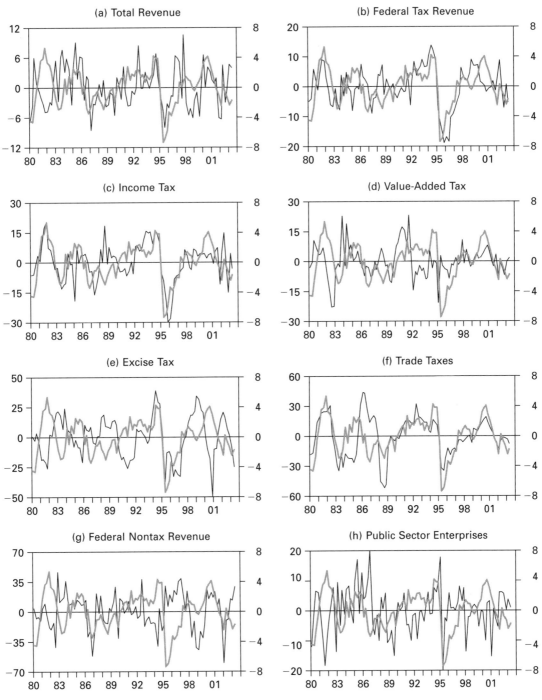

Source: Authors' calculations.

Notes: Deviations from trend are measured in percent (left axis) and are indicated by black lines. Gray lines indicate the cyclical component of real GDP (right axis).

Table 6.5: Cyclical Properties of Public Sector Revenue and Expenditure, 1980 Q1–2003 Q2

Cyclical component of	Standard deviation		Correlation with GDP
	Percent	× share of GDP	
Revenue	4.2	1.1	0.23
Federal tax revenue	6.5	0.7	0.56
Income tax	9.5	0.4	0.57
VAT	8.1	0.2	0.08
Excise tax	17.5	0.3	0.06
Trade taxes	19.9	0.1	0.59
Other taxes	17.8	0.1	0.14
Federal nontax revenue	21.2	1.1	−0.11
Oil rights	26.0	1.0	−0.12
Other	28.8	0.4	0.07
Revenue of PSEs	7.5	0.7	0.01
PEMEX	19.4	0.7	−0.14
Other	6.0	0.4	0.28
Expenditure	7.0	2.0	0.22
Primary expenditure	7.4	1.6	0.61
Wages and salaries	7.4	0.4	0.51
Materials and other	10.8	0.6	0.28
Transfers to states	8.3	0.2	0.42
Transfers to PSEs	19.2	0.3	0.12
Other transfers	15.0	0.8	0.44
Capital expenditure	13.0	0.4	0.38
Interest	23.1	1.7	−0.35
Memo item: oil revenue	10.8	0.9	−0.25

Sources: Raw fiscal data are from Banco de México. GDP data are from INEGI. Statistics are based on authors' calculations using quarterly data.

Notes: PEMEX, Petroleos Mexicanos; PSEs, public sector enterprises.

movements of total revenue were not that highly correlated with output, with a correlation of only 0.23. Revenue was also somewhat more volatile than output, with a standard deviation of 4.2 percent (representing about 1.1 percent of GDP), as opposed to 2.6 percent for GDP.

A different picture emerges once components of revenue are considered. Federal tax revenue, shown in figure 6.5b, grew substantially from 1980 to 2003, and its trend is much more consistent with that of GDP: slow growth in the early to mid-1980s, followed by accelerated real growth that was interrupted by the 1995 recession. Overall, as table 6.4 indicates, tax revenue rose slightly as a percentage of GDP, and represents a much larger percentage of total revenue than in the past: 46.5 percent of revenue in 1989–2002, as opposed to 36.2 percent of revenue in 1980–8. Also, tax revenue (shown by table 6.5) is more highly correlated with real activity than is overall revenue: The correlation of the HP cycle in tax revenue with that of GDP is 0.56.

Within tax revenue, the trends and cycles across various tax categories exhibit some interesting differences. Figures 6.5c–f show the most important components of tax revenue: income, value-added, and excise taxes, and taxes on international trade (mainly taxes on imports).

As table 6.4 indicates, income taxes and value-added taxes (VATs) have become increasingly important parts of revenue, rising from a combined 25.6 percent of revenue in the period 1980–8, to a combined 33.9 percent of revenue in the period 1989–2002. In fact, by 2002, income taxes and VATs represented 22.6 and 15.5 percent of all revenue, respectively, versus just 12.4 and 9.5 percent of all revenue in 1985. Excise taxes have also grown in importance since 1995, with most of this attributable to increased gasoline taxes. Meanwhile, trade taxes, which increased in importance into the early 1990s, have been cut substantially: In 2002 they represented less than 2 percent of overall revenue. The declining reliance on import duties and the slow expansion of income taxation and the VAT as sources of revenue are typical of countries at Mexico's stage of industrialization.

Regarding cyclical properties, figures 6.6c–f show the cyclical components of the components of tax revenue. Income taxes are clearly highly procyclical (table 6.5 indicates that the correlation with the cyclical component of GDP is 0.57), though clearly more volatile than the business cycle itself. Value-added and excise taxes are not particularly procyclical; their correlations with the cyclical component of GDP are just 0.08 and 0.06, respectively. Revenue from trade taxes is highly procyclical; the correlation with GDP is 0.59, reflecting the highly procyclical nature of imports.

Real nontax revenues displayed an upward trend in real terms, but they have remained at a fairly stable share of overall revenue (about 20 percent). Table 6.4 indicates that most nontax revenues are derived from oil rights, though these have declined somewhat in importance as a source of revenue. As table 6.5 shows, nontax revenue is the most volatile source of income for the government: The standard deviation of its cyclical component is 21 percent. Table 6.5 also indicates that nontax revenue is roughly acyclical. The volatility and acyclicality of nontax revenue are largely a reflection of the fact that oil prices are volatile and are roughly uncorrelated with Mexico's overall business cycle.

The remaining source of public sector revenue is the revenue of public sector enterprises. The single largest public sector enterprise in Mexico is PEMEX, the state oil company, whose revenue represented about 11 percent of overall revenue in 2002, but almost 25 percent of revenue in the mid-1980s.

6

As indicated by table 6.4, revenue from other public sector enterprises (PSEs) has also declined over time as a share of both GDP and overall revenue. PEMEX's revenues are roughly uncorrelated with the cyclical component of GDP, again reflecting the fact that oil prices are roughly uncorrelated with Mexico's overall business cycle. As table 6.5 indicates, revenue from other PSEs is moderately procyclical.

To assess Mexico's overall dependence on oil-based revenue, one can sum gasoline taxes, revenue from oil rights, and the revenues of PEMEX. As table 6.4 illustrates, Mexico's dependence on oil revenue has declined over time. In the mid-1980s, oil revenue represented between 40 and 45 percent of total revenue, but by 2002, it represented less than 30 percent. And as table 6.5 indicates, the cyclical component of oil revenue is somewhat negatively correlated with the business cycle. This explains why Mexico's overall revenue is less cyclically sensitive than the revenue of governments in economies at a similar stage of development that lack oil resources.

Expenditure

On the expenditure side of the public sector budget, one should distinguish between interest on public debt and other forms of spending, referred to as primary expenditure. Primary expenditure peaked at about 30 percent of GDP in 1981. Thereafter, it fell steadily, and has remained below 20 percent of GDP since 1989, except in 1994 and 2002. The result of this fiscal contraction is that—despite the decline in overall revenue as a share of GDP—the public sector has moved to a stronger primary surplus position. The average primary balance in the period 1980–8 was 2.3 percent of GDP; after 1988 it was 3.8 percent of GDP.

Post-1988 there was also a substantial decline in interest expenditure as a share of GDP. In the period 1980–8, rapid inflation and a significant stock of domestic debt implied an average interest burden of 11.7 percent of GDP. In the post-1988 period this declined to just 4.6 percent of GDP.

Interestingly, primary expenditure is highly procyclical, as indicated by table 6.5. The correlation of its cyclical component with the cyclical component of GDP is 0.61, and it is substantially more volatile than GDP, with a standard deviation of 7.4 percent. The procyclical behavior of expenditure actually offsets the procyclical behavior of revenue and tends to make the primary budget countercyclical. As a recent study by the Inter-American Development Bank indicates (Gavin and others 1996), from a Keynesian perspective, the public sector in Mexico thus acts much less as a stabilizer than it does in other OECD economies. Once expenditure is divided into its components, an even clearer picture emerges. Wages and salaries in the public sector, depicted in figure 6.7b, declined steadily in real terms from 1980 through 1996. Since then they have increased steadily in real terms and have stabilized at around 4 percent of GDP. Figure 6.8b and table 6.5 indicate that wages and salaries have been highly procyclical. Most of this procyclical behavior is not due to the federal government wage bill but is largely determined by the behavior of wages within public sector enterprises.

Expenditure on materials and supplies, as well as other nontransfer current spending, has declined sharply in importance, from 28.3 percent of revenue in the period 1980–8 to just 20.1 percent of revenue in the period after 1988. This pattern is confirmed by figure 6.7c. Materials and supplies expenditures are only slightly procyclical, as indicated by figure 6.8c and table 6.5. The correlation of their cyclical component with GDP is just 0.28.

Transfers have become an increasingly significant component of the overall public sector budget, as shown by figures 6.7d–f. In 2002 they represented 58.6 percent of public sector revenue, as opposed to just 41 percent in 1980. Although government transfers to public sector corporations in Mexico have declined in importance, there have been substantial increases in social programs and revenue-sharing transfers to state governments.

The expenditure category "other transfers" is interesting because it represents transfers to households and the private sector, as opposed to transfers destined for state governments and public sector enterprises. Although transfers to state governments might be expected to be procyclical since they represent revenue-sharing, it is perhaps surprising that other transfers are also highly procyclical (see table 6.5, and figure 6.8f). One might expect these other transfers to include aid and social assistance, and that such spending would be countercyclical. But as it turns out, only a relatively small fraction of the government's transfer spending is on social programs with this characteristic.

The federal government shares a substantial portion of its revenue with the states, and this revenue-sharing has increased in importance over time, as shown by table 6.4. Not surprisingly, this expenditure is procyclical; its cyclical component has a correlation of 0.42 with the cyclical component of GDP. This is similar in magnitude to the correlation of overall tax revenue with GDP.

Capital expenditure has declined significantly: in real terms, by about 75 percent from its peak in 1982 (figure 6.7g). As a percentage of GDP,

6

Figure 6.7: Public Sector Expenditure in Mexico, 1980–2003

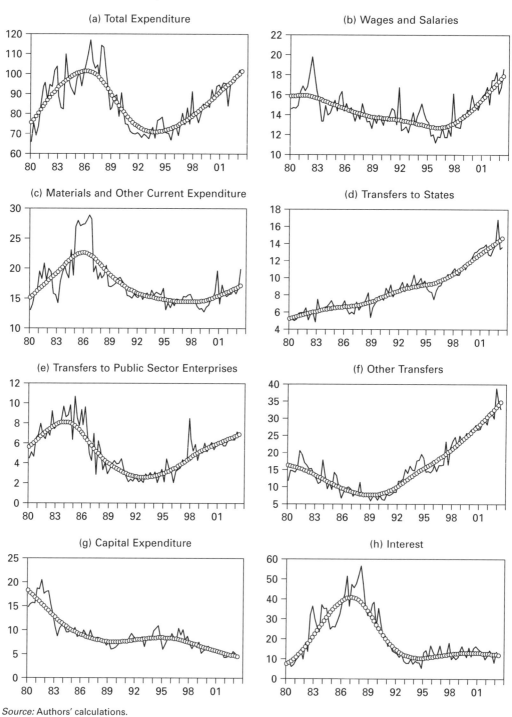

Source: Authors' calculations.

Notes: Each series is measured in billions of 1993 pesos. Dotted lines indicate the HP trend of each series.

Figure 6.8: Cyclical Components of Public Sector Expenditure, 1980–2003

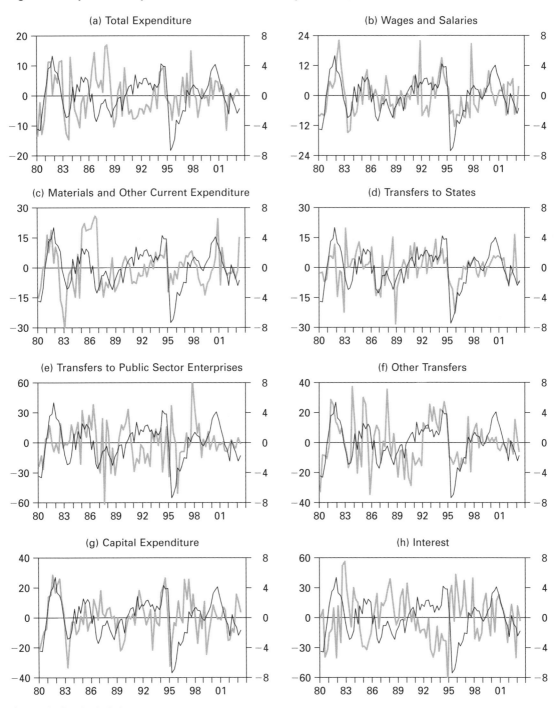

Source: Authors' calculations.

Notes: Deviations from trend are measured in percent (left axis) and are indicated by black lines. Gray lines indicate the cyclical component of real GDP (right axis).

capital expenditure has declined from a peak of 7.4 percent in 1981, to just 1.2 percent in 2002; and as a percentage of revenue, from a peak of 30.6 percent in 1981 to just 5.4 percent in 2002. Capital spending is quite procyclical, as shown by figure 6.8g. Its cyclical correlation with GDP was 0.38 (table 6.5) from 1980 through 2002.

The final expenditure item is interest, which is illustrated in figure 6.7h. Inflation effects are the driving force behind changes in the size of interest flows. Interest expenditure shot up in 1982 and 1986, not only because public sector debt increased, but mainly because inflation accelerated dramatically. High real interest rates in the stabilization period after 1988 kept interest expenditure at high levels, but declining debt stocks and lower real interest rates eventually brought interest spending down. Interest expenditure again rose in significance during 1995 (as inflation accelerated during the peso crisis), but by 1995 the public sector's overall level of indebtedness was much lower than in the early 1980s. After the peso crisis, the interest burden once again moderated. Interest expenditure is countercyclical, its correlation with GDP being −0.35 (table 6.5), largely because inflation in Mexico has tended to be highest during periods of recession.

Interest expenditure plays little role in the subsequent analysis, which focuses mainly on the primary budget balance (revenue minus primary expenditure).

2   Constructing the Cyclically Adjusted Budget Surplus in Mexico

To construct a historical time series for the cyclically adjusted budget balance, one can use the methodology described in chapter 5.

For the purposes of this chapter, all revenue categories were considered for adjustment. In addition, transfers to the states and other transfers were also considered for adjustment. All revenue categories were candidates for adjustment, since there seem to be sound a priori reasons for expecting each of them to behave procyclically. In the case of transfer payments to the states, these are a form of revenue-sharing, so one might expect them to behave similarly to tax revenue. In a sense, transfers to the states represent a reduction in the central government's revenue that behaves much as revenue does. However, one might expect other transfers to be countercyclical, under the assumption that the government has countercyclical social programs.

Estimates of the elasticities of these revenue and expenditure categories with respect to the cyclical component of output are presented in table 6.6. As chapter 5 describes in greater detail, these elasticities are estimated by running ordinary least squares (OLS) regressions of the following form:

$$r_t^c = ey_t^c + \varepsilon_t, \qquad\qquad (2.1)$$

where r_t^c and y_t^c are, respectively, the cyclical components of a revenue category and real GDP, as defined by the HP filter.

As table 6.6 shows, revenue from the income tax is significantly procyclical, and the elasticity of its cyclical component with respect to that of output is 2.19. Hence, income tax revenue can be adjusted in constructing the cyclically adjusted budget balance.

Table 6.6: Estimates of Revenue and Expenditure Elasticities

Revenue/ expenditure category		Estimated elasticities				
		All revenue		*Non-oil revenue*	*Oil revenue*	
	Output	*Output*	*Oil price*	*Output*	*Oil price*	
Income taxes	2.19* (0.33)	...	...	...	...	
VATs	0.27 (0.34)	...	...	...	...	
Excise taxes	0.40 (0.73)	−0.40 (0.65)	−0.51* (0.09)	−0.36 (0.76)	−0.55* (0.14)	
Trade taxes	4.67* (0.67)	...	...	...	...	
Other taxes	0.98 (0.74)	...	...	...	...	
Nontax revenue	−0.93 (0.88)	0.07 (0.77)	0.64* (0.11)	0.85 (1.20)	0.97* (0.11)	
PSE revenue	0.03 (0.32)	0.07 (0.32)	0.03 (0.05)	0.67* (0.24)	0.24* (0.11)	
Oil revenue	...	...	...	...	0.41* (0.05)	
Transfers to states	2.64* (0.56)	...	...	...	...	
Other transfers	1.39* (0.31)	...	...	...	...	

Sources: Raw fiscal data are from Banco de México. GDP data are from INEGI. Data on oil prices are from the Federal Reserve Bank of St. Louis and exchange rate data are from the IFS. Statistics are based on authors' calculations using quarterly data.

Notes: Estimates were computed using ordinary least squares. Standard errors appear in parentheses. *indicates significance at the 5 percent level. ... indicates "not applicable." IFS, International Financial Statistics; PSE, public sector enterprises; VATs, value-added taxes.

However, the low correlation between VAT revenues and output (see table 6.5) ends up being reflected in an insignificant and small estimate of the elasticity of the VAT's cyclical component with respect to that of output. As a result, the VAT revenue is not adjusted in constructing the cyclically adjusted budget balance.

Excise tax revenue, like VAT revenue, is not highly correlated with aggregate activity (see table 6.5). This also is reflected in a positive but insignificant estimate of its elasticity with respect to the cyclical component of output. Since gasoline taxes represent about two-thirds of excise tax revenue, now estimate an additional regression of the form:

$$r_t^c = e_y \, y_t^c + e_p \, p_t^c + \varepsilon_t, \tag{2.2}$$

where p_t^c is the cyclical component of the relative price of oil defined by the HP filter.[3] When estimating (2.2), as table 6.6 indicates, no significant correlation with output is found; but, interestingly, a significant *negative* correlation with the relative price of oil is found. To explore the data further, split the excise tax data into the nongasoline tax and gasoline tax components, and run separate regressions. As table 6.6 indicates, the non-oil component of excise tax revenue remains uncorrelated with output. Yet, the gasoline tax continues to be significant and negatively correlated with the relative price of oil. As figure 6.9a indicates, the overall negative relationship between gasoline taxes and the relative price of oil within the sample studied is not stable across time. In the 1980s, gasoline taxes tended to move with the oil price, but beginning in the 1990s, this pattern of correlation was reversed. Given these overall results, the excise tax revenue is not adjusted with respect to output in constructing the cyclically adjusted budget balance.

When one examines trade taxes, these are found to be significantly procyclical. The authors' estimate of the elasticity of trade taxes with respect to the cyclical component of output is 4.67. This result is not surprising given that most trade taxes are on imports, which not only have a big investment and durable consumption component but also are highly sensitive to business conditions. So trade tax revenue is adjusted in constructing the cyclically adjusted budget balance.

An examination of other taxes found these to be slightly procyclical (see table 6.5). The authors' estimate of the elasticity of other taxes with respect to the cyclical component of output is 0.98. Although this estimate is not significant at the 5 percent level, other tax revenue is adjusted in constructing the cyclically adjusted budget balance.

Figure 6.9: Cyclical Components of Oil-Based Revenue in Mexico, 1980–2003

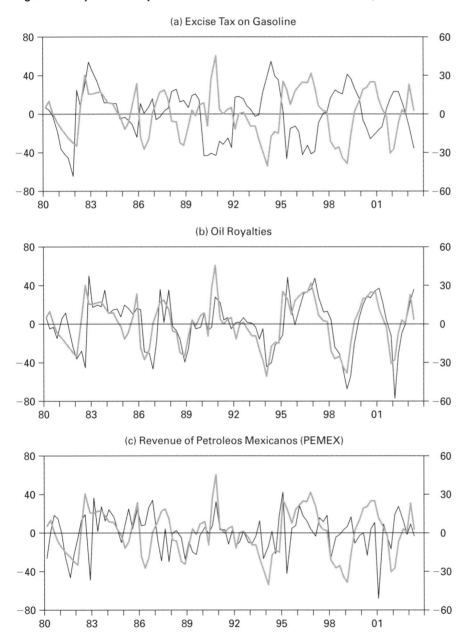

Source: Authors' calculations.

Notes: Deviations from trend are measured in percent (left axis) and are indicated by black lines. Gray lines indicate the cyclical component of the relative price of oil (right axis).

Nontax revenue is not highly correlated with aggregate activity. In fact, it is slightly negatively correlated with real activity (see table 6.5). This is reflected in a negative but insignificant estimate of its elasticity with respect to the cyclical component of output. Since oil royalties represent about two-thirds of nontax revenue, regressions of the form (2.2) were estimated. As table 6.5 shows, there is still no significant correlation with output—but there is a strong correlation with the relative price of oil. To explore the data further, split nontax revenue into its oil royalties and other components, and run separate regressions. As table 6.6 indicates, the non-oil component of nontax revenue is still not significantly positively correlated with output. Oil royalties, however, are highly significant and positively correlated with the relative price of oil. This relationship is shown to be stable over the sample studied, as figure 6.9b indicates. Given these results, nontax revenues are not adjusted with respect to output in constructing the cyclically adjusted budget balance.

Revenue from public sector enterprises is not highly correlated with aggregate activity (see table 6.5). This is reflected in an insignificant estimate of the elasticity of PSE revenues with respect to the cyclical component of output (see table 6.6). Since revenue from PEMEX represents more than a third of this revenue, regressions of the form (2.2) were also estimated. As table 6.6 indicates, no significant correlation was found with output or with the relative price of oil. To explore further, the data were split into revenue from PEMEX and revenue from the other public sector enterprises, and separate regressions were run. As table 6.6 shows, revenue from the other PSEs is significantly and positively correlated with output, with an estimated elasticity of 0.67 with respect to the cyclical component of output. The revenue of PEMEX is significantly and positively correlated with the relative price of oil, with an estimated elasticity of 0.24. This relationship is shown in figure 6.9c. Given these results, the revenue of the non-PEMEX public sector enterprises is adjusted with respect to output in constructing the cyclically adjusted budget balance.

On the expenditure side of the fiscal accounts, transfers to the states were considered first. These transfers essentially deliver part of federal tax revenue to the state and local governments, and one might expect the transfers to be procyclical, given the overall procyclical pattern of revenue. Indeed, this was found to be the case, with the estimated elasticity of transfers to the states being a highly significant 2.64. Hence, transfers to the states were adjusted when constructing the cyclically adjusted budget balance.

In addition to transfers to states, there are also transfers to public sector enterprises. Because there seems to be no particular reason to think that these would be procyclical on structural grounds, they are not considered for cyclical adjustment. As discussed earlier, the remaining transfers, which presumably go to the private sector (via private firms or households), might be expected to be countercyclical. One might expect there to be a variety of social expenditure programs which, due to their structure, would require larger government payouts during recessions. As table 6.5 indicates, however, the pattern of correlation of these other transfers with the cyclical component of output is positive, not negative. Table 6.6 shows that the elasticity of these transfers with respect to output is 1.39—and highly significant. Despite this, other transfers were not adjusted when constructing the cyclically adjusted budget balance, because there seems to be no compelling reason why transfer programs should display this behavior.

Finally, an overall measure of oil-based revenue was considered. This is the sum of gasoline tax revenue, oil royalties, and the revenue of PEMEX. As table 6.4 indicates, in the sample studied, oil revenue represents about one-third of the public sector revenue in Mexico. There is some question as to whether the cyclically adjusted budget measures should take into account the sensitivity of this portion of revenue to oil prices, which, as table 6.6 indicates, is highly significant, with an estimated elasticity of 0.41. If one wants to make adjustments that purely reflect the effect of the business cycle on the budget, one would make no adjustments to oil-based revenue. If, however, the purpose of estimating a cyclically adjusted fiscal surplus is to isolate those components of the budget that are driven by the discretionary decisions of policymakers, correcting for oil prices seems justified. As a result, two alternative measures of the cyclically adjusted budget surplus are presented. One makes no adjustment for oil prices, while the other does.

The cyclically adjusted primary budget balance is defined as

$$\Delta_t^A = \Delta_t + \text{adjustment}$$
$$= (R_t - X_t) - \left(\sum_{j=1}^{4} R_{jt}\left[1 - \exp\left(-\hat{e}_{Rj}\, y_t^c\right) \right] - X_{1t}\left[1 - \exp\left(-\hat{e}_{X1}y_t^c\right) \right] \right),$$

$$(2.3)$$

where R_t is revenue; X_t is primary expenditure; $\Delta_t = R_t - X_t$, R_{1t} represents income tax revenue; R_{2t} is trade tax revenue; R_{3t} is other tax revenue; R_{4t} is revenue from the non-PEMEX public sector enterprises; $\hat{e}_{R1}$, $\hat{e}_{R2}$, $\hat{e}_{R3}$, and $\hat{e}_{R4}$

are the corresponding output elasticities; X_{1t} is transfers to the states; and $\hat{e}_{X1}$ is the corresponding output elasticity.

The oil and cyclically adjusted primary budget balance is defined as

$$\Delta_t^B = \Delta_t^A - R_{Ot}\left[1 - \exp\left(-\hat{e}_O p_t^c\right)\right], \qquad (2.4)$$

where R_{Ot} is oil-based revenue, and $\hat{e}_O$ is the elasticity of oil-based revenue with respect to the relative oil price.

Figure 6.10a presents data on the public sector's primary surplus measured as a percentage of the HP trend of GDP. Note that in the early 1980s, the public sector was in such a large primary deficit position that it was forced to reverse as of 1982, with the onset of the debt crisis. Throughout the rest of the 1980s, the 1990s, and into the new century, the government remained in a strong primary surplus position. From 1983 through 1992, the primary surplus was usually higher than 5 percent of GDP. As inflation was stabilized and the government's debt problems were gradually resolved, the government no longer needed to run such a large primary surplus, and it was scaled back to less than 5 percent for most of the later period (apart from a period of fiscal austerity after the 1994 crisis).

The overall balance, which includes nominal interest payments, is illustrated in figure 6.10b. This paints a different picture, but as argued earlier, the overall balance is deceptive, because during periods of high inflation, interest flows largely reflect compensation for inflation rather than real income to the recipient. For this reason, the overall balance is not the focus of the subsequent analysis.

The cyclically adjusted primary balance is illustrated in figure 6.10c. At first glance, the cyclically adjusted balance and the standard measure of the primary balance appear to be similar. The difference between the two measures is plotted in figure 6.10e, and at times it is substantial, though it is never larger than 1 percent of GDP in absolute value. When the difference is positive, it indicates that fiscal policy was more contractionary than indicated by the standard primary surplus; when it is negative, fiscal policy was more expansionary than indicated by the standard primary surplus. Note, for example, that fiscal policy looks more contractionary during the period 1995–6, when the adjusted budget figures are considered.

Adjustments for changes in oil prices can also be substantial. Oil-based revenue moves closely with the world oil price, which is highly volatile. Figure 6.10f shows that adjustments of revenue for exogenous movements in

6

Figure 6.10: Measures of the Cyclically Adjusted Budget Balance in Mexico, 1980–2003

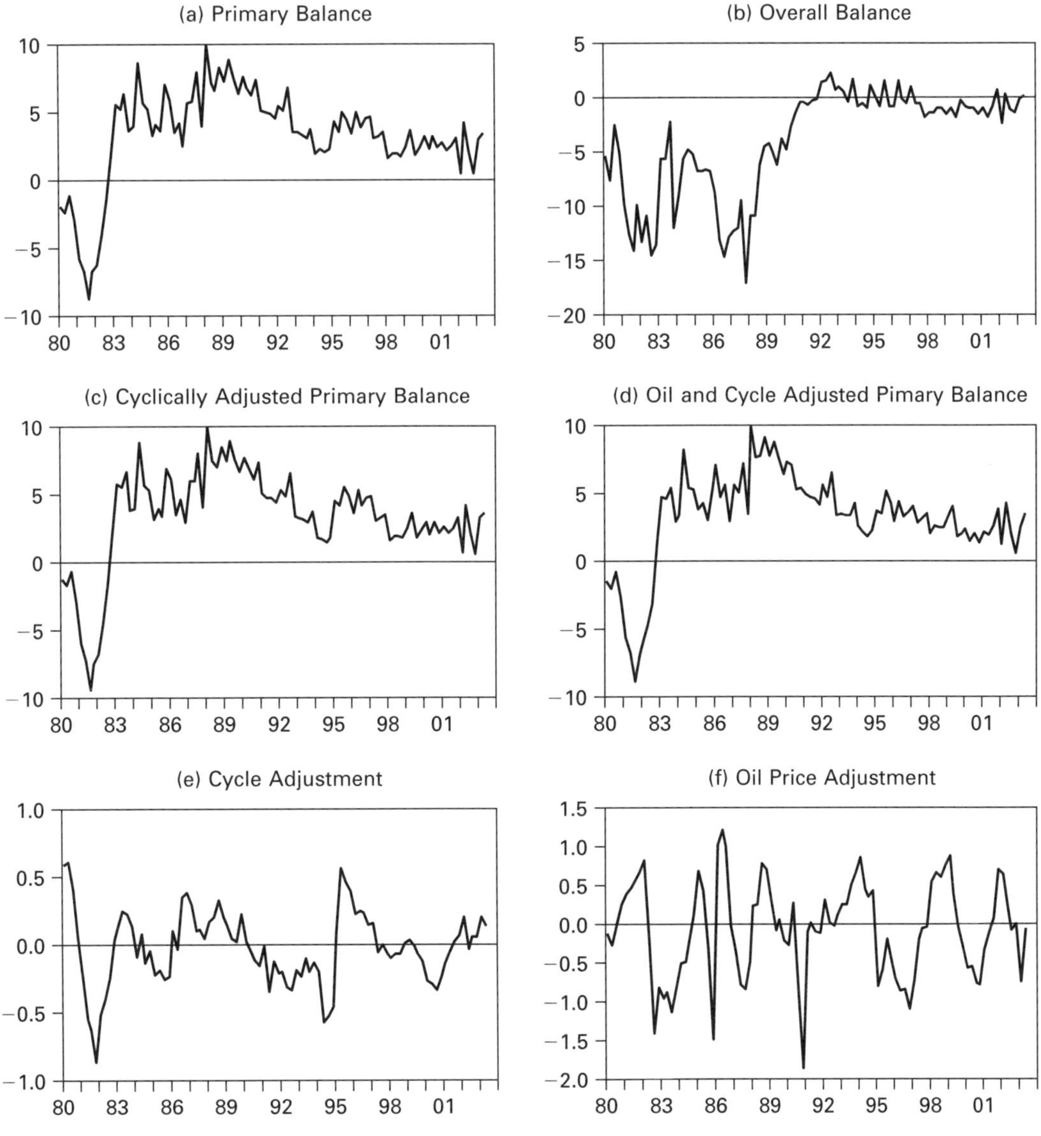

(a) Primary Balance

(b) Overall Balance

(c) Cyclically Adjusted Primary Balance

(d) Oil and Cycle Adjusted Pimary Balance

(e) Cycle Adjustment

(f) Oil Price Adjustment

Source: Authors' calculations.

Note: All variables are measured in percentage of the trend level of GDP.

oil prices have amounted to as much as 2 percent of GDP. For example, oil revenue shot up in 1991 because of the Gulf War. Removing this effect from the data requires an adjustment in the amount of 2 percent of GDP. However, figure 6.10d shows that the overall picture of the budget balance is changed only a little by taking into account movements in oil-based revenue due to changing oil prices. Other factors dominate movement in the primary balance.

3   Characterizing Fiscal Policy

Using the primary balance as a summary measure, one can characterize Mexico's fiscal policy as procyclical for the following reasons. Countercyclical policy, or leaning against the wind, is usually described as running deficits during recessions and surpluses during expansions. In other words, policy is countercyclical when the budget surplus is procyclical. However, the correlation between Mexico's primary surplus as a percentage of trend GDP and the cyclical component of GDP from 1980 through mid-2003 is –0.30. This indicates that Mexico has tended to run bigger surpluses during hard times and smaller surpluses or deficits during good times.

The cyclical adjustment of the primary surplus makes this fact more obvious. The correlation between the cyclically adjusted primary surplus and GDP is –0.36. This suggests that rather than leaning against the wind, discretionary policy appears to lean quite strongly with the wind.[4]

The finding here is consistent with the discussion in Gavin and others (1996) and Talvi and Végh (2000). Gavin and others study a number of Latin American countries and find that in the typical country, fiscal policy is much more procyclical than in the OECD. Both revenue and expenditure are typically much more sensitive to the business cycle than in the OECD, but the expenditure effect is stronger. Talvi and Végh's findings are similar for a broader sample of 56 countries. They contrast fiscal policy in the G7 countries (where, consistent with Barro's tax-smoothing proposition, policy appears to be countercyclical) and policy in industrializing countries (where spending and tax revenue are both highly procyclical).[5]

Interpretations of findings of procyclical policy vary. Gavin and others argue that during recessions, the public sector in many Latin American countries faces a hard budget constraint. They argue that discretionary spending cannot be expansionary in the traditional sense, because the

6

government is liquidity-constrained during recessions. But this begs the question: How did the government become liquidity-constrained in the first place? Was procyclical fiscal policy itself the culprit?

A similar explanation of procyclical fiscal policy is offered by Caballero and Krishnamurthy (2004), who argue that the lack of financial depth in emerging markets is responsible for the cyclical behavior of government budgets. They suggest that if governments in emerging markets were to attempt to borrow in recessions, they would severely crowd private borrowers out of the already limited supply of foreign lending.

Talvi and Végh, in contrast, argue that the procyclicality of government spending is itself a function of the variability of government revenue. They suggest that tax revenues in industrializing countries are more variable and more highly procyclical than in industrialized countries. As a result, the government of an industrializing country faces political pressure to increase government spending during expansions. However, Talvi and Végh do not account for the different patterns of behavior of government spending within the G7 and industrializing economies through differences in political pressure across countries. Instead, they argue that countries with more procyclical spending have more strongly procyclical revenue.

Does Talvi and Végh's story work for Mexico? One problem, as table 6.5 shows, is that public sector revenue is not that strongly procyclical in Mexico. The correlation between the cyclical components of revenue and output is only 0.23. Another problem is that primary expenditure is not only procyclical but it is much more strongly procyclical than is revenue. The correlation between the cyclical components of expenditure and output is 0.61. A further problem with their theory is that when oil prices rise, and, as has been shown, revenues derived from oil rise, primary expenditure tends to fall.[6] This suggests that revenue windfalls from oil are used to retire debt, while increases in revenue associated with the business cycle are more than fully spent.

Consistent with the International Monetary Fund methodology described in greater detail in chapter 5, the *discretionary primary budget balance* was calculated for Mexico. If Δ is the primary balance, then the discretionary balance is defined as

$$\Delta^D = \Delta - (tY - xY^*), \qquad (3.1)$$

where t and x are the sample averages of revenue and primary expenditure as fractions of GDP, Y is real GDP, and Y^* is the HP trend of real GDP. Figure 6.11a presents the discretionary primary budget balance expressed as

Figure 6.11: The Discretionary Balance and the Fiscal Impulse, 1980–2003

(a) Alternative Measures of the Primary Balance

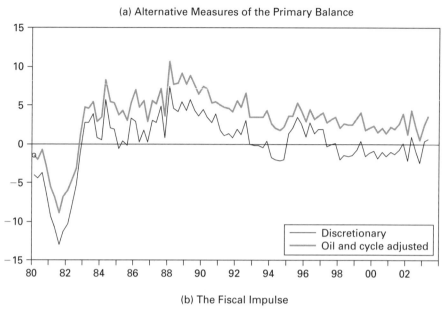

(b) The Fiscal Impulse

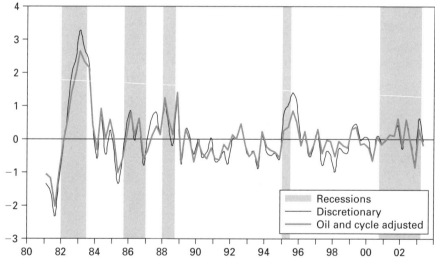

Source: Authors' calculations.

Note: All series are measured in percentage of the trend level of GDP.

a percentage of the trend level of real GDP. Comparing this to the oil price and cycle-adjusted budget balance also shown in figure 6.11a, one sees that the two series are highly correlated—although they have a different level. In fact, the correlation between the two series is 0.979.[7]

As mentioned in chapter 5, the fiscal impulse, $\Delta_t^D - \Delta_{t-1}^D$, in some sense, measures the change in the stance of fiscal policy. Whenever it is positive, policy is moving toward a more expansionary position. Figure 6.11b shows the fiscal impulse calculated using the discretionary budget balance and the oil and cycle-adjusted budget surplus. Both series are expressed as backward-looking, four-quarter, moving averages, because the quarterly observations are extremely volatile. The two measures are highly correlated, and both indicate that there is a tendency for fiscal policy to move toward a more contractionary stance during recessions.

4   The Impact of Fiscal Policy on Real Activity

Ideally, one would like to assess the impact of Mexico's fiscal policy on real activity. And from the perspective of the Keynesian textbook theory discussed in chapter 5, this could be done quite easily. The negative correlation of Mexico's cyclically adjusted primary balance with real activity could be taken to indicate that fiscal policy creates an additional stimulus to real activity during expansions, and exacerbates downturns by reducing domestic demand during recessions. The Keynesian interpretation relies on two assumptions: first, that all movements in the cyclically adjusted primary balance can be treated as indicators of exogenous and discretionary policy decisions, and second, that the Keynesian framework is the right one in which to assess the likely impact of changes in the budget balance.

Ideally, one would also prefer to measure the impact of fiscal policy on real activity without reference to a particular theoretical framework; that is, analysts would like to use a more data-based approach. However, the first point cannot be avoided: Even a data-based approach requires the identification of exogenous changes in the stance of fiscal policy. And it is not obvious that the cyclically adjusted primary balance represents a measure of exogenous policy.

A vector autoregressive approach is now used to assess the impact of fiscal policy on output. In order to do this, one must make identifying assumptions that isolate exogenous changes in policy. Many studies of the U.S. economy have grappled with the question of how to isolate exogenous shifts in fiscal policy using scalar autoregressive or VAR models, and all of the issues raised in the literature are not addressed in this chapter.[8] However, these issues are identified as they arise.

A small VAR model of the Mexican economy is now estimated in an effort to address the following questions: How does discretionary policy affect economic activity? And what were the fiscal impulses to output in historical episodes? The time series included in the VAR is defined and followed by identifying assumptions and answers to these two questions.

A Small VAR Model of the Mexican Economy

Here a quarterly VAR model for a 6×1 vector of time series, z_t, is specified, where z_t consists of:

- The logarithm of the world price of oil (expressed in constant 1993 pesos per barrel)
- The logarithm of real GDP in the United States (measured in constant 1996 chained dollars)
- The U.S. federal funds rate (measured in percent per year)
- The oil- and cyclically adjusted primary balance of the Mexican public sector (measured in percent of trend GDP)
- The logarithm of real GDP in Mexico (measured in constant 1993 pesos)
- The logarithm of the real Mexico-U.S. exchange rate.

The logarithm of the oil price, p_{Ot}, is included not only because oil prices affect the public sector budget balance, but also because they largely determine Mexico's terms of trade. Oil prices may, therefore, have an effect on economic activity as well as the real exchange rate. The logarithm of real GDP in the United States, y_{Ut}, is included because it can be used as an exogenous indicator of the demand for Mexican exports. The U.S. federal funds rate, r_{Ut}, is used as an indicator of monetary policy in the United States. Because Mexico's ability to borrow funds might well depend on conditions in the world financial market, American monetary policy is likely to play some role in business cycle fluctuations in Mexico.

The oil- and cyclically adjusted primary balance as a percentage of trend GDP, δ_t^B, is used as the indicator of fiscal policy in Mexico. The logarithm

6

of Mexican real GDP, y_t, is included to examine the feedback between the fiscal surplus and output. Finally, the logarithm of the real exchange rate, s_t^*, is included because it may be a useful indicator of other shocks that affect the Mexican economy, such as productivity shocks with wealth effects, as well as short- and medium-term changes in Mexican monetary policy. The logarithm of the real exchange rate is measured as $s_t^* = \ln(S_t P_t^*/P_t)$, where S_t is the nominal exchange rate in pesos per dollar, P_t^* is the U.S. GDP deflator, and P_t is the Mexican GDP deflator.

So

$$x_t = \begin{pmatrix} p_{Ot} \\ y_{Ut} \\ r_{Ut} \end{pmatrix} \quad w_t = \begin{pmatrix} \delta_t^B \\ y_t \\ s_t^* \end{pmatrix} \quad \text{and } z_t = \begin{pmatrix} x_t \\ w_t \end{pmatrix}.$$

The vector z_t stacks the *external variables*, x_t, above the *internal variables*, w_t. A "structural" VAR model of z_t is set to permit contemporaneous feedback among the variables:

$$B z_t = A(L) z_{t-1} + \varepsilon_t, \tag{4.1}$$

where B is a nonsingular square matrix, $A(L) = A_1 L + A_2 L^2 + \cdots + A_k L^k$ is a kth-ordered polynomial in the lag operator, and ε_t is a vector of mutually orthogonal serially uncorrelated shocks. Premultiplying (4.1) by B^{-1} one obtains

$$z_t = C(L) z_{t-1} + u_t, \tag{4.2}$$

where $C(L) = B^{-1} A(L)$ is a kth-ordered polynomial in the lag operator, and $u_t = B^{-1} \varepsilon_t$ is a vector of potentially correlated error terms. The standard procedure for estimating VARs is to choose k, and then simply run OLS regressions for each equation implicit in (4.1). Notice that these assumptions about ε_t imply that its covariance matrix is some diagonal matrix D. The covariance matrix of u_t is $\Sigma = B^{-1} D B$. The matrix B can be backed out from an estimate of Σ if sufficient identifying restrictions are placed on B.

Consistent with the partition of z_t into x_t and w_t, one can write (4.1) as

$$\begin{pmatrix} B_{xx} & B_{xw} \\ B_{wx} & B_{ww} \end{pmatrix} \begin{pmatrix} x_t \\ w_t \end{pmatrix} = \begin{pmatrix} A_{xx}(L) & A_{xw}(L) \\ A_{wx}(L) & A_{ww}(L) \end{pmatrix} \begin{pmatrix} x_{t-1} \\ w_{t-1} \end{pmatrix} + \varepsilon_t. \tag{4.3}$$

Because the variables in x_t are (arguably) believed to have been determined by factors outside the Mexican economy, these restrictions are imposed: $B_{xw} = 0$ and $A_{xw}(L) = 0$. The diagonal elements of B_{xx} and B_{ww} are normalized to 1.

It is arguable that world oil prices are determined exogenously and do not depend on contemporaneous or lagged feedback from any of the other variables—the restriction that the 1,2 and 1,3 elements of B_{xx} and $A_{xx}(L)$ are 0 is imposed.

As in Christiano, Eichenbaum, and Evans (1999), here it is assumed that the U.S. Federal Reserve observes current economic activity before setting its federal funds rate target. For this reason, a restriction is imposed: that the 2,3 element of B_{xx} is 0.

The most important identifying assumptions are probably the following: Assume that the oil- and cyclically adjusted fiscal balance, δ_t^B, reacts contemporaneously to the external variables, x_t, but not to the internal variables, that is, the other elements of w_t. This is considered to be a reasonable assumption, as it is considered unlikely that discretionary fiscal policy is able to respond to domestic economic conditions within a short time horizon (one quarter). This means that the 1,2 and 1,3 elements of B_{ww} are set equal to zero. Although these assumptions are believed to be reasonable, one should be sensitive to the possibility that strictly exogenous movements in the budget have not been isolated via these identifying assumptions. Finally, the restriction that the real exchange rate responds contemporaneously to real output is imposed, but not vice versa. This means that the 2,3 element of B_{ww} is set equal to zero. This last assumption is not very important for the results, as the main focus here is on the effects of fiscal policy shocks.

Given these identifying assumptions, the model can be estimated by OLS. The equations are estimated in levels, with a linear time trend included on the right-hand side of each equation.

The Effect of Fiscal Policy on Real Activity

Figure 6.12 presents impulse response functions with respect to a fiscal shock. These are computed by solving for the moving average representation of z_t in terms of ε_t:

$$
\begin{aligned}
z_t &= [I - B^{-1}A(L)L]^{-1}B^{-1}\varepsilon_t \\
&= \Psi_0\varepsilon_t + \Psi_1\varepsilon_{t-1} + \Psi_2\varepsilon_{t-2} + \cdots = \Psi(L)\varepsilon_t.
\end{aligned} \tag{4.4}
$$

The matrices Ψ_k can be calculated once (4.1) has been estimated.

Figure 6.12: Impulse Response Functions

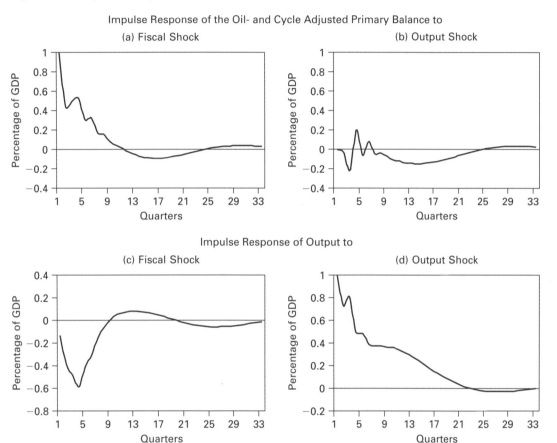

Source: Authors' calculations.

Note: The output shock is an unanticipated 1 percent increase in Mexico's output. The fiscal shock is an unanticipated 1 percent of GDP improvement in the oil- and cyclically adjusted fiscal surplus.

The response of the fiscal balance, z_4, to a fiscal shock, ε_4, is given by $\partial E_t z_{4t+k}/\partial \varepsilon_{4t} = \Psi_k(4,4)$. The response of output, z_5, to a fiscal shock, ε_4, is given by $\partial E_t z_{5t+k}/\partial \varepsilon_{4t} = \Psi_k(5,4)$. Notice, from figure 6.12a, that a shock to the fiscal balance of 1 percent of GDP has a persistent effect on the fiscal balance, but that the fiscal balance returns to its previous value after about two years. Figure 6.12c shows how output responds. It shows that within about three quarters of the shock's occurrence, output falls by about –0.6 percent. This is a substantial decline, but after this output recovers, and within about two years the effects of the shock on output are negligible. The response of output appears to be consistent with basic Keynesian theory.

In terms of policy design, the response of output to unanticipated fiscal shocks matters; but how the response of output to other shocks is affected by the behavior of the fiscal surplus also matters. For example, does the fiscal surplus insulate output from the effects of other shocks? There is no simple way to address this issue, because it pertains to experiments on the feedback rule for fiscal policy. The VAR identifies one feedback rule prevailing during one sample period, but it cannot, strictly speaking, be used to answer questions about the possible impact of alternative feedback rules.

To expand on the noninsulating properties of fiscal policy, compute the response of the fiscal balance at period $t + k$ to each of the shocks at period t, $\partial E_t z_{4t+k}/\partial \varepsilon_{jt}$, $j = 1, \ldots, 6$, and compare this to the response of output to the same shock, $\partial E_t z_{5t+k}/\partial \varepsilon_{jt}$. When the response of output is positive, the shock is expansionary. If the response of the fiscal balance is also positive, one could think about this as policy *leaning against the wind*, because fiscal policy would be taking a contractionary stance in response to a shock that has an expansionary effect.

The VAR model includes six shocks, for which the responses were computed out to $k = 24$ (a six-year horizon). Of course, this choice is arbitrary. Thus, there are 150 responses of output and the fiscal surplus (at 25 different dates, to six different shocks). In only 31 of these cases do the responses of output and the fiscal surplus have the same sign. In 119 (or about 80 percent) of the cases the responses move in opposite directions. This suggests a strong tendency of fiscal policy to magnify, not dampen, the effect of shocks on output, given the presumption that improvements in the fiscal balance are contractionary.

Another way to judge the importance of different shocks is the variance decomposition. The variance decomposition breaks the forecast error for z_t into components corresponding to innovations in each element of ε_t. If one were forecasting output j periods ahead, the forecast error $e_{t,t+j} = z_{t+j} - E_t z_{t+j}$ would be given by

$$e_{t,t+j} = \Psi_0 \varepsilon_{t+j} + \Psi_1 \varepsilon_{t+j-1} + \cdots + \Psi_{j-1}\varepsilon_{t+1}.$$

The variance decomposition of, say, y_t, at horizon j, would decompose the variance of the fifth element of $e_{t,t+j}$ into six components representing the contribution to the variance by each of the six elements of $\varepsilon_{t+1}, \varepsilon_{t+2}, \ldots, \varepsilon_{t+j}$.

The relative importance of the six shocks will vary depending on the forecast horizon. If a shock is relatively important at short horizons, then it is a shock that has relatively short-lived but important effects on output; however, if a shock is relatively important at long horizons, then it has more of a long-run impact. Table 6.7 illustrates the variance decomposition for Mexican GDP at different forecasting horizons. The table indicates that fiscal shocks are an important source of fluctuations in GDP, especially at horizons of about three to eight quarters, where they account for a maximum of 16 percent of the variance in GDP. In an earlier study, fiscal shocks were found to be even more important (Burnside 2001); but that study considered only data up to 1998. This suggests the possibility that fiscal shocks have become smaller or less important to the Mexican economy since that time.

Another way to examine the importance of the budget for output is to compute a historical decomposition of fluctuations in GDP into their sources. This can be done quite easily as a by-product of the VAR estimation. The decomposition divides all deviations of GDP from a linear trend

6

Table 6.7: Variance Decomposition of Output
(percentage of variance of the forecast error)

Forecast horizon (quarter)	Percentage of variance due to shocks to					
	Oil price	U.S. GDP	Federal funds rate	Fiscal balance	GDP	Real exchange rate
1	0.0	6.7	5.2	2.2	86.0	0.0
2	5.0	8.4	3.3	9.5	60.1	13.8
3	4.9	11.3	1.8	12.7	48.3	20.9
4	5.1	13.4	1.3	16.2	36.8	27.2
6	6.4	13.1	4.0	15.2	29.6	31.8
8	6.3	12.2	9.3	13.1	27.4	31.8
12	5.6	10.6	18.2	11.1	26.4	28.2
16	6.3	9.4	24.7	10.0	24.6	25.1
∞	11.2	8.6	30.4	8.3	20.0	21.4

Sources: Raw fiscal data are from Banco de México. Mexican data on GDP and the GDP deflator are from INEGI. Data on oil prices and the federal funds rate are from the Federal Reserve Bank of St. Louis. Exchange rate data are from the IFS. U.S. data on GDP and the GDP deflator are from the U.S. Department of Commerce. Statistics are based on authors' calculations using quarterly data.

Notes: IFS, International Financial Statistics; INEGI, Instituto Nacional de Estadística Geografia e Informática).

Figure 6.13: Deviations of Output from Trend, and the Estimated Component Due to Fiscal Shocks, 1981–2003

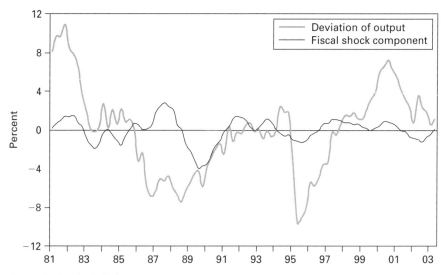

Source: Authors' calculations.

into seven components: one part due to conditions at the beginning of the sample period, and six parts each due to the six different shocks in the VAR. Figure 6.13 plots the portion of GDP caused by fiscal shocks. Note that the fiscal shocks have typically contributed a small portion of the variation in output, and that the fiscal shock component tends to be positively correlated with the overall deviation of output from trend. However, with the exception of the period 1989–90 there is no episode in which shocks to the fiscal balance itself appear to be the most important factor. So one might conclude by arguing that innovations in the fiscal balance seem to have played a relatively small role in driving business cycle fluctuations in Mexico. However, shocks to the fiscal balance do appear to have important short-run effects on real activity consistent with Keynesian theory. Furthermore, and perhaps more important, fiscal policy appears not to lean against the wind. When output is affected by other shocks, fiscal policy tends to respond to those shocks in ways that intensify their effects on output.

5 Conclusion

In this chapter, the cyclical properties of the budget balance in Mexico have been explored and a number of conclusions reached.

First, Mexico's fiscal policy tends to be procyclical, as the cyclically adjusted budget balance is negatively correlated with real activity. This reflects the strongly procyclical character of government spending, even when transfers to states are factored out of the analysis. In this way, Mexico resembles many countries in Latin America.

One explanation is that Mexico's automatic stabilizers are weak. In most OECD countries, taxes and social programs act as natural stabilizers of the business cycle. Tax revenue and, in some cases, even marginal tax rates tend to accelerate during cyclical upturns. Spending on social programs such as unemployment insurance and welfare increases during cyclical downturns. These factors tend to make the fiscal surplus move with the business cycle, so that fiscal policy has a natural, and automatic, tendency to dampen business cycle fluctuations from the perspective of Keynesian theory. However, in Mexico these automatic stabilizers are weak. While income tax revenue, taxes on imports, and some other categories of tax revenue move procyclically, they represent only a fraction of the public sector's revenue. Furthermore, transfer payments to the private sector are procyclical. This presumably indicates that little social assistance spending has cyclical sensitivity.

Not only are automatic stabilizers weak in Mexico, but the rest of the budget has tended to be strongly procyclical. Cyclical upturns are an opportunity to expand public sector investment and other forms of discretionary spending, while cyclical downturns bring austerity. These effects likely exacerbate the business cycle.

Automatic stabilizers can be improved. Part of the problem for Mexico is that close to one-third of all revenue comes from petroleum in one form or another, and oil prices have tended to be countercyclical. Mexico is relying less and less on oil revenue, and has moved toward more broadly targeted taxation of economic activity. This has strengthened stabilizers on the revenue side. But if transfer programs designed to soften the blow of cyclical fluctuations were enhanced, this would help as well.

Mexico could also improve its discretionary fiscal policy. Discretionary spending, especially the public sector wage bill and public investment, is highly volatile and highly sensitive to the business cycle.

6

Notes

1. This chapter builds on the results in Burnside (1999), which provides a similar analysis of fiscal policy in Mexico for the period 1980–98.
2. The X11 algorithm implemented as a software package by Estima was used to seasonally adjust the data. (See http://www.estima.com/x11info.shtml.)
3. A quarterly measure of the relative price of oil was constructed from the spot U.S. dollar per barrel price of West Texas Intermediate crude oil (from the Federal Reserve Bank of St. Louis), multiplied by the quarterly average peso-to-dollar exchange rate (from the International Financial Statistics), divided by the Mexican GDP deflator (from INEGI).
4. The further oil-price adjustment makes this correlation –0.34. Even if one excludes the period 1980–2, which was an exceptional period of large primary deficits, the correlation of the primary balance with real activity remains negative (–0.20). The correlation for the cyclically adjusted balance becomes –0.32, while for the oil-price and cycle-adjusted balance it is –0.28.
5. Barro's (1979) tax-smoothing argument is that, for welfare reasons, governments are likely to desire relatively smooth paths for government spending and tax rates. Such behavior implies a pattern of procyclical budget surpluses.
6. A regression of the cyclical component of primary expenditure on the cyclical components of output and the relative price of oil delivers the following results: The coefficient on output is 1.64, while the coefficient on the oil price is –0.10. Both coefficients are significant at the 5 percent level.
7. Even over the 1983–2003 subsample period, the correlation is 0.94.
8. See, for example, Christiano and Eichenbaum (1992), Braun (1994), McGrattan (1994), Ohanian (1997), Ramey and Shapiro (1998), Edelberg, Eichenbaum, and Fisher (1999), and Burnside, Eichenbaum, and Fisher (2004).

References

Barro, Robert J. 1979. "On the Determination of Public Debt." *Journal of Political Economy* 87 (5, Pt. 1): 940–71.

Braun, Anton R. 1994. "Tax Disturbances and Real Economic Activity in the Postwar United States." *Journal of Monetary Economics* 33 (3): 441–62.

Burnside, Craig. 2001. "Fiscal Policy, Business Cycles, and Growth in Mexico." In *Mexico: Fiscal Sustainability* (vol. 2). Background papers, Report No. 20236-ME, Latin America and Caribbean Region. Washington, DC: World Bank.

Burnside, Craig, Martin Eichenbaum, and Jonas D. M. Fisher. 2004. "Fiscal Shocks and Their Consequences." *Journal of Economic Theory* 115 (1): 89–117.

Caballero, Ricardo, and Arvind Krishnamurthy. 2004. "Fiscal Policy and Financial Depth." NBER Working Paper 10532, National Bureau of Economic Research, Cambridge, MA.

Christiano, Lawrence J., and Martin Eichenbaum. 1992. "Current Real Business Cycle Theories and Aggregate Labor Market Fluctuations." *American Economic Review* 82 (3): 430–50.

Christiano, Lawrence J., Martin Eichenbaum, and Charles L. Evans. 1999. "Monetary Policy Shocks: What Have We Learned and to What End?" In John B. Taylor and Michael Woodford, eds. *Handbook of Macroeconomics*, volume 1a. Amsterdam: Elsevier Science Publishers.

Edelberg, Wendy, Martin Eichenbaum, and Jonas Fisher. 1999. "Understanding the Effects of Shocks to Government Purchases." *Review of Economic Dynamics* 2 (1): 166–206.

Gavin, Michael, Ricardo Hausmann, Roberto Perotti, and Ernesto Talvi. 1996. "Managing Fiscal Policy in Latin America and the Caribbean: Volatility, Procyclicality, and Limited Creditworthiness." Working Paper 326, Office of the Chief Economist, Inter-American Development Bank, Washington, DC.

McGrattan, Ellen R. 1994. "The Macroeconomic Effects of Distortionary Taxation." *Journal of Monetary Economics* 33 (3): 573–601.

Newey, Whitney K., and Kenneth D. West. 1987. "A Simple, Positive Semi-Definite, Heteroskedasticity and Autocorrelation Consistent Covariance Matrix." *Econometrica* 55 (3): 703–8.

Ohanian, Lee E. 1997. "The Macroeconomic Effects of War Finance in the United States: World War II and the Korean War." *American Economic Review* 87 (1): 23–40.

Ramey, Valerie, and Matthew D. Shapiro. 1998. "Costly Capital Reallocation and the Effects of Government Spending." *Carnegie Rochester Conference Series on Public Policy* 48: 145–94.

Talvi, Ernesto, and Carlos Végh. 2000. "Tax Base Variability and Procyclical Fiscal Policy." NBER Working Paper 7499, National Bureau of Economic Research, Cambridge, MA.

6

Data Sources

Banco de México. Data on revenues and expenditure of the public sector. http://www.banxico.gob.mx.

Federal Reserve Bank of St. Louis. Data on the spot price of West Texas Intermediate crude oil and the federal funds rate. FRED database. http://research.stlouisfed.org/fred2/.

IFS (International Financial Statistics). Information on the Mexican peso/U.S. dollar exchange rate. International Financial Statistics database.

INEGI (Instituto Nacional de Estadística Geografia e Informática). National income accounts data (GDP and Real GDP). http://www.inegi.gob.mx/inegi/default.asp.

United States Department of Commerce. U.S. national income accounts data. Bureau of Economic Analysis. http://www.bea.doc.gov/.

6

Chile's Fiscal Rule

Norbert Fiess

O23 E62

F34 E32

H63   E23

Unlike the debate on fiscal policy in Europe, which generally focuses on how to facilitate the workings of automatic stabilizers while achieving fiscal consolidation, the discussion on fiscal policy in the Latin America and Caribbean region (LAC) concentrates predominantly on long-term sustainability issues, largely ignoring the effects of the economic cycle (Perry 2003). This may come as a surprise to some, as LAC economies are more volatile than their European counterparts and have typically applied procyclical fiscal policies that may have exacerbated volatility. Some analysts and policymakers appear to believe that countercyclical fiscal policies are a luxury that only developed countries can afford or, at least, that LAC countries should address adjustment and solvency issues before attempting to reduce the highly procyclical nature of their fiscal policies. Perry (2003) argues that this approach is a mistake, however, because the costs of procyclical fiscal policies in LAC are enormous in terms of growth and welfare, especially for the poor. Furthermore, procyclical policy tends to lead to a deficit bias and is therefore unsustainable and noncredible.

The procyclical bias of fiscal policy in LAC countries has been attributed to limited access to capital markets in downturns and to lack of fiscal discipline in upturns (due to the political economy of fiscal policy in the presence of weak budgetary institutions in upturns). Gavin and others (1996), Gavin and Perotti (1997), and Talvi and Végh (2000) show that fiscal policy in Latin America is procyclical. During expansions, government consumption increases and taxes fall, while the opposite is true during recessions. Gavin and others relate procyclical fiscal policy in developing economies to imperfect access to capital markets during bad times, whereas Talvi and Végh primarly blame the inability of domestic finance institutions to generate a large enough surplus during good times. Fiscal rules tied to the cyclically adjusted balance can help reduce political pressure for procyclical expenditure, ensuring that surpluses generated in good times are saved for bad times.

Calderón and Schmidt-Hebbel (2003) and Kaminsky, Reinhart, and Végh (2004) are two recent studies that use cross-country data to analyze the pro- and countercyclicality of fiscal policies in emerging markets. Using a cross-section of 11 emerging market countries, Calderón and Schmidt-Hebbel contradict the traditional view that fiscal policy is procyclical in emerging markets. They find that only countries with high country-risk spreads exhibit procyclical policies, while emerging markets with better fundamentals are capable of countercyclical policies. However, Kaminsky, Reinhart, and Végh (2004), in a comprehensive study of 105 countries, report strong evidence of procyclical fiscal policies across all groups of developing countries. In particular, middle- to high-income countries stand out as the most procyclical—and their procyclical fiscal policies appear to be intrinsically linked and reinforced by a boom-bust cycle of capital flows.

In an effort to eliminate a procyclical bias of fiscal policy, many countries have begun implementing rule-based fiscal policies. The intended effect is that rule-based fiscal policies will allow automatic stabilizers to work freely during the cycle and help keep any surplus in good times out of reach from the political process in normal discretionary budgetary decisions.

In 2000, the government of President Ricardo Lagos introduced a fiscal rule based on a structural surplus of 1 percent of GDP, to reaffirm and intensify Chile's commitment to fiscal responsibility. Chile has established a reputation for fiscal discipline and running sustainable public sector deficits. The debt of the central government has been declining for some time now, falling to 16 percent of GDP (from 43 percent in 1990). Thus, Chile's new approach to fiscal policy represents an attempt to structure and signal its policies over a medium-term horizon; it is not an emergency effort to acquire fiscal policy credibility. The new fiscal rule is supposed to allow automatic stabilizers in the budget to work uninhibited, thus avoiding the fine-tuning of fiscal policy to the phases of the cycle.

This chapter describes Chile's fiscal policy rule and assesses its implications for social expenditure. It is organized as follows. Section 1 discusses fiscal rules in some detail and introduces the concept of the structural balance; section 2 describes Chile's new fiscal rule and offers some critical observations; and section 3 assesses the implications of Chile's new fiscal rule for social expenditure within the insurance framework of Ehrlich and Becker (1972).

Chile's fiscal rule targets a structural rather than an actual balance, so it is difficult to assess potential implications for the size and composition of future public or social expenditure. However, it is possible to show that the fiscal rule helps smooth public and social expenditure over the cycle. Because Chile's new fiscal rule has not stood the test of time, analysis presented here must be viewed as preliminary and based on limited econometric evidence.

1   Fiscal Rules and the Concept of the Structural Balance

The main motivation behind rule-based fiscal policy is that discretionary fiscal policy can harm macroeconomic stability. In a recent study of a cross-section of 51 countries, Fatás and Mihov (2003) provide evidence that discretionary fiscal policy amplifies business cycle fluctuations and reduces the rate of growth, while rule-based fiscal policies help to lower output volatility and positively affect growth.

Fiscal Rules

The term *fiscal rule* is loosely defined. In the widest sense, fiscal rules refer to "budgetary institutions" (Alesina and Perotti 1999), or a set of rules and regulations according to which budgets are drafted, approved, and implemented. In a more narrow sense, the term refers to legislated restrictions on fiscal policy that set specific limits on fiscal indicators such as the fiscal balance, debt, expenditure, or taxation.

Fiscal rules differ according to whether they are legislated, specify numerical targets, and/or apply to various definitions of the public sector. They have been applied to:

- ensure macroeconomic stability (post-World War II Japan);
- enhance the credibility of the government's fiscal policy and help in debt consolidation (Canadian provinces);

7

- ensure long-term sustainability of fiscal policy (New Zealand);
- minimize negative externalities within a federation or an international arrangement (Maastricht Treaty); and
- reduce procyclical bias in fiscal policy (Chile).

Fiscal rules per se do not guarantee fiscal discipline. Milesi-Ferretti (2000) shows that if a government has a margin for "creative accounting," the imposition of a fiscal rule may entail a trade-off between costly "window-dressing" and true fiscal adjustment. Mattina and Delorme (1996) show that fiscal discipline imposed by market mechanisms can be just as effective as fiscal rules. They based their results on estimates of nonlinear credit supply curves, where the deficit is modeled as a function of the yield spread and the debt-to-GDP ratio.

In order for a fiscal rule to be efficient, it should therefore be:

- flexible (when needed for countercyclical policy);
- credible (viewed as permanent); and
- transparent (easy to monitor and difficult to manipulate).

There is an obvious conflict between flexibility and credibility. Credibility demands rigidity, but a rule that is too rigid may become nonviable if perceived as unsustainable. Perry (2003) points further to a dichotomy in objectives between fiscal policies that focus exclusively on avoiding a deficit bias and those that focus exclusively on reducing a procyclical bias. A fiscal rule that emphasizes avoiding a deficit bias and ignores the potential effects of shocks and the economic cycle can be counterproductive if it accentuates the procyclicality of fiscal policies. However, a rule that attempts to support countercyclical fiscal policies but is not designed to achieve long-term debt sustainability will be equally unsustainable and further noncredible. A well-designed rule should therefore attempt both to facilitate the operation of automatic stabilizers (or even permit a limited active countercyclical fiscal policy) and to avoid a deficit bias.

Empirical evidence on the effectiveness of fiscal rules is mixed, because most rules have not passed the test of time. While Alesina and Perotti (1999) find a significant negative relation between the stringency of a rule and the size of the primary deficit for 20 LAC countries from 1980 to 1992, Kennedy and Robbins (2001) show that having a legislated fiscal rule is not a necessary condition for successful fiscal consolidation within Organisation of Economic Co-operation and Development (OECD) countries. Bayoumi and Eichengreen

(1995) and Levinson (1998) show that for the United States, fiscal rules decrease the ability of subnational governments to use fiscal policy to smooth the business cycle and can, therefore, lead to a significant increase in output volatility. Alesina and Bayoumi (1996), using similar data, find no significant relationship between GDP volatility and the stringency of fiscal controls. Fatás and Mihov (2003), using a cross-country analysis of 51 countries, find that the volatility of output induced by discretionary fiscal policy lowers economic growth by 0.6 percentage point for every percentage point increase in volatility, while automatic stabilizers tend to reduce output volatility.

The Structural Balance

Traditionally, fiscal policy is seen as a stabilizer of the business cycle. Fiscal policy is typically designed to be expansionary during recessions and contractionary during expansions. Two instruments are used for this purpose: automatic stabilizers and discretionary fiscal policy. Automatic stabilizers are budget components that respond automatically to the business cycle without any explicit government action. Income tax revenues and unemployment benefit expenditures, for example, respond, respectively, positively and negatively to the business cycle. Discretionary fiscal policy consists of active policy measures meant to stimulate the economy during bad times.

The actual budget balance reflects cyclical or transitory influences on the budget, as well as structural or permanent influences, so a failure to distinguish between structural and cyclical influences creates the risk that policymakers may over- or underadjust fiscal policy in response to budget developments. To overcome the limitations of traditional budget accounting, the concept of the structural balance has been proposed. This approach attempts to factor out cyclical components from the actual budget balance in order to provide less "noisy" indicators to guide fiscal policy. Within this concept, it is useful to think of the actual balance, B, as a composition of a structural, B^s, and a cyclical component, B^c:

$$B = B^s + B^c. \tag{1.1}$$

Generally, the construction of the structural balance follows two steps. The first step involves the construction of a reference path for real GDP to obtain a measure of potential output in the absence of cyclical fluctuations. The difference between the "actual" and the "potential" output measures the output gap in a particular year. In the second step, these output gaps (together with government revenue and expenditure elasticities) are used to calculate the level of public revenue and expenditure if potential output is at the reference path level. The impact of automatic stabilizers and a progressive tax system are thus accounted for. The resulting cyclically adjusted or structural budget balance corresponds to the underlying budgetary position implied by the path of potential output.

The structural balance per se is not a fiscal rule but more a means to an end. The structural balance can, however, be useful in defining a medium-term *fiscal target*. Since the economy and fiscal balances are subject to transitory shocks, reference to the structural balance can help policymakers avoid unnecessary and often procyclical policy adjustments. Transitory shocks to fiscal balances require no adjustments because they will be reversed over the course of the business cycle, but permanent shocks need attention. The structural balance can also be interpreted as an *indicator for discretionary fiscal policy*. If the business cycle leads to nondiscretionary changes in fiscal policy through automatic stabilizers, but the business cycle itself is partially driven by discretionary fiscal policy measures, the structural balance should be a better indicator of shifts in the discretionary fiscal policy stance. Finally, as in the case of Chile, the structural balance can also be the basis for a *fiscal rule*, by setting budget target levels based on the structural rather than the actual budget balance.

While the decomposition in (1.1) seems intuitive, it is important to remember that the structural balance (unlike the actual balance) is an *unobservable concept*. It represents the fiscal balance that would have occurred if all temporary influences on the budget had been absent. The biggest problem in calculating the structural balance is related to correctly identifying cyclical and structural components such as cyclical and potential output. Although a variety of methods exist for calculating potential output and corresponding output gaps, all have major shortcomings (see, for example, Deutsche Bundesbank 1997). An additional caveat is that estimates of the structural balance are usually based on the assumption of constant revenue and expenditure elasticities over time. Although a less serious problem for mature economies, this is of greater concern to emerging economies that still face substantial structural changes.

The most commonly used approaches are based on a production function, as applied by the OECD and the International Monetary Fund (IMF), and Hodrick-Prescott (HP) filtering, as applied by the European Commission. Brunila, Hukkinen, and Tujula (1999) show that when the main focus is on estimating the level of the structural balance, the production function approach provides a better measure than the HP filter-based approach. If the focus is, however, on changes in the fiscal policy stance, the choice of method matters less. Formulating a fiscal policy based on a specific level of the structural balance as opposed to a change in the structural balance is, therefore, more difficult.

Finally, the level of the structural balance is sensitive not only to the underlying estimation method but also to the accounting methodology. For example, if a very narrow definition of the public sector is applied and too many accounts are excluded (such as state enterprises), the level of the structural balance loses meaning for fiscal sustainability, because the base for assessing fiscal sustainability becomes too narrow.

As such, the usefulness of the structural balance in formulating fiscal targets depends crucially on correct identification of temporary and permanent shocks. Shocks that are assumed to be permanent but later turn out to be transitory might cause unnecessary tightening of the fiscal stance. However, if a transitory shock turns out to be permanent, necessary adjustments will have been delayed. The appropriateness of the structural balance as an indicator of discretionary fiscal policy additionally requires a correct distinction between discretionary and nondiscretionary fiscal policy.[1]

2   The Chilean Experience

In 2000, the government of President Ricardo Lagos introduced a fiscal rule based on a structural surplus of 1 percent of GDP—to reaffirm and intensify Chile's commitment to fiscal responsibility. The new method of preparing the budget is believed to deliver indicators for identifying the fiscal stance, avoid a procyclical policy bias in public finances, allow an evaluation of the macroeconomic impact of fiscal policy, and ensure fiscal discipline and sustainability. The decision to implement a new approach to fiscal policy was taken after the structural balance for 1999 showed a deficit for the first time in 10 years.

Chile's Fiscal Rule

The fiscal rule in Chile does not qualify as a fiscal rule in the stricter sense, as it is not stated in law. It is a self-imposed measure by the Lagos government to guide fiscal policy from 2001 to 2005. The rule is extremely rigid as a target value, for the structural surplus is specified and no escape clauses are mentioned. Despite not being legally binding, the rule is perceived as highly credible in light of Chile's good track record of fiscal discipline. The rule applies only to the central government, and the following public sector flows are excluded from the new structural balance:

- the quasi-fiscal deficit of the central bank (about 1 percent of GDP over the past 10 years);
- the balances of nonfinancial public enterprises;
- the balances of the military sector (only the funds transferred to the military from the central government are included); and
- the balances of municipalities.

Taken together, the public sector flows excluded from the structural balance are substantial. But this does not necessarily imply a reduction in transparency or a dilution of incentives for fiscal discipline. The quasi-fiscal deficit of the central bank has been about 1 percent of GDP over the past 10 years, but has declined more recently. Municipalities are bound by borrowing constraints that imply an overall zero budget balance requirement. The quasi-fiscal deficit of the nonfinancial public sector has been about 0.5 to 1 percent of GDP and does not pose a direct threat to the solvency of the public sector. As long as figures from state enterprises are made public, transparency is provided (see IMF 2001).

The calculation of the structural balance in Chile follows the IMF and OECD methodology.[2] But two adjustments have been made to capture particularities of the Chilean economy. First, only revenues (not expenditures) are adjusted for the business cycle. Second, given the high importance of copper revenues for public finances in Chile, structural revenues are adjusted for fluctuations in copper prices. Finally, to better capture changes in the net-worth of the central government, some accounting adjustments are made to the actual balance—before the structural and cyclical components are calculated.[3]

The structural balance reflects the amounts of revenue and expenditure that would be achieved if the economy operated at full potential and the price of copper were at the long-term price. The structural balance, therefore, factors out the cyclical and random effects of both GDP and the copper price.

To summarize, the calculation of the structural balance in Chile consists of the following three steps:

- Adjustment of the actual balance according to the concept of net worth variation of the central government.
- Estimation of the impact of cyclical budget components (tax revenues and the price of copper). The cyclical component of tax revenues, T^c, is obtained by adjusting observed tax revenues, T, using an estimated output elasticity, ε, of 1.05:

$$T^c = T - T(Y^*/Y)^\varepsilon.$$

  Cyclical output is defined as the difference between actual output, Y, and potential output, Y^*, where potential output is derived from a production function linking output to capital, labor, and total factor productivity. Potential output is calculated as the level of output at which capacity utilization rates are at normal levels, labor input is consistent with the natural rate of unemployment, total factor productivity is at its trend level, and the price of copper is at its long-term level.

  Cyclical adjustment to the copper price is based on the gap between the actual export price reported by CODELCO (Corporacion Nacional del Cobre Chile) and an estimated reference price, which is close to a long-term moving average.[4]

- Construction of the structural balance, by subtracting the cyclical components of tax revenue and copper income from the adjusted balance constructed in the first step. Potential output and the long-term copper price are key inputs for the construction of the structural balance. However, as both variables are unobservable, their estimation is subject to methodological debate. In the case of Chile, these two variables are obtained by two panels of experts (one for potential output and one for the copper price). Both panels are appointed by the minister of finance and are asked to provide projected estimates of the relevant variables for the coming five years. The averages of the experts' estimates are then used to construct the structural balance.

Figure 7.1 shows the actual, adjusted, structural balance, and total cyclical components of Chile's budget. During 1987 and 2000, the adjusted balance indicates an average surplus of 1 percent of GDP; the structural balance averaged 0 percent of GDP. The total cyclical component measures the

7

Figure 7.1: Actual, Adjusted, and Structural Balance and Total Cyclical Budget Components, 1987–2002
(as a percentage of GDP)

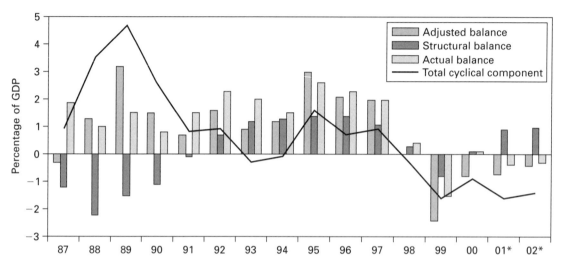

Source: Marcel and others 2001a.
Note: Values for 2001 and 2002 are estimates.

7

difference between the adjusted and structural balances, so it averaged 1 percent of GDP during 1987–2000. When comparing the different budget concepts, it is interesting to note that the actual balance showed a surplus of 1.5 percent in 1989, while the structural balance showed a deficit of –1.5 percent. The adjusted balance was 3.2 percent. These numbers were reversed in 2000, when the structural balance showed a slight surplus of 0.1 percent and the actual and adjusted balances were in deficit.

The large difference between the actual and adjusted balances is due to the different treatment of the copper stabilization fund (CSF) in the new accounting concepts. In the traditional accounting used for the CSF, withdrawals (during periods of lower copper prices) were treated as revenues, and deposits into the fund (during periods of higher copper prices) were deducted from revenues. But this is no longer the case for the calculation of the adjusted balance. This approach causes the adjusted balance to be more volatile than the actual balance, and the smoothing of the balance previously accomplished by the CSF is now accomplished by factoring out the cyclical component of the copper price when calculating the structural balance.

Some Observations on Chile's Fiscal Rule

This section provides some general observations regarding adjustment for the copper cycle in Chile's fiscal rule.

Adjustment for the Copper Cycle

The copper-related adjustment to the structural balance is substantial—and much larger than the tax revenue adjustment related to the output gap (see figure 7.2). As such, the copper reference price is central for the derivation of the structural balance and the fiscal rule. Within the fiscal framework, the copper price is treated as mean-reverting. This justifies treating fluctuations in copper prices as temporary. Empirical evidence, however, does not lean toward mean-reversion in copper prices (Mainardi 1998), suggesting that all copper price changes should be treated as permanent. While empirical evidence on mean-reversion suffers from the usual problem of the low power of unit root tests, it is nonetheless true that even if copper prices are mean-reverting, the process of mean-reversion seems to take a rather long time, indicating a near-unit root process.[5] Engel and Valdes (2002) estimate a half-life of price shocks of four years; Cashin and others (1999) report an

7

Figure 7.2: Decomposition of Total Cyclical Component, 1987–2000
(percentage of GDP)

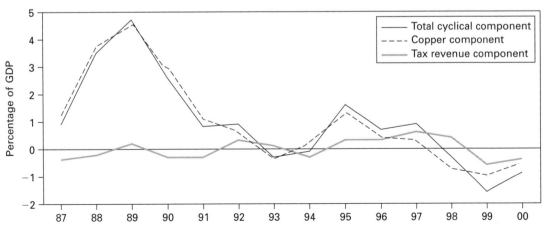

Source: Marcel and others 2001a.

Figure 7.3: Copper Price, 1900–2000

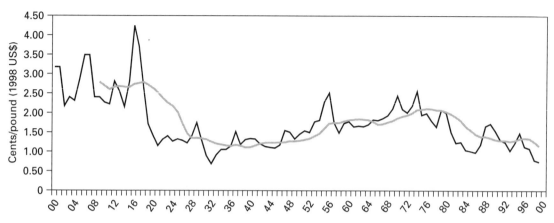

Source: United States Geological Survey.

even higher half-life of about 6.5 years, indicating that the actual copper prices could stay below the reference price for a substantial period of time.[6]

From the mid-1980s to 2000, the reference price of copper has been rather smooth compared to the market price (see figure 7.3). The calculation of the structural balance has therefore treated nearly all copper price fluctuations as transitory (nearly all copper price fluctuations have been removed from the fiscal balance). While this procedure yields a much clearer indicator of changes in fiscal discipline, it is uncertain to what extent this adjustment aids in assessing fiscal sustainability.

Lack of Adjustment on the Expenditure Side

Automatic stabilizers act on both the revenue and expenditure sides of a budget, so when calculating structural balances for OECD countries, cyclical adjustments are made on both sides. In the case of Chile, no cyclical adjustment is made to the expenditure side, because no significant relation between public expenditure and output has been established. The Chilean authorities explain that this is due to underdeveloped unemployment and severance benefit systems, which do not act as automatic stabilizers (see Marcel and others 2001a). But because the structural balance is adjusted only for cyclical revenue fluctuations, there is the danger that the scale of automatic stabilizers allowed by the Chilean structural balance target is limited. If, for example, the government introduces temporary employment programs or other types of social spending during an economic downturn, this additional expenditure must be offset by tightening elsewhere (see IMF 2001).

By construction, Chile's fiscal rule achieves a smoothing of expenditures over the cycle—and the intention is to help create stable conditions for the development of long-term social and investment programs. De Ferranti and others (2000) argue that social expenditure should at least be kept constant throughout the cycle and that, ideally, it should be countercyclical. From a social protection point of view it might, therefore, be useful to introduce explicit automatic stabilizers on the expenditure side. This would enforce Chile's ability to run nondiscretionary countercyclical fiscal policy.

Calculation of the Output Gap Is Sensitive to Methodology

As mentioned earlier, no generally accepted methodology of calculating the cyclically adjusted budget balance exists. The results tend to be fairly sensitive to the method of calculation. This, of course, raises questions about both the accuracy of the measure and the importance of estimation errors. The latter become a problem only if estimation errors are systematically related to the cycle. The Chilean authorities provide a sensitivity analysis using different output elasticities (0.7, 1.05, and 1.25), as well as a 10 percent confidence interval around the estimated output gap, and show that their results are fairly robust. However, Nadal-De Simone uses Hodrick-Prescott and Kalman filtering and finds substantially different estimates of the output gaps (see IMF 2001).[7] As box 7.1 shows for Argentina, different measures of the output gap can lead to quite different measures of the structural balance. The production-function-based output gap with two simple measures of output gaps derived from two different Hodrick-Prescott filters is later contrasted, using a smoothing parameter of 100 and a smoothing parameter of 30. As can be seen from figure 7.4, the level estimates of the output gap differ substantially, even though they are not very sensitive to the choice of smoothing parameter for the HP filter. However, all three methods identify the same directional pattern. As such, when evaluating the stance of Chile's fiscal policy, methodological differences seem to matter less—a result that is also found by Brunila, Hukkinen, and Tujula (1999) for Finland.

7

Box 7.1: A Structural Balance for Argentina—Sensitivity to Methodology

Perry and Servén (2003) present estimates of a structural economic balance for Argentina. Estimates of the structural balance are found to vary greatly with assumed time path for potential GDP. Figure 7B.1 shows estimates of potential GDP based on an HP filter and a linear trend. The different estimates express different views about developments in Argentina since 1998. According to the linear trend estimate, the Argentine economy experienced a pronounced recession in the late 1990s, while the HP filter suggests a downward revision in potential output.

Figure 7B.1: Argentina: Potential and Actual GDP, 1979 Q4–2001 Q4

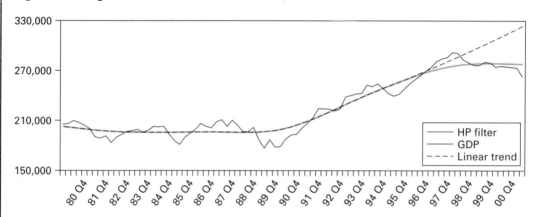

The different potential GDP estimates translate directly into different estimates of the structural balance (figure 7B.2). These differences in the estimates would lead to starkly different interpretations with respect to the magnitude of the structural balance and the fiscal stance.

Figure 7B.2: Argentina: Structural Economic Balance, 1995–2001
(as percentage of potential GDP)

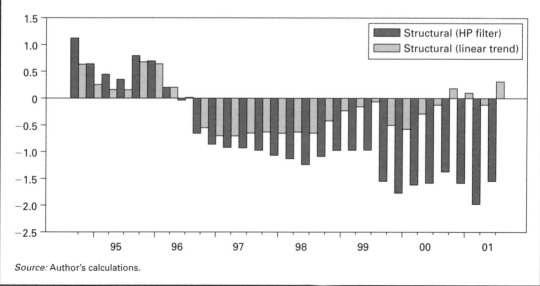

Source: Author's calculations.

Figure 7.4: Output Gap, 1986–2000
(percentage of potential GDP)

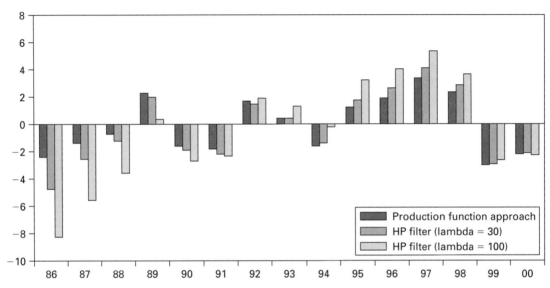

Source: Author's calculations.

7

Countercyclicality of the Structural Rule

Chile's fiscal rule targets a maximum structural balance of 1 percent of GDP. The working of the rule is illustrated in a simplified way in the left-hand side of figure 7.5. Even though fiscal revenues fluctuate with the economic cycle (upward-sloping sine curve), the government must set expenditure (gray trend line) in a way that tracks the path of structural revenue (black trend line). The relative constancy of the structural balances implies that during a boom, the actual surplus is high; during a recession, the actual surplus is low. The development of the actual balance over the cycle is represented by the horizontal sine curve (revenues minus expenditures).

The new rule implies that adjusted public expenditure grows with the same slope as structural revenues, although at a lower level. This is meant to enable Chile to generate large surpluses in good times and thus avoid a procyclical bias in fiscal policy, something that has been prevalent in the past. Talvi and Végh (2000) and Bergoeing and Soto (2002) provide estimates of procyclicality before the introduction of the fiscal rule. According to Talvi

Figure 7.5: Deficit and Surplus Bias

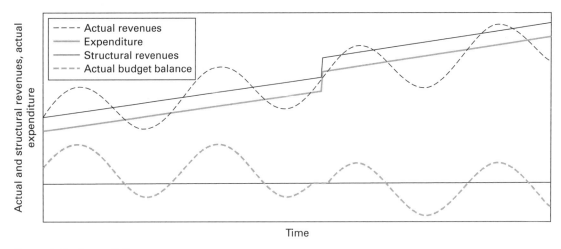

Source: Author's compilation.

7

and Végh (2000), the correlation coefficient of government spending and output in Chile during 1970 and 1994 was 0.59 (Latin American average: 0.53). Bergoeing and Soto (2002) report a correlation coefficient of 0.34, based on quarterly data from 1986 to 1998.

The mechanism works well if structural revenues are estimated correctly. However, the right-hand side of figure 7.5 simulates the effect of a systematic overestimation of structural revenues, for example, due to an overestimated copper reference price or a larger output gap. The consequence is that projected structural revenues, which build the basis for the calculation of actual expenditure, will be overestimated. Overestimation of structural revenues accommodates more expenditure, and thus introduces a more expansionary fiscal stance. If structural revenues are systematically overestimated, a *potential* deficit bias is introduced in the actual balance. And since public sector borrowing requirements need to be met on the basis of actual rather than structural balances—as with debt sustainability—a financing problem could arise. This problem would be amplified for emerging economies, where debt sustainability and actual deficits have a great deal of relevance when evaluating country risk. Lagos and Costa (2002), therefore, suggest that Chile's fiscal rule be modified by placing restrictions on both the size of the actual deficit and the number of consecutive deficits allowed before the rule is modified.

3 Self-Insurance and Self-Protection at the Country Level

Volatility leads to instability, uncertainty, and risk. And macroeconomic volatility has long been a trademark of economies in LAC, where economic risk prevails at both aggregate and individual levels. For individuals, economic instability translates directly into risk of unemployment or loss of income. At the aggregate level, macroeconomic volatility has a direct negative impact on long-term growth (Fatás and Mihov 2003). It appears, therefore, to be rational for both individuals and governments to insure against risk. Within the comprehensive insurance framework developed by Ehrlich and Becker (1972), self-insurance, self-protection, and risk-pooling are the possible risk insurance mechanisms (see table 7.1). These mechanisms have different implications for the ultimate probability of incurring a loss, and for the extent of the loss itself. And these implications derive from the decisions of economic agents regarding how much to insure against loss and how much to lower the probability of loss.

Self-insurance and risk-pooling transfer income from good to bad states of the world but do not reduce the likelihood that these transfers will be required (that is, that the bad state will occur). Self-protection does, however, reduce the probability of a bad state, yet does not limit the size of a loss. The following section attempts to assess how Chile's fiscal rule relates to

Table 7.1: Chile's Fiscal Rule within the Ehrlich-Becker Insurance Framework

Self-insurance		Self-protection
Micro risk	*Macro risk*	*Macro risk*
Public expenditure smoothing reduces pro-cyclicality of safety nets	Countercyclical fiscal policy Surplus bias	Sustainable debt management Lower cost of external financing Lower risk of financial contagion

Source: Author's compilation.

the concept of self-insurance and self-protection at the country level, as detailed in De Ferranti and others (2000).

Sustainable Debt Management and Reduction of Contagion Risk

Gill and Ilahi (2000) identify precautionary fiscal targets and contingent fiscal rules as mechanisms for self-insurance at the country level. According to this classification, Chile's new fiscal rule can be seen as a measure of country-level self-insurance. The fiscal rule adjusts for the business cycle and for cyclical fluctuations in the copper price and thus, like a stabilization fund, transfers resources from good to bad states. By pursuing debt sustainability and communicating a clear signal of fiscal discipline to the markets, the new fiscal framework should also help to protect against fiscal crises and help to lower the costs of external financing. As such, Chile's fiscal rule can also be seen as a measure to self-protect. By signaling fiscal discipline to the markets, the rule should also reduce the risk of financial contagion. The fact that, despite an actual fiscal deficit, sovereign bond spreads in Chile declined substantially during 2001 (and the fact that the correlation with other emerging market spreads has been falling for some time) provides evidence that a credible and efficient fiscal rule can serve as a measure to self-protect against macroeconomic risk.

Public and Social Expenditure Smoothing

De Ferranti and others (2000) try to quantify the causes of excess volatility in LAC and find that nearly one-third of the volatility was due to exogenous shocks. Terms of trade are more volatile in LAC than elsewhere, due to concentration in a few commodity exports; and capital flows are more volatile as well, though not so much as is usually believed. They attribute another third of the volatility in LAC to insufficient financial integration and development of domestic financial markets, and the final third to procyclical volatility in macro policies (fiscal and monetary). So the importance of volatile monetary policy has been reduced over time, but that is not the case with fiscal policy. Fiscal policy remains highly procyclical, as found by Gavin and others (1996), among others, and tends to accentuate the cycle.

Procyclical fiscal policies not only accentuate the cycle but they are also especially harmful for the poor. De Ferranti and others (2000) show that in LAC, social expenditures as a percentage of GDP are at best held constant during downturns. Further, the more targeted social expenditures tend to fall as a percentage of GDP—when they should instead expand as the number of poor people increases. As a consequence, in a typical downturn social expenditures for each poor person are reduced by 2 percent for each 1 percent of reduction in output. By contrast, social expenditures usually grow as a percentage of GDP in upturns—when they are less needed. This procyclicality of safety nets adds substantial policy risk to income risk for the poor in these areas. A fiscal rule that reduces procyclicality in social expenditure fits into the Ehrlich-Becker insurance framework as a self-insurance strategy at the country level, and thus helps to reduce the income risk of the poor.

Chile has an outstanding track record in reducing poverty. Due to a combination of strong growth and well-directed social programs, poverty was cut in half during the period 1987–8, from 40 percent to 17 percent (World Bank 2001). Social policies in Chile during the past decade also had a significant impact on reducing income inequality. This reduction in inequality coincided with a general increase in social expenditure during the period, prompting the interesting question of whether the new fiscal framework imposes a limit on social expenditure. Might further gains from equality and poverty reduction be achieved only through better targeting of government programs?

We now attempt to evaluate the potential impact of the new fiscal rule on social protection. The Chilean fiscal rule has yet not stood the test of time (and is still in a period of transition), so this exercise can only be considered as preliminary.

Potential Impact on Social Expenditure

Chile's fiscal rule is a structural *surplus* rule; it does not target a specific budget level. If taxes are increased or the tax base expanded, structural revenues will increase. And since the fiscal rule implies that expenditures follow the path of structural revenues, actual expenditures will increase as well. So unlike fiscal rules that specify a budget balance target such as a balanced budget rule or expenditure ceiling, it is difficult to identify the implications

7

of this rule for either the size and composition of future public or social expenditures or reductions in poverty inequality.

As mentioned earlier, any misestimation of structural revenues or the copper reference price can make fiscal policy more expansionary or contractionary than intended, further complicating an a priori assessment of the size and composition of future public and social expenditures.

The fiscal rule implies that expenditure should follow the relatively smooth path of structural revenues. Public expenditure should, therefore, be less volatile and achieve a smoothing of social expenditure over the cycle.

Figures 7.6 and 7.7 illustrate the cyclical component of GDP as estimated in Marcel and others (2001a) against the cyclical components of total and social expenditures. Both variables are expressed as percentage deviations from their trend components. A value close to zero implies that the cyclical component is close to its trend level. The cyclical components of the expenditure categories are derived using the Hodrick-Prescott (HP) filter. The focus is on the directional change and less on the size of the deviation from trend of the expenditure variables, which makes methodological differences in estimation less important.

As can be seen from figures 7.6 and 7.7, total expenditure has remained close to its trend level since the implementation of the structural surplus rule

Figure 7.6: Cyclical Components of GDP and Total Expenditure, 1989–2001

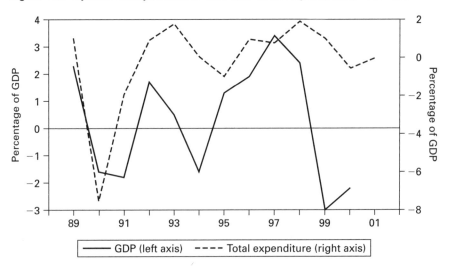

Source: Author's calculations.

Figure 7.7: Cyclical Components of GDP and Social Expenditure, 1989–2001

Source: Author's calculations.

and the variance in the changes of expenditure has decreased substantially. This finding is even more evident for social expenditure. Figures A7.1–5 in the annex to this chapter show the results for the different subcomponents of social expenditure. The reduced volatility at the aggregate level does not translate to the disaggregated level. The increase in expenditure on education, housing, and social security was offset by a decrease in subsidies and other social expenditures. It is interesting to note that the cyclical deviation of the different expenditure categories from their trend levels has decreased since the fiscal rule was implemented. The exception is subsidies, which show a strong decline. However, this can be explained by the declining importance of severance payments. The current severance system was replaced in 2002 by an individual accounts-based severance insurance system, where the fiscal impact is now independent of the unemployment rate.

4   Conclusion

Although it is too early to fully evaluate the impact of the fiscal rule adopted by Chile in 2000, the experience to date has been positive. In 2001, Chile continued its fiscal consolidation effort while pursuing countercyclical fiscal policy (to the extent of the difference between the structural surplus of 1 percent and the realized balance of –0.3 percent).

Within the risk-insurance framework of Ehrlich and Becker (1972), Chile's rule represents a successful attempt to self-insure against macroeconomic risk at the country level. The fiscal rule adjusts for the business cycle and for cyclical fluctuations in the copper price and thus, like a stabilization fund, transfers resources from good to bad states. By pursuing debt-sustainability and communicating a clear signal of fiscal discipline to the markets, the new fiscal framework should help to protect against fiscal crises and help lower the costs of external financing. To the extent that the Chilean rule signals credible fiscal discipline to financial markets, it also has the potential to serve as a self-protection measure against financial contagion.

Chile's fiscal rule is a structural *surplus* rule, not a structural *balance* rule; that is, the rule does not target a specific budget level. So even though it is difficult to assess potential implications on the size and composition of future public or social expenditure under the rule, it is possible to show that the rule will render public expenditure less volatile and, as such, achieve a smoothing of social expenditure over the cycle. This should, in turn, help reduce aggregated macroeconomic volatility and foster long-term economic growth.

The concept of the structural balance takes center-stage in Chile's new fiscal rule. Any fiscal rule that is based on the structural balance rather than the actual balance is novel, and not without problems. Here it is important to remember that the structural balance is a *latent* concept. Neither the structural balance nor its main determinants (potential output and the long-run copper price) are observable. Hence, there is no unique way to measure the structural balance, and different estimation techniques will derive different estimates.

Given the importance of the structural balance as a measure of the fiscal stance, the choice of the "correct" methodology is more than a technicality. Transparency is vital in calculating the structural balance. And though the Chilean authorities have opted for a fairly transparent and simple fiscal rule, there is still room for discretion with respect to potential output and the copper reference price. The Chilean authorities are delegating the calculation of potential output and the copper reference price to an independent panel of experts (which helps to increase transparency); but this does not necessarily increase predictability if these two variables follow random walks. This is another important point to remember when formulating fiscal policy lessons for other countries. An overestimate of potential output and/or an overestimate of the long-run copper price will facilitate a more expansionary fiscal policy yet not violate a set structural surplus target.[8] This chapter has also argued that if structural revenues are systematically overestimated, a potential deficit bias is introduced in the actual balance.

Since public sector borrowing requirements must be met on the basis of the actual (not structural) balance—and the same holds for debt sustainability—a financing problem could arise if actual deficits persist despite structural surpluses. This problem is amplified for emerging economies, where debt sustainability and actual deficits are highly relevant in evaluating country risk. To avoid a potential deficit bias that could lead public finances down an unsustainable path, it may be best to consider including a time limit on how long an actual deficit is allowed before the fiscal rule must be revised.

5 Annex

7

Figure A7.1: Cyclical Components of GDP and Housing Expenditure

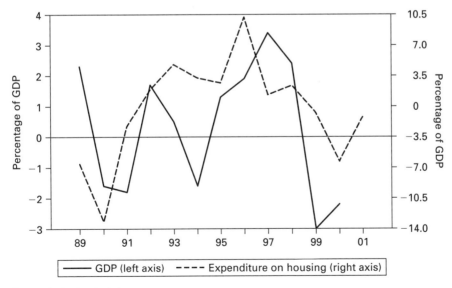

Source: Author's calculations.

Figure A7.2: Cyclical Components of GDP and Social Security Expenditure

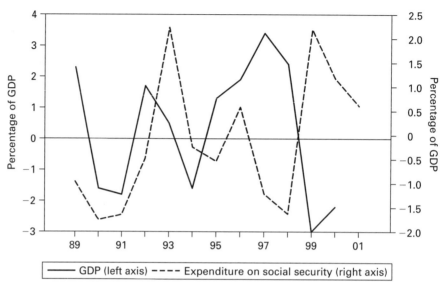

Source: Author's calculations.

7

Figure A7.3: Cyclical Components of GDP and Education Expenditure

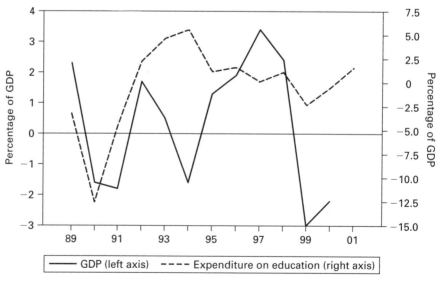

Source: Author's calculations.

Figure A7.4: Cyclical Components of GDP and Expenditure on Subsidies

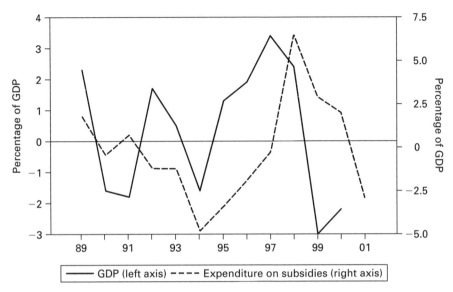

Source: Author's calculations.

Figure A7.5: Cyclical Components of GDP and Other Social Expenditure

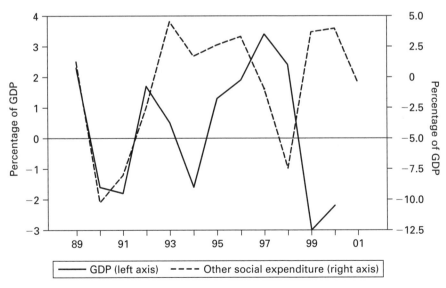

Source: Author's calculations.

Notes

1. When cyclically adjusting the budget, it is important to decide which expenditures and revenues fall into the "automatic" and "discretionary" categories. The assumption is that the business cycle causes automatic stabilizers to adjust, while the business cycle itself is caused by discretionary components. If all components of the budget were adjusted for cyclicality, the resulting structural budget would be, by construction, completely uncorrelated with the business cycle (Burnside 2000). Hagemann (1999) and others point out that the conceptual classification of fiscal policy in discretionary and nondiscretionary components is not unambiguous.

2. See Marcel and others (2001a, 2001b).

3. These adjustments include approximating the actual fiscal balance to the variation in the net-worth of the central government. This requires a reclassification of items that represent deficit financing of the central government but which do not necessarily modify the government's net-worth position. For this purpose, on the revenue side, privatization receipts and other flows related to purchases of bonds and securities and sales of financial assets are subtracted, while deposits (or drafts) in the Copper Stabilization Fund are added (or subtracted). On the expenditure side, adjustments are made to ensure accrual-based treatment of Pension Recognition Bonds (see Marcel and others 2001a, 2001b).

4. While the Copper Stabilization Fund operated in tranches (and as such was not able to fully exploit the cyclical fluctuations in the copper price), the copper price adjustment within the new fiscal rule captures cyclical variations of the copper price more efficiently from a fiscal point of view. This is because the structural balance is adjusted for the absolute difference between the copper price and the copper reference price.

5. Using data from 1990 to 2000, we find that Augmented Dickey Fuller (ADF) unit root tests cannot reject a unit root in the copper price series, while Phillips-Perron (PP) tests reject nonstationarity

Test type	Statistic	5 percent critical value
ADF test: no constant, no trend	−1.57	−1.95
ADF test: constant, no trend	−1.62	−2.86
ADF test: constant, trend	−1.88	−3.41
PP test: no constant, no trend	−2.04	−1.95
PP test: constant, no trend	−2.42	−2.86
PP test: constant, trend	−2.70	−3.41

6. Or in a different context: If mean-reversion of commodity prices is slow, commodity-based stabilization funds must be rather large in order to be effective.

7. Harvey (2002) shows a substantial difference between business cycle estimates based on the Hodrick-Prescott filter, the Baxter-King filter, and a structural time-series model. Estimates based on structural time-series modeling and quarterly GDP data from 1960 to 2000 show that the preferred model for Chilean GDP has two cycles: the first with a duration of 10.66 years, and the second of just under 3 years. The long-run cycle picks up the major recessions during this period. In monthly data from 1982 to 2001, Harvey identifies only the short cycle (with a frequency of just under 3 years).

8. If the long-run price of copper is assumed to be higher than the "true" price, estimated revenues will be higher; and since estimated revenues are the basis for the actual expenditure, expenditures will increase, resulting in a higher actual deficit.

References

7

Alesina, Alberto, and Tamim Bayoumi. 1996. "The Costs and Benefits of Fiscal Rules: Evidence from the United States." NBER Working Paper No. 5614. Cambridge, MA: National Bureau of Economic Research.

Alesina, Alberto, and Roberto Perotli. 1999. "Budget Deficits and Budget Institutions." In James M. Poterba and Jurgen von Hagen, eds., *Fiscal Institutions and Fiscal Performance*. Chicago: NBER/University of Chicago Press.

Bayoumi, Tamim, and Barry Eichengreen. 1995. "Restraining Yourself: The Implications of Fiscal Rules for Economic Stabilization." *IMF Staff Papers* 42 (1): 783–91.

Bergoeing, Raphael, and Raimundo Soto. 2002. "Testing Real Business Cycle Models in an Emerging Economy." Working Paper 159, Central Bank of Chile, Santiago, Chile.

Brunila, Anne, Juhana Hukkinen, and Mika Tujula. 1999. "Indicators of the Cyclically Adjusted Budget Balance: The Bank of Finland's Experience." Bank of Finland Discussion Papers, 1/99. Helsinki, Finland.

Budnevich L., Carlos L. 2002. "Countercyclical Fiscal Policy: A Review of the Literature, Empirical Evidence and Some Policy Proposals."

Discussion Paper 2002/41, World Institute for Development Economics Research. Helsinki, Finland.

Burnside, Craig. 2000. "Fiscal Policy, Business Cycles, and Growth in Mexico." Background paper prepared for *Mexico: Fiscal Sustainability*. Report No. 20236-ME, Latin America and Caribbean Region. Washington, DC: World Bank, 2001.

Calderón, César, and Klaus Schmidt-Hebbel. 2003. "Macroeconomic Policies and Performance in Latin America." *Journal of International Money and Finance* 22 (7): 895–923.

Cashin, Paul C., John McDermott, and Alasdair Scott. 1999. "Booms and Slumps in World Commodity Prices." IMF Working Paper 99/155, International Monetary Fund, Washington, DC.

de Ferranti, David, Guillermo E. Perry, Indermit S. Gill, and Luis Servén. 2000. "Securing Our Future in a Global Economy." World Bank Latin American and Caribbean Studies. The World Bank, Washington, DC.

Deutsche Bundesbank. 1997. "Problems Associated with Calculating 'Structural' Budget Deficits." *Monthly Report* (April): 31–45.

Ehrlich, Isaac, and Gary S. Becker. 1972. "Market Insurance, Self-Insurance and Self-Protection." *Journal of Political Economy* 80 (4): 623–48.

Engel, Eduardo, and Rodrigo Valdes. 2002. Preciendo el precio de cobre: mas alla del camino aleatorio? Mimeo. Yale University, New Haven, CT. http://cowles.econ.yale.edu/~engel/pubs/pub_100.pdf

Fatás, Antonio, and Ilian Mihov. 2003. "The Case for Restricting Fiscal Policy Discretion." *Quarterly Journal of Economics* 118 (4): 1419–47.

Gavin, Michael, and Roberto Perotti. 1997. "Fiscal Policy and Private Saving in Latin America in Good Times and Bad." In Ricardo Hausmann and Helmut Reisen, eds. *Promoting Savings in Latin America*. Inter-American Development Bank and Development Centre of the Organisation for Economic Co-Operation and Development, Paris.

Gavin, Michael, Ricardo Haussman, Roberto Perotti, and Ernesto Talvi. 1996. "Managing Fiscal Policy in Latin America and the Caribbean: Volatility, Procyclicality, and Limited Creditworthiness." Working Paper 326, Office of the Chief Economist, Inter-American Development Bank, Washington, DC.

Gill, Indermit S., and Nadeem Ilahi. 2000. "Economic Insecurity, Individual Behaviour and Social Policy," Manuscript, LCSHD, World Bank, Washington, DC. http://wbln0018.worldbank.org/LAC/

7

LACInfoClient.nsf/o/3ee47810770452658525694b003cd4ea/$FILE/ Gill_Ilahi.pdf

Hagemann, Robert P. 1999. "The Structural Budget Balance: The IMF's Methodology." IMF Working Paper 99/95, International Monetary Fund, Washington, DC.

Harvey, Andrew. 2002. "Trends, Cycles and Convergence." In Norman Loayza and Raimundo Soto, eds., *Economic Growth: Sources, Trends, and Cycles.* Santiago: Central Bank of Chile.

IMF (International Monetary Fund). 2001. "Chile: Selected Issues." IMF Country Report 1/120. International Monetary Fund, Washington, DC.

Kaminsky, Graciela L., Carmen M. Reinhart, and Carlos A. Végh. 2004. "When It Rains, It Pours: Procyclical Capital Flows and Macroeconomic Policies." *NBER Macroeconomics Annual* 19: 11–53.

Kennedy, Suzanne, and Janine Robbins. 2001. "The Role of Fiscal Rules in Determining Fiscal Performance." Department of Finance Working Paper 2001–16, Government of Canada, Ottawa.

Lagos, Luis F., and Rosanna Costa. 2002: Es necesario modificar la regla fiscal, http://www.lyd.com/ biblioteca/revistas/regla_fiscal.html.

Levinson, Arik. 1998. "Balanced Budgets and Business Cycle: Evidence from the States." *National Tax Journal* 51 (4): 715–32.

Mainardi, Stefano. 1998. "Non-stationarity and Structural Breaks in Mineral Price and Supply Historical Series." *Prague Economic Papers* 3/1998, 263–75.

Marcel, Mario, Marcelo Tokman, Rodrigo Valdes, and Paula Benavides. 2001a. Balance estructural del gobierno central: metodología y estimaciones para Chile: 1987–2000, Ministerio de Hacienda, Santiago, Chile. (http://www.dipres.cl/publicaciones/Balance%20MH_1.pdf)

_____. 2001b. Balance estructural: La base de la nueva regla de policita fiscal chilena. *Economia Chilena* 4 (3).

Mattina, Todd, and Francois Delorme. 1997. "The Impact of Fiscal Policy and the Risk Premium of Government Long-Term Debt: Some Canadian Evidence." Working Paper No. 97–01, Queen's University, Ontario, Canada.

Milesi-Ferretti, Gian Maria. 2000. "Good, Bad or Ugly? On the Effects of Fiscal Rules with Creative Accounting." IMF Working Paper 00/172, International Monetary Fund, Washington, DC.

Perry, Guillermo. 2003. "Can Fiscal Rules Help Reduce Macroeconomic Volatility in the Latin America and Caribbean Region?" Policy Research Working Paper 3080, World Bank, Washington, DC.

7

Perry, Guillermo, and Luis Servén. 2003. "The Anatomy of a Multiple Crisis: Why Was Argentina Special and What Can We Learn from It?" Policy Research Working Paper 3081, World Bank, Washington, DC.

Talvi, Ernesto, and Carlos A. Végh. 2000. "Tax Base Variability and Procyclical Fiscal Policy." NBER Working Paper 7499, National Bureau of Economic Research, Cambridge, MA.

World Bank. 2001. "Chile: Poverty and Income Distribution in a High Growth Economy: The Case of Chile 1987–98." Report No. 22037-CH, Latin America and the Caribbean Region. World Bank, Washington, DC.

7

Chapter 8

205-32

(selected countries)

Currency Crises and Fiscal Sustainability

Craig Burnside, Martin Eichenbaum, and Sergio Rebelo

F33

O19
O23 E62

H62

O16

8

This chapter discusses the relation between fiscal sustainability and the sustainability of a fixed exchange rate regime. At the most general level, fiscal sustainability simply corresponds to the notion that a government's intertemporal budget constraint holds without explicit default on its debt. This requires that the initial real value of a government's debt be equal to the real present value of its future primary surpluses plus the present value of inflation-related revenues such as seigniorage. In contrast, sustainability of a fixed exchange rate regime requires that the government not raise any inflation-related revenues.[1] So under such a regime, fiscal sustainability reduces to the condition that the real value of a government's initial debt must equal the real present value of its primary fiscal surpluses.

The classic example of a fixed exchange rate regime that is not sustainable is analyzed in the seminal papers of Krugman (1979) and Flood and Garber (1984). These authors consider a situation in which a government is running persistent primary deficits. A key implicit assumption of their analyses is that future primary surpluses will not be large enough to balance the government's intertemporal budget constraint. Since it is infeasible to indefinitely borrow and repay the resources needed to cover the ongoing deficits, the government will eventually have to print money to raise seigniorage revenues. This means that the fixed exchange rate regime is not sustainable. As is shown later, the precise timing of the fixed exchange rate collapse depends on various assumptions about government behavior and the demand for domestic money. But collapse it will. Precise timing aside, in this scenario an analyst would observe large ongoing deficits and rising debt levels prior to the collapse of the fixed exchange rate regime.

One might be tempted to conclude that large primary deficits are a necessary symptom of fiscal nonsustainability under a fixed exchange rate regime. But that is not the case. Unless the assumptions of the Krugman-Flood-Garber analyses hold, it is difficult to assess whether a given country is on a fiscally sustainable path using historical data on standard macroeconomic aggregates like deficits. Deciding whether a fixed exchange rate regime is sustainable necessarily involves forecasting the *future* values of government purchases, transfers, and tax revenues. This is particularly difficult in a world where governments incur large contingent liabilities. Such liabilities often arise because governments are committed to bailing out large sectors of the economy (banks and other large financial institutions, for example) should they fail. A government that is running substantial fiscal surpluses may switch to a fiscally nonsustainable path, once large contingent liabilities are triggered. This happens when the government does not have a credible way of raising future primary surpluses to pay for the activated liabilities. Under these circumstances, activated contingent liabilities translate into prospective deficits that the government must fund via inflation-related revenues. It follows that the fixed exchange rate regime is no longer sustainable. Again, the precise time at which the collapse occurs depends on various assumptions. But as in the Krugman-Flood-Garber case, the collapse is inevitable.

In the examples presented here (motivated by the Asian currency crises of the 1990s), the fixed exchange rate regime collapses before the government begins to pay the activated liabilities, incurs primary deficits, or prints money. In such a situation, primary deficits are obviously a poor indicator of fiscal nonsustainability. Instead, the analyst must carefully assess the nature of a government's contingent liabilities, the probability that those liabilities will be activated, and the extent to which the government is willing to raise revenues not related to inflation to pay for its prospective expenditures. In practice, such an assessment will involve detailed institutional information about the country in question. Statistical analysis of standard macroeconomic data—no matter how well-informed by economic theory—will not suffice.

The remainder of this chapter is organized as follows. Section 1 provides a simple version of the government budget constraint. A more realistic version of the budget constraint that is useful for organizing data and analyzing particular episodes appears in chapter 9. Here the crucial issue will be whether or not the government needs to raise resources via inflation-related revenues. Sections 2 and 3 consider the classic Krugman-Flood-Garber experiment. Section 4 explores the case of currency crises triggered by prospective deficits and argues, on empirical grounds, that this case provides a good description of the origins of the Asian currency crises. Section 5 briefly reviews the shortcomings of this analysis and serves as an introduction to chapter 9.

1   The Government's Intertemporal Budget Constraint

This section develops a simplified version of the government's intertemporal budget constraint. The key simplification is that the only inflation-related source of revenue available to the government is printing money. Additional sources of inflation-related revenue are discussed in chapter 9: deflating the real value of outstanding nonindexed nominal debt and reducing the real value of government expenditures via an *implicit* fiscal reform. The latter means that the government can deflate the real value of its outlays that are fixed, at least temporarily, in nominal terms (for example, civil servant wages or social security payments).

To proceed, assume that there is a single good whose domestic currency price is P_t. The foreign currency price of this good is P_t^*, and purchasing power parity (PPP) holds:

$$P_t = P_t^* S_t. \tag{1.1}$$

Here S_t is the exchange rate expressed in units of local currency per unit of foreign currency (so a depreciation means a rise in S_t). For simplicity, assume that $P_t^* = 1$, so that $P_t = S_t$.

The government can borrow and lend in international capital markets at a constant real interest rate r. It also has assets in the form of foreign reserves that earn the real interest rate r. Now denote the dollar value of the government's debt net of foreign reserves by b_t. Net government debt evolves according to

$$\dot{b}_t = r b_t - (\tau_t - g_t - v_t) - \dot{M}_t / S_t. \tag{1.2}$$

The variable g_t represents real government spending on goods and services, v_t represents real transfers, and τ_t represents real tax revenues. The term $\tau_t - g_t - v_t$ represents the real government surplus, while M_t denotes the level of the money supply. One can use the notation $\dot{x}$ to represent the derivative of x with respect to time, dx/dt.

Equation (1.2) assumes that the government's real debt and the supply of money evolve smoothly over time.[2] In currency crisis models there are typically points in time at which M and b change discretely; one such point in time is the instance at which the exchange rate regime is abandoned. One can denote the set of such points in time by I. At these points (that is, at any $t \in I$) the change in government debt is given by

$$\Delta b_t = -\Delta(M_t/S_t). \tag{1.3}$$

Assuming no default on the government debt, using (1.2), the condition $\lim_{t\to\infty} e^{-rt} b_t = 0$, and allowing for discrete jumps in government debt, yields the government's intertemporal budget constraint:

$$b_0 = \int_0^\infty (\tau_t - g_t - v_t)e^{-rt}\,dt + \int_0^\infty (\dot{M}_t/S_t)e^{-rt}\,dt + \sum_{t\in I}\Delta(M_t/S_t)e^{-rt}. \tag{1.4}$$

According to (1.4) the initial level of the government's debt must be equal to the present value of future primary surpluses, $\int_0^\infty (\tau_t - g_t - v_t)e^{-rt}\,dt$, plus the present value of seigniorage, $\int_0^\infty (\dot{M}_t/S_t)e^{-rt}\,dt + \sum_{t\in I}\Delta(M_t/S_t)e^{-rt}$. One can say that a set of monetary and fiscal policies is fiscally sustainable as long as (1.4) holds.

Fiscal sustainability is much more stringent in an economy operating under a fixed exchange rate regime. Abstracting from foreign inflation the price level must be constant in a fixed exchange rate regime, because otherwise PPP would not hold. Abstracting from growth in the demand for real balances (due to growth in output or consumption) this last condition requires that the money supply be constant, so that seigniorage revenues are zero.[3] It follows that (1.4) reduces to

$$b_0 = \int_0^\infty (\tau_t - g_t - v_t)e^{-rt}\,dt. \tag{1.5}$$

The key point here is that sustainability of a fixed exchange rate regime requires that the government balance its intertemporal budget constraint without resorting to inflation-based revenues. The forward-looking nature of (1.5) makes clear why it is so difficult to determine from real-time data whether a country is on a fiscally sustainable path. There is no way to evaluate fiscal sustainability without forecasting the future paths of expenditures

Table 8.1: Fiscal Surplus, 1995–9
(percentage of GDP)

Country	1995	1996	1997	1998	1999
Indonesia	0.0	0.8	1.2	−0.7	−1.9
Korea, Rep. of	1.0	1.3	1.0	−0.9	−4.0
Malaysia	3.3	2.2	2.1	4.0	−1.0
Philippines	−1.8	−1.4	−0.4	−0.8	−2.7
Thailand	1.9	3.0	2.5	−0.9	−2.5
Hong Kong (China)	−0.3	2.2	6.1	−1.8	0.8
Singapore	13.9	12.3	9.3	9.4	3.6
Taiwan (China)	0.2	0.4	−0.7	−0.6	0.9
Japan	−2.3	−3.6	−4.2	−3.4	−4.3
United States	−3.8	−3.3	−2.4	−1.2	−0.1

Source: Burnside, Eichenbaum, and Rebelo (2001).

and taxes. For example, a country could run a sustained deficit for a period of time, yet (1.5) could still hold, because the government has credible plans to run future surpluses that will offset the deficits. In contrast, a country could run a surplus but have future deficits so large that (1.5) does not hold.

This last possibility is more than a theoretical curiosity. Table 8.1 presents data on the fiscal surpluses for the United States and several Asian countries. Notice that the countries involved in the Asian currency crisis of 1997 (Indonesia, Republic of Korea, Malaysia, the Philippines, and Thailand) were running either surpluses or modest deficits. At the same time, the United States, which did not suffer large adverse movements in its exchange rate, was running a fiscal deficit. This example will be revisited later, in a discussion on the importance of contingent liabilities and their impact on government budget constraints.

2   Fiscal Sustainability and Speculative Attacks

When the sustainability condition, (1.5), does not hold, it is inevitable that a fixed exchange rate regime will be abandoned. The only questions are: When will it happen, and what will the aftermath look like? The answers to these questions depend on three elements of the model: (1) the nature of money demand, (2) the rule for abandoning the fixed exchange rate, and (3) post-crisis monetary policy. These elements are now added to the analysis in a discussion of two experiments. In the first case there is an immediate increase in government transfers, which induces the government to begin running a deficit. In the second case agents find out that there will be an increase in future government transfers, say, because contingent liabilities to a failing banking system have been activated. This will induce prospective but not current deficits.

Money Demand

A standard specification for the demand for domestic money is now adopted, due to Cagan (1956):

$$M_t = \theta Y P_t e^{-\eta R_t}, \qquad (2.1)$$

where θ and η are positive constants. According to (2.1), the demand for domestic money depends positively on domestic real income, Y, and depends negatively on the opportunity cost of holding money, that is, the nominal interest rate, R_t. The parameter η represents the semi-elasticity of money demand with respect to the interest rate. For the sake of simplicity, assume that domestic real output is constant over time.

In the absence of uncertainty, the nominal interest rate is equal to the real rate of interest, r_t, plus the rate of inflation, $\pi_t = \dot{P}_t/P_t$:

$$R_t = r_t + \pi_t. \qquad (2.2)$$

Combining (2.1) and (2.2) one obtains a differential equation in P_t:

$$\log(M_t) = \log(\theta Y) + \log(P_t) - \eta(r + \dot{P}_t/P_t). \qquad (2.3)$$

The solution to this equation is

$$\ln P_t = \eta r - \ln(\theta Y) + \frac{1}{\eta} \int_t^\infty e^{-(s-t)/\eta} \ln(M_s)\, ds.$$

Consistent with classic results in Sargent and Wallace (1973), equation (2.3) implies that the current price level is an increasing function of current and future money supplies. To see the intuition behind this result, suppose that at time t the economy is under a floating exchange rate regime. Higher growth rates of money in the future translate into higher rates of inflation and a higher nominal interest rate. This, in turn, lowers the demand for real balances at time t. Under floating exchange rates, M_t is exogenously determined by the central bank. So the only way for real balances to fall in equilibrium is for the price level to rise.

Equation (2.3) also holds while the exchange rate is fixed. Suppose, first, that the fixed exchange rate regime is sustainable. Then inflation is zero, and $P_t = S$. The money supply, which is endogenous, must equal the quantity demanded given S:

$$M = S\theta Y \exp(-\eta r). \qquad (2.4)$$

When the value of M is constant, equation (2.3) reduces to

$$\ln P_t = \eta r - \ln(\theta Y) + \ln M. \qquad (2.5)$$

If the level of the money supply is given by (2.4), then $P_t = S$.

If the government tried to print more money than the level M given by (2.4), private agents would simply trade it in at the fixed exchange rate for foreign reserves or government debt. Thus, as long as the country is in a fixed exchange rate regime, the government cannot generate seigniorage revenues.[4]

The interpretation of (2.3) is more complicated when the exchange rate is fixed at time t, but agents know that at some future date t^* the economy will let the exchange rate float. After t^*, the path of the money supply is determined by the central bank, so the intuition for (2.3) is as described earlier. Before t^*, the money supply is endogenously determined by the behavior of private agents. To understand the role played by equation (2.3) before t^*, one must first identify the determinants of t^*. This task is now explained.

8

The Rule for Abandoning the Fixed Exchange Rate

It is standard in the literature to assume that the government follows a threshold rule for abandoning the fixed exchange rate regime: The regime is abandoned in the first period, t^*, in which the government's debt reaches some finite upper bound, $\bar{b}$. This rule turns out to be equivalent to another rule to be used in this analysis: The fixed exchange rate is abandoned when the amount of domestic money sold by private agents in exchange for foreign reserves exceeds some percentage of the initial money supply, that is, when the money demand falls to $e^{-\chi}M$, for some $\chi > 0$.

To see why the two rules are equivalent, it is important to recognize that in any equilibrium where the fixed exchange rate regime is abandoned, the inflation rate rises discretely at the time this occurs. Agents, anticipating this, will discretely reduce their domestic money balances an instant before the exchange rate regime is abandoned. Under the fixed exchange rate regime, agents go to the government and exchange domestic money for dollars at the exchange rate S. This reduces the government's reserves, thus raising its net debt. So the rise in debt that sets off the government's threshold rule and the fall in money demand occur simultaneously.

In addition to being a good description of what happens in actual crises, the threshold rule can be interpreted as a short-run borrowing constraint on the government: It limits the amount of reserves that the government can borrow to defend the fixed exchange rate.[5] Rebelo and Végh (2002) discuss the circumstances in which it is optimal for a social planner to follow a threshold rule.[6] While they use a general equilibrium model, the Rebelo and Végh framework is similar in spirit to the model used here.

Post-crisis Monetary Policy

Finally, one can adopt the following specification of post-crisis monetary policy: In period T the government engineers a one-time increase in the money supply relative to its pre-crisis level, that is, $M_T = e^\gamma M$. Thereafter, the money supply grows at the rate μ. This formulation for post-crisis money supply decouples the time of the speculative attack (which will be computed later) from the time at which the government starts to print money. It also nests as a special case the specification used by Krugman (1979) and Flood and Garber (1984) according to which money starts growing at a constant rate μ as soon as a fixed exchange rate is abandoned. Finally, this specification is simple enough that one can provide intuition about the timing of the speculative attack.

As is shown, in general, given the threshold rule and our assumptions about monetary policy, the fixed exchange rate regime will be abandoned prior to time T. As will be established, the fixed exchange rate regime is abandoned when the money supply falls by χ percent, so the post-crisis behavior of the money supply can be summarized as follows:

$$M_t = \begin{cases} e^{-\chi}M, & \text{for } t^* \le t < T \\ e^{\gamma+\mu(t-T)}M, & \text{for } t \ge T. \end{cases} \tag{2.6}$$

With these elements in place, one can now discuss the timing of the speculative attack—once agents become aware at time zero that the fixed exchange rate regime is unsustainable.

Determining the Timing of the Crisis

Note that just before t^*, the exchange rate and the price level are still fixed. This means that instantaneous inflation is zero ($\pi_t = 0$ for $t < t^*$) and equation (2.5) holds; that is, $P_t = S$ for $t < t^*$. An instant after time t^*, the exchange rate is floating and the price level is given by (2.3). In order for P_t to be continuous, equations (2.5) and (2.3) must both imply that $P_{t^*} = S$.[7] Given this fact, and given (2.6), it is clear that the demand for real balances falls discontinuously at time t^*, from M/S to $e^{-\chi}M/S$. This is accomplished by private agents exchanging domestic currency for dollars at t^* at the exchange rate S. It is precisely this flight from local currency into dollars that activates the government's rule for abandoning the fixed exchange rate.

If one takes the post-crisis growth rate of money, μ, as given, it is possible to solve for t^* by (1) computing P_{t^*} using (2.3) and the path for the money supply, (2.6) and (2) combining this with the fact that $P_{t^*} = S$. The annex to this chapter shows that this yields the following expression for the time of the speculative attack:

$$t^* = T - \eta \ln\left(\frac{\chi + \gamma + \mu\eta}{\chi}\right). \qquad (2.7)$$

If the value of t^* implied by (2.7) is less than 0, the attack happens immediately; that is, $t^* = 0$. In this case, the exchange rate is discontinuous at time zero. It is also possible for the crisis to happen at time T, but only if γ is negative; more specifically, it requires that $\gamma = -\chi$ and $\chi = \mu\eta$. The annex considers these special cases in greater detail.

Other things equal, t^* is larger the longer the government delays implementing its new monetary policy (the larger is T) and the more willing the government is to accumulate debt; one can see that the higher χ is, the more debt the government accumulates before the crisis occurs. In addition, the higher the interest rate elasticity of money demand (the larger is η) and the more money the government prints in the future (the higher are γ and μ), the smaller is t^*. The intuition underlying these results is as follows. Once the fixed exchange rate regime is abandoned, inflation rises in anticipation of the increase in the money supply that occurs from time T forward. A higher elasticity of money demand (η) makes it easier for the money supply to fall by χ percent. This means that the threshold rule is activated sooner, thus reducing the value of t^*. Higher values of μ and γ also reduce t^* because they lead to higher rates of inflation, making it possible for a drop of χ percent in the money supply to happen sooner.

Some caution is required in interpreting these results, because the parameters on the right-hand side of (2.7) cannot be changed independently of each other. When one parameter is varied, either γ or μ must be adjusted to ensure that the government budget constraint continues to be satisfied. To fully characterize t^*, one must solve for the combination of γ and μ, so that (1.4) holds.

One natural question is: Why doesn't the attack happen at time zero, when people find out that the government will run either ongoing or prospective deficits? To understand why the collapse generally occurs after time zero, two issues must be kept in mind. First, as long as the government has access to foreign reserves and is willing to use them, it can fix the price of its currency. It does so by exchanging domestic money for foreign reserves at the fixed price S. In this model, the government is willing to do this until the level of domestic money falls by χ percent. Stated differently, a fixed exchange rate regime is a price-fixing scheme that will endure as long as the government has the ability and the willingness to exchange domestic currency for dollars. If the government were not willing to endure any increases in its debt (it was unwilling to buy back any of the domestic money supply at $S_t = S$), then the exchange rate regime would collapse at $t = 0$. Given the government's willingness to buy back no more than χ percent of the money supply, the key determinant of when the fixed exchange rate regime collapses is when money demand falls by χ percent. Second, as a result of the discrete increase in money supply at time T, inflation is monotonically increasing between t^* and time T. This reflects the fact that in standard Cagan money demand models, the price level at time t is a function of discounted current and future money supplies. An important feature of this function is that the further out in time the increase in the money supply is, the lower its impact on the initial price level [see (2.3)]. In general, inflation is too low at time zero to produce a fall in money demand large enough to trigger the government's threshold rule. This would be the case only if the demand for real balances at time zero fell by at least χ percent, and this would happen only if γ, μ, and η were sufficiently large. If so, there would be a discontinuous jump in the exchange rate at time zero.

As the previous discussion makes clear, the timing of the devaluation is deterministic—everybody knows the precise time at which the fixed exchange rate regime will collapse. This shortcoming can be remedied by introducing some element of uncertainty into the model, such as money demand shocks.[8] One can abstract from uncertainty since it complicates the analysis considerably but does not change the basic message about fiscal sustainability.

In the following two experiments, the first considers the classic Krugman-Flood-Garber case, in which the government begins to run ongoing deficits that make the fixed exchange rate regime unsustainable. The key feature of this example is that the deficits would be a real-time indicator of fiscal nonsustainability. A version of the analysis in Burnside, Eichenbaum, and Rebelo (2001) is then considered, in which private agents come to expect that the government will run future deficits that will not be offset by future primary surpluses. The analysis will show that this results in a collapse of the fixed exchange rate regime, after agents receive information about the higher future deficits, but before the government starts to run those deficits or print money. So, here, past deficits would be a useless indicator of fiscal sustainability.

3   Ongoing Deficits

Consider an economy that is initially in a sustainable fixed exchange rate regime—that is, (1.5) holds—with a constant primary surplus, $\tau - g - v$. The level of government debt is constant and equal to

$$b_0 = (\tau - g - v)/r. \tag{3.1}$$

At time zero, information arrives that there has been a permanent rise in government transfers to a new level $\bar{v}$. In order for the fixed exchange rate regime still to be sustainable, the government must adjust its taxes or government spending so that (1.5) continues to hold. This requires that

$$(\bar{v} - v)/r = \int_0^\infty [(\bar{\tau}_t - \tau) - (\bar{g}_t - g)]e^{-rt}\,dt, \tag{3.2}$$

where $(\bar{v} - v)/r$ is the increase in the present value of government transfers, while $\bar{\tau}_t$ and $\bar{g}_t$ denote the new values of taxes and government spending. Notice that since this is a constraint on the present value of transfers and taxes, fiscal sustainability is consistent with a persistent ongoing primary deficit. Of course, that deficit must be offset, at some point, by a persistent ongoing primary surplus in the future.

The assumption here is that the government does not change the path of taxes of government spending, so that $\bar{\tau}_t = \tau$ and $\bar{g}_t = g$. Given these assumptions, the primary surplus declines by $\bar{v} - v$ and the stock of debt is no longer constant. Furthermore, for (1.4) to hold, the government must, at some point, print money. Thus, the fixed exchange rate regime is not sustainable, although the exchange rate will remain fixed until the government's threshold rule for floating the exchange rate is activated by a sufficient rise in its debt (or an equivalent drop in money demand).

While the economy remains under a fixed exchange rate regime, the government's debt evolves according to

$$b_t = b_0 + \frac{\bar{v} - v}{r}(e^{rt} - 1), \quad \text{for } t < t^*. \tag{3.3}$$

Note that the stock of debt rises at an increasing rate while the economy remains in the fixed exchange rate regime:

$$\dot{b}_t = (\bar{v} - v)e^{rt}, \quad \text{for } t < t^*.$$

Immediately prior to time t^*, the debt stock will have risen to the level $b_0 + (\bar{v} - v)(e^{rt^*} - 1)/r$. As shown in the annex, at time t^* the inflation rate rises discretely to χ/η. This occurs in anticipation of the higher and faster growing money supply path that will prevail in the future. This discrete rise in inflation causes agents to use the last few seconds of the fixed exchange rate regime to reduce their money balances from M to $Me^{-\chi}$. This is accomplished by swapping domestic money for reserves. So at time t^* the debt stock rises, consistent with (1.3), by $\Delta b_{t^*} = (M - Me^{-\chi})/S$, so that

$$b_{t^*} = b_0 + \frac{\bar{v} - v}{r}(e^{rt^*} - 1) + \frac{M - Me^{-\chi}}{S}. \tag{3.4}$$

It is this final jump in debt that sets off the government's threshold rule. The precise timing of the attack (that is, the solution for t^*) is determined by making $b_{t^*} = \bar{b}$. The annex presents formal proof that there is an equivalence between a threshold rule described in terms of debt rising to the level $\bar{b}$, and a rule described in terms of money demand falling to the level $Me^{-\chi}$.

Since the money supply remains constant between t^* and T, seigniorage is zero and debt continues to rise according to

$$\dot{b}_t = r(b_t - b_0) + \bar{v} - v > 0. \tag{3.5}$$

At date T there is another jump, but this time it is downward. The government increases the supply of money to Me^{γ} by buying back government debt. So, other things equal, the effect of this operation is to reduce the level of debt by $(Me^{\gamma} - Me^{-\chi})/S_T$. It follows from this and (3.5) that b_T is given by

$$b_T = b_0 + \frac{\bar{v} - v}{r}(e^{rT} - 1) + \frac{M - Me^{-\chi}}{S}e^{r(T-t^*)} - \frac{Me^{\gamma} - Me^{-\chi}}{S_T}. \quad (3.6)$$

As equation (3.6) shows, three factors determine the change in the government's debt between period 0 and period T. First, from time 0 forward, the government's primary deficit is larger by the amount $\bar{v} - v$. This increase in the primary deficit causes debt to accumulate. At time t^* there is a jump up in the level of debt due to the decline in money balances during the speculative attack. Finally, at time T the government's debt stock jumps down as it engineers a discrete increase in money balances.

From time T forward the money supply expands at rate μ. As shown in the annex, this implies that for $t \geq T$, the exchange rate is given by $S_t = e^{\gamma + \mu(\eta + t - T)}S$, the inflation rate is μ, real balances are constant at the level

$$\frac{M_T}{S_T} = \theta Y e^{-\eta(r+\mu)} = e^{-\eta\mu}\frac{M}{S},$$

and the government receives a constant seigniorage flow of: $\mu e^{-\eta\mu}M/S$.

Recall that the level of μ must ensure that the government's intertemporal budget constraint, (1.4), holds. For $t > T$, the sum of the primary surplus and the flow of seigniorage revenue is constant over time. It is easy to see that (1.4) holds if the sum of the primary surplus and the flow of seigniorage revenue equals the interest payments on the debt accumulated by date T:

$$\tau - g - \bar{v} + \mu e^{-\eta\mu}\frac{M}{S} = rb_T. \quad (3.7)$$

Given the expression for b_T, (3.6), the government must set μ so that (3.7) is satisfied. Notice, however, given the expression for b_T, that (3.7) is equivalent to the lifetime budget constraint for period 0:

$$\frac{\bar{v} - v}{r} = e^{-rt^*}\frac{Me^{-\chi} - M}{S} + e^{-rT}\frac{Me^{\gamma} - Me^{-\chi}}{S_T} + e^{-rT}\frac{\mu e^{-\eta\mu}}{r}\frac{M}{S}. \quad (3.8)$$

In this form, it is clear that the increase in the present value of transfers must be financed with increased seigniorage revenue.

Table 8.2: Parameters for the Numerical Examples

$\eta = 0.5$	Interest elasticity of money demand
$\chi = 0.12$	Threshold rule parameter
$S = 1$	Initial exchange rate
$\theta = 0.06$	Constant in the money demand function
$r = 0.05$	Real interest rate
$Y = 1$	Constant level of output
$(\bar{v} - v)/r = 0.24$	Present value of new transfers
$b_0 = 0$	Initial debt level
$T = 1$	Time of switch to new monetary policy
$\gamma = 0.12$	Percentage of increase in M at T relative to $t = 0$

A Numerical Example

To discuss the properties of the model, it is useful to present a numerical example. The parameter values used here, summarized in table 8.2, are loosely based on Korean data. For reasons discussed earlier, arguably the Krugman-Flood-Garber analysis does not apply to Korea. But the Korean example is taken more seriously in the context of the following section, in the discussion of prospective deficits. So to conserve space, the parameter values used in both examples are now discussed. These parameters are taken from the analysis in Burnside, Eichenbaum, and Rebelo (2001).

Normalize real income, Y, and the initial exchange rate, S, to 1. Then set the semi-elasticity of money demand with respect to the interest rate, η, equal to 0.5. This is consistent with the range of estimates of money demand elasticities in developing countries provided by Easterly, Mauro, and Schmidt-Hebbel (1995). Set the constant $\theta = 0.06$ so that in the initial steady state, the model is consistent with the ratio of the monetary base to GDP in Korea in the late 1990s. Set the real interest rate, r, to 5 percent. This is roughly consistent with U.S. dollar interest rates in Korea during the 1990s. For convenience, set $b_0 = \tau - g - v = 0$.

Now assume that $\bar{v} = v + 0.012$, which implies that the present value of the increase in transfer spending is $(\bar{v} - v)/r = 0.012/0.05 = 0.24$, or 24 percent of GDP. Then set $\chi = 0.12$, $\gamma = 0.12$, and $T = 1$. The rationale for choosing these parameter values will become clear in the following section. Given these parameter values, solve (6.2) from the technical annex and (3.8) simultaneously for t^* and μ, which turn out to be 0.45 and 0.24, respectively.

Figure 8.1 displays the paths for the exchange rate, nominal and real money, inflation and money growth, as well as real government debt. A number of features emerge. First, as anticipated, government debt begins to rise from time zero due to the increase in transfers and the primary deficit to

Figure 8.1: Equilibrium Paths for Crisis Models

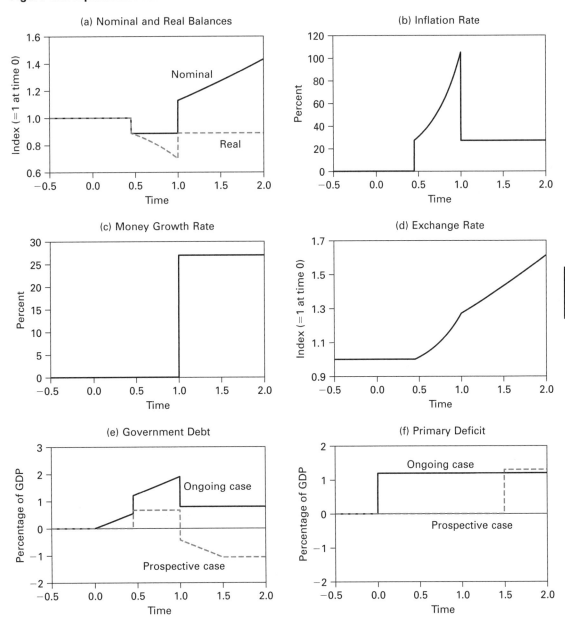

new, permanently higher, levels. The speculative attack takes place at $t^* = 0.49$, at which time the debt jumps discontinuously as agents trade domestic money for reserves. The debt grows smoothly between times t^* and T, at which point it drops discontinuously as the government increases the money supply and starts to generate seigniorage revenues. Second, the exchange rate rises in a continuous way from t^* to T and then depreciates at a constant rate μ. Finally, note that in this example the money supply does not grow before the speculative attack. The only indicator of the crisis to come is the increase in the deficit and the accumulation of increasing amounts of debt.

4   Prospective Deficits

Now consider an example in which the deficit is not a good leading indicator for a currency crisis. In this example agents know that there will be future deficits that make the fixed exchange rate regime unstable. This example is motivated by the 1997 currency crises in Indonesia, Korea, Malaysia, the Philippines, and Thailand. In the authors' view—exposited in Burnside, Eichenbaum, and Rebelo (2001)—these governments were faced with large *prospective* deficits associated with implicit bailout guarantees to failing banking systems. The expectation that these future deficits would, at least in part, be financed by seigniorage revenues led to a collapse of the fixed exchange rate regimes in Asia.[9] Of course, market participants could have believed that governments would fund their obligations by raising taxes or cutting expenditure. But in the authors' view, this was not credible. The state of the world in which financial intermediaries would suffer grievous losses is exactly the state of the world in which current and prospective real output and tax revenues would fall. While not modeled in this chapter, raising distortionary taxes or lowering government purchases under those circumstances could well be politically unacceptable or socially undesirable relative to the alternative: monetizing the prospective deficits and receiving aid from international agencies like the International Monetary Fund. But this alternative is incompatible with maintaining a fixed exchange rate.

As before, consider an economy that is initially in a sustainable fixed exchange rate regime with a constant government primary surplus, $\tau - g - v$, and a constant level of government debt given by (3.1).

At time zero information arrives that from time $T' > T$ on there will be a permanent rise in government transfers to a new level $\bar{v}$. In order for the fixed exchange rate regime to still be sustainable, taxes or government spending must adjust so that (1.5) continues to hold. This requires that

$$e^{-rT'}(\bar{v} - v)/r = \int_0^\infty [(\bar{\tau}_t - \tau) - (\bar{g}_t - g)]e^{-rt}\, dt. \qquad (4.1)$$

Also, as before, assume that the government does not change the path of taxes or government spending, so that $\bar{\tau}_t = \tau$ and $\bar{g}_t = g$. This implies that (4.1) does not hold, so that the fixed exchange rate regime is not sustainable.

Given these assumptions, $\dot{b}_t = 0$ for $t < t^*$. Government debt remains constant until the time of the speculative attack, because the increase in transfers does not occur immediately: $b_t = b_0$, for $t < t^*$.

As in the Krugman-Flood-Garber case, the level of debt jumps discretely at t^*, as agents reduce their money balances from M to $Me^{-\chi}$:

$$b_{t^*} = b_0 - (Me^{-\chi} - M)/S.$$

Since the money supply remains constant between t^* and T, seigniorage is zero and the evolution of the stock of debt is given by $b_t = b_0 - e^{r(t-t^*)}$ $(Me^{-\chi} - M)/S$, for $t^* < t < T$. At time T the government increases the supply of money by γ percent so the level of debt at time T is given by

$$b_T = b_0 - e^{r(T-t^*)}\frac{Me^{-\chi} - M}{S} - \frac{Me^{\gamma} - Me^{-\chi}}{S_T}.$$

From time T through time T' there is no increase in the primary deficit, but the money supply expands at the rate μ, implying that the government receives a seigniorage flow of $\mu M_T/S_T$. This implies that the stock of debt evolves according to

$$b_t = b_0 - e^{r(t-t^*)}\frac{Me^{-\chi} - M}{S} - e^{r(t-T)}\frac{Me^{\gamma} - Me^{-\chi}}{S_T} - \frac{e^{r(t-T)} - 1}{r}\mu\frac{M_T}{S_T}.$$

After time T' transfers increase permanently to the level $\bar{v}$. This implies that after date T' the stock of debt will evolve according to

$$b_t = b_0 - e^{r(t-t^*)}\frac{Me^{-\chi} - M}{S} - e^{r(t-T)}\frac{Me^{\gamma} - Me^{-\chi}}{S_T}$$
$$- \frac{e^{r(t-T)} - 1}{r}\mu\frac{M_T}{S_T} + \frac{e^{r(t-T')} - 1}{r}(\bar{v} - v).$$

8

The lifetime budget constraint is satisfied if $\lim_{t\to\infty} e^{-rt}b_t = 0$. From the previous equation it is clear that the lifetime budget constraint is satisfied if debt is constant at the level $b_{T'}$ and

$$e^{-rT'}\frac{\bar{v}-v}{r} = e^{-rt^*}\frac{Me^{-\chi}-M}{S} + e^{-rT}\frac{Me^{\gamma}-Me^{-\chi}}{S_T} + \frac{e^{-rT}}{r}\mu\frac{M_T}{S_T}.$$

This equation is equivalent to (3.8) as long as the present value of the increase in transfers remains the same across the two examples. In this case, the paths of the exchange rate are identical across the two examples, as is the timing of the speculative attack. Other things equal, all that matters is the present value of the new transfers, which are financed by seigniorage.

In the previous section it was assumed that $\bar{v} = v + 0.012$. Notice that this implied that the present value of the increase in transfer spending was $(\bar{v}-v)/r = 0.24$, or 24 percent of GDP. This corresponds to a conservative estimate of the fiscal cost of Korea's banking crisis relative to its GDP.[10] In this section, the present value of the increase in transfer spending is $e^{-rT'}(\bar{v}-v)/r$. Now set $T' = 1.5 > T = 1$. In order that the increase in the present value of transfers should still be 0.24, set $\bar{v} - v = 0.24re^{rT'} = 0.0129$. In the previous section, $\chi = 0.12$. This corresponds to the fall in Korea's monetary base between December 1996 and December 1997. The value of γ was also set to 0.12. This corresponds to the ratio of the average value of the monetary base in the second half of 1999 versus the first half of 1997.

Figure 8.1 displays the paths for the exchange rate, nominal and real money, as well as real government debt and the primary deficit. These paths are the same as in the case of ongoing deficits, with the exception of the paths for the deficit and the stock of government debt. The key features of the example are as follows. First (as with the first example), the collapse of the fixed exchange rate regime occurs after the new information about the deficit arrives but before the new monetary policy is implemented at time T. Second, inflation begins to rise at t^*, before the change in monetary policy. So consistent with classic results in Sargent and Wallace (1981), future monetary policy affects current inflation.

Note that, in this example, the currency crisis is preceded by neither a rise in government debt nor an increase in the primary deficit, nor an increase in the money supply. This is consistent with the view that past deficits and past money growth rates are not reliable predictors of currency crises or fiscal sustainability.[11] The analysis here suggests that, in many

8

Table 8.3: Changes in Banking Sector Stock Market Values
(7/1/97 = 100)

Country	Pre- 7/1/97 peak Date	Pre- 7/1/97 peak Value	7/1/97 Value	Peak to 7/1/97 % change Level	Peak to 7/1/97 % change Relative to nonfinancials	12/31/97 Value	Peak to 12/31/97 % change Level	Peak to 12/31/97 % change Relative to nonfinancials
Indonesia	2/28/97	103.2	100.0	−3.1	−3.2	26.3	−74.5	−65.0
Korea, Rep. of	11/7/94	207.3	100.0	−51.8	−34.4	62.5	−69.8	−27.7
Malaysia	2/25/97	121.6	100.0	−17.7	−4.0	36.3	−70.1	−48.0
Philippines	1/31/97	136.8	100.0	−26.9	−13.2	56.4	−58.8	−34.7
Thailand	1/31/96	281.1	100.0	−64.4	−29.6	60.1	−78.6	−48.9

Source: Burnside, Eichenbaum, and Rebelo (2001).

cases, analysts should focus their attention on the magnitude of a government's prospective liabilities.

To conclude, consider the evidence in Burnside, Eichenbaum, and Rebelo (2001) regarding key assumptions in this example as they pertain to the Asian currency crisis. First, the exchange rate crises in Asia were preceded by publicly available signs of imminent banking crises. Table 8.3 displays stock market-based measures of the values of the financial and nonfinancial sectors in the crisis-affected countries. These data show that in Korea and Thailand, and to a lesser extent in Malaysia and the Philippines, the value of the financial sector had been declining, in both absolute and relative terms, well before the currency crises. For example, by July 1, 1997 and December 31, 1997, the stock market value of the Korea banking sector had declined by roughly 52 percent and 70 percent, respectively, relative to its previous peak value. In contrast, by December 31, 1997, the noncrisis countries' banking sectors had not declined significantly relative to their nonfinancial sectors. This suggests that markets were not particularly concerned about the banks in the noncrisis countries.

Second, failing financial sectors in Asia were associated with large prospective government deficits. Table 8.4 uses information on pre- and post-currency crisis loan default rates to generate rough estimates of eight governments' total implicit liabilities to the financial sector. According to these estimates, nonperforming loan rates were substantially higher in the crisis countries. Finally, table 8.5 depicts estimates of the size of the prospective deficits associated with the need to recapitalize banks in Indonesia, Korea, Malaysia, and Thailand.

Table 8.4: Estimated Nonperforming Loans, June 1997

Country	Domestic bank lending	Private nonbank foreign borrowing	Total lending	Nonperforming credit (as a percentage of)		
	(Percentage of GDP)			All loans	GDP	Government revenue
Indonesia	54.6	14.7	69.3	14	9.7	65.8
Korea, Rep. of	129.9	5.1	135.0	19	25.7	128.0
Malaysia	143.0	6.7	149.7	12.5	18.7	79.9
Philippines	56.4	5.5	61.9	20.5	6.5	33.8
Thailand	135.9	7.3	143.1	24.5	35.1	194.7
Hong Kong (China)	166.1	14.8	180.9	2	3.6	18.3
Singapore	113.9	8.5	122.4	4	4.9	12.5
Taiwan (China)	149.5	1.1	150.5	4	6.0	50.4

Source: Burnside, Eichenbaum, and Rebelo (2001).

Table 8.5: Costs of Restructuring and Recapitalizing the Banking System

Country	Percentage of GDP	Date of estimate
Indonesia	65	November 1999
Korea, Rep. of	24	December 1999
Malaysia	22	December 1999
Thailand	35	June 1999

Source: Burnside, Eichenbaum, and Rebelo (2001).

5 Conclusion

This chapter explored the connection between fiscal sustainability and fixed exchange rates. The discussion first focused on the fact that the sustainability of a fixed exchange rate regime requires that a government satisfy its intertemporal budget constraint without recourse to inflation-related revenues. Second, it was argued that ongoing deficits are neither a necessary nor a sufficient condition for the nonsustainability of a fixed exchange rate regime. The 1997 currency crises in Asia are a good illustration of this point.

In the model used to make these points, the only inflation-related revenues available to the government were seigniorage revenues. As a result, the model predicts high inflation rates and money growth in the aftermath of a devaluation. In addition, given the purchasing power parity assumption, the rate of inflation is equal to the rate of devaluation. There are many crises in which these predictions are false. Chapter 9 considers why inflation and money growth are often low in the aftermath of a currency crisis. A closely related question is addressed there as well: How do governments actually pay for the fiscal costs associated with the currency crisis?

6   Technical Annex

The Timing of the Crisis

A Crisis between 0 and T

To begin, solve for the time, t^*, at which the speculative attack occurs and the exchange rate is floated. Notice that (2.3) implies that

$$\ln P_{t^*} = \eta r - \ln(\theta Y) + \frac{1}{\eta} \int_{t^*}^{T} e^{-(s-t^*)/\eta} \ln(e^{-\chi}M)\, ds$$

$$+ \frac{1}{\eta} \int_{T}^{\infty} e^{-(s-t^*)/\eta} \ln(e^{\gamma + \mu(s-T)}M)\, ds$$

$$= \eta r - \ln(\theta Y) + \ln M + (\chi + \gamma + \mu\eta)e^{(t^*-T)/\eta} - \chi$$

$$= \ln S + (\chi + \gamma + \mu\eta)e^{(t^*-T)/\eta} - \chi. \qquad (6.1)$$

Since it is known that $P_{t^*} = S$, this implies that

$$\chi = (\chi + \gamma + \mu\eta)e^{(t^*-T)/\eta},$$

or, equivalently, that

$$t^* = T + \eta \ln[\chi/(\chi + \gamma + \mu\eta)]. \qquad (6.2)$$

A Crisis at Time 0

When $\chi < e^{-T/\eta}(\chi + \gamma + \mu\eta)$, the expression in (6.2) implies that $t^* < 0$. In this case, the crisis must happen at $t^* = 0$ and the price level jumps at time 0 to the level implied by (6.1):

$$P_0 = S \exp\lfloor(\chi + \gamma + \mu\eta)e^{-T/\eta} - \chi\rfloor > S.$$

A Crisis at Time T

It is also possible that $t^* = T$; that is, the crisis and the switch in monetary policy have the same timing. This occurs if $\gamma = -\chi$. Notice that in this case, (2.3) implies that

$$\ln P_{t^*} = \eta r - \ln(\theta Y) + \frac{1}{\eta}\int_T^\infty e^{-(s-T)/\eta}\ln(e^{-\chi+\mu(s-T)}M)\,ds$$

$$= \eta r - \ln(\theta Y) + \ln(M) - \chi + \mu\eta$$

$$= \ln S - \chi + \mu\eta.$$

Since $P_{t^*} = S$ when $t^* > 0$, then $\chi = \mu\eta$. That is, the crisis can only happen at time T if the government's threshold rule parameter $\chi = \mu\eta$ is determined by the speed of post-crisis money growth and the interest elasticity parameter.

Ongoing Deficits

Crisis Happens at $0 < t^* < T$

To see the equivalence between a threshold rule based on money demand and one based on the government's debt stock, suppose one assumed that for $t^* \le t < T$ the stock of money remained constant at the level M_{t^*}, its level immediately after the government floats the exchange rate. For $t^* \le t < T$, the price level, given by (2.3), would be given by

$$\ln P_t = \eta r - \ln(\theta Y) + (1 - e^{(t-T)/\eta})\ln M_{t^*} + e^{(t-T)/\eta}(\gamma + \ln M + \mu\eta).$$

Notice that this implies that the money supply (and demand) must fall to some level less than M at the time the fixed exchange rate regime is abandoned. If it did not, notice that one would have

$$\ln P_{t^*} \ge \ln S + e^{(t^*-T)/\eta}(\gamma + \mu\eta),$$

which would imply a jump in the exchange rate at time t^*. Denote the lower level of money demand at time t^* as $Me^{-\chi}$ with $\chi > 0$.

8

Notice that $\dot{b}_t = rb_t - (\tau - g - \bar{v})$ for $0 < t < t^*$. Since $\tau - g - v = rb_0$, one can rewrite this as $\dot{b}_t = r(b_t - b_0) + (\bar{v} - v)$ for $0 < t < t^*$. Hence,

$$b_t = b_0 + \frac{\bar{v} - v}{r}(e^{rt} - 1) \quad \text{for } 0 < t < t^*.$$

So

$$\lim_{t \uparrow t^*} b_t = b_0 + \frac{\bar{v} - v}{r}(e^{rt^*} - 1).$$

It has been shown that there must be a jump in nominal balances, to some lower level $Me^{-\chi}$, at time t^*, implying that

$$b_{t^*} = \lim_{t \uparrow t^*} b_t + \frac{M - Me^{-\chi}}{S} = b_0 + \frac{\bar{v} - v}{r}(e^{rt^*} - 1) + \frac{M - Me^{-\chi}}{S}.$$

If the fixed exchange rate regime is abandoned at time t^*, this means that b_{t^*} must be equal to the threshold level of debt, $\bar{b}$. So

$$\bar{b} = b_0 + \frac{\bar{v} - v}{r}(e^{rt^*} - 1) + \frac{M - Me^{-\chi}}{S}.$$

But it is also known that if money demand falls by a factor $e^{-\chi}$ at the time of the attack, then t^* is given by (6.2). Hence,

$$\bar{b} = b_0 + \frac{\bar{v} - v}{r}(e^{r\{T + \eta \ln[\chi/(\chi + \gamma + \mu\eta)]\}} - 1) + \frac{M - Me^{-\chi}}{S}.$$

This shows that there is a one-to-one mapping between $\bar{b}$ and χ. Therefore, one can parameterize the threshold rule in terms of debt or in terms of money demand.

For $t^* \le t < T$, notice that $\dot{b}_t = rb_t - (\tau - g - \bar{v})$. Hence,

$$b_T = e^{r(T - t^*)}b_{t^*} + \frac{e^{r(T - t^*)} - 1}{r}(\bar{v} + g - \tau) - \frac{Me^{\gamma} - Me^{-\chi}}{S_T}.$$

If one substitutes in the expression for b_{t^*}, then

$$b_T = b_0 + (e^{rT} - 1)\left(\frac{\bar{v} - v}{r}\right) + e^{r(T - t^*)}\frac{M - Me^{-\chi}}{S} - \frac{Me^{\gamma} - Me^{-\chi}}{S_T}.$$

Given values of T, χ, γ, and μ, it is clear that t^*, $S_T = Se^{\gamma + \mu\eta}$ and b_T are determined.

From date T forward the government prints money according to $M_t = e^{\gamma + \mu(t - T)}M$, so that $\dot{M}_t = \mu M_t$. From (2.3) it is straightforward to show that $S_t = Se^{\gamma + \mu(\eta + t - T)}$ for $t \ge T$. Hence, $\dot{M}_t / S_t = \mu e^{-\mu\eta}M/S$ for $t \ge T$, where

$M/S = \theta Y e^{-\varpi}$. This implies that if $\lim_{t \to \infty} e^{-rt} b_t = 0$, then

$$b_T = \int_T^\infty (\tau - g - \bar{v}) e^{-r(t-T)} \, dt + \int_T^\infty \mu e^{-\mu\eta} \frac{M}{S} e^{-r(t-T)} \, dt.$$

This can be rewritten as

$$r b_T = \tau - g - \bar{v} + \mu e^{-\mu\eta} M/S. \tag{6.3}$$

Given T, χ, and γ, this is an implicit equation in μ.

Crisis Happens at $t^* = 0$

As shown above, if the crisis happens at time 0, then S_0 jumps to the level

$$S_0 = S \exp\left[(\chi + \gamma + \mu\eta) e^{-T/\eta} - \chi \right].$$

During the crisis, the government's debt rises as it exchanges money for debt at the exchange rate S. Hence, immediately after the crisis, the government's debt stock is $b_0 + (M - Me^{-\chi})/S$. Similar to what was shown in the previous section,

$$b_T = b_0 + (e^{rT} - 1)\left(\frac{\bar{v} - v}{r}\right) + e^{rT} \frac{M - Me^{-\chi}}{S} - \frac{Me^\gamma - Me^{-\chi}}{S_T}.$$

Given T, χ, γ, and μ, $S_T = Se^{\gamma+\mu\eta}$ and b_T are determined. Given T, χ, and γ, (6.3) becomes an implicit equation in μ. Once this equation is solved for μ, one would need to check whether, in fact, $t^* = 0$.

Crisis Happens at $t^* = T$

Given the same logic as in the previous subsection, but imposing $t^* = T$ and $\gamma = -\chi$, one has

$$b_T = b_0 + \frac{\bar{v} - v}{r}(e^{rT} - 1) + \frac{M - Me^{-\chi}}{S}.$$

Given values of T and χ, b_T is determined.

From date T forward the government prints money according to $M_t = e^{-\chi+\mu(t-T)}M$ so that $\dot{M}_t = \mu M_t$. From (2.3) it is straightforward to show that $S_t = Se^{-\chi+\mu(\eta+t-T)}$ for $t \geq T$. As shown earlier, since there can be no jump in the exchange rate at time $t^* = T$, this means $\mu = \chi/\eta$. Since μ is pinned down by χ, this implies that the threshold rule parameter, χ, is not a free parameter. It must adjust to satisfy the government's lifetime budget constraint, (6.3).

Prospective Deficits

One has $\dot{b}_t = rb_t - (\tau - g - v) = 0$ for $0 < t < t^*$. Hence, $b_t = b_0$ for $0 < t < t^*$. There is a jump in nominal balances, to some lower level $Me^{-\chi}$, at time t^*, implying that

$$b_{t^*} = b_0 + \frac{M - Me^{-\chi}}{S}.$$

For $t^* \leq t < T$, notice that $\dot{b}_t = rb_t - (\tau - g - v)$. Hence,

$$b_T = e^{r(T-t^*)}b_{t^*} + \frac{e^{r(T-t^*)} - 1}{r}(v + g - \tau) - \frac{Me^{\gamma} - Me^{-\chi}}{S_T}.$$

If one substitutes in the expression for b_{t^*}, then

$$b_T = b_0 + e^{r(T-t^*)}\frac{M - Me^{-\chi}}{S} - \frac{Me^{\gamma} - Me^{-\chi}}{S_T}. \tag{6.4}$$

Given values of T, χ, γ, and μ, one can see that t^*, $S_T = Se^{\gamma+\mu\eta}$ and b_T are determined.

As above, for $t \geq T$, $M_t = e^{\gamma+\mu(t-T)}M$, $\dot{M}_t = \mu M_t$, $S_t = Se^{\gamma+\mu(\eta+t-T)}$, and $\dot{M}_t/S_t = \mu e^{-\mu\eta}M/S$. This implies that if $\lim_{t\to\infty} e^{-rt}b_t = 0$, then

$$b_T = \int_T^\infty (\tau - g)e^{-r(t-T)}\,dt - \int_T^\infty v_t e^{-r(t-T)}\,dt + \int_T^\infty \mu e^{-\mu\eta}\frac{M}{S}e^{-r(t-T)}\,dt.$$

Given that $v_t = v$ for $t < T'$ and $v_t = \bar{v}$ for $t > T'$, one can rewrite this as

$$b_T = \int_T^\infty (\tau - g)e^{-r(t-T)}\,dt - \int_T^{T'} ve^{-r(t-T)}\,dt - \int_{T'}^\infty \bar{v}e^{-r(t-T)}\,dt$$

$$+ \int_T^\infty \mu e^{-\mu\eta}\frac{M}{S}e^{-r(t-T)}\,dt$$

or

$$b_T = \frac{\tau - g - v}{r} + e^{r(T-T')}\frac{v - \bar{v}}{r} + \frac{1}{r}\mu e^{-\mu\eta}\,M/S. \tag{6.5}$$

Given T, χ, and γ, this is an implicit equation in μ.

As above, given T, χ, and γ, (6.5) is an implicit equation in μ which can be solved while noting that b_T is given by (6.4).

Notes

1. Here one can abstract from growth in the demand for domestic money and foreign inflation.

2. Technically, (1.2) applies when b and M are differentiable functions of time.

3. If the exchange rate is fixed at some value S, notice that the PPP condition, (1.1), implies that $P_t = SP_t^*$. If one assumes that money demand is of the form $M_t^d = P_t \Phi(R_t, Y_t)$, and that the nominal interest rate is $R_t = r + \pi_t$, where $\pi_t = \dot{P}_t/P_t$, the money demand can be rewritten as $M_t^d = SP_t^* \Phi(r + \dot{\pi}_t^*, Y_t)$, where $\dot{\pi}_t^*$ is the foreign inflation rate. In the absence of foreign inflation or real growth, this implies that the money supply must be constant to maintain the fixed exchange rate.

4. If there were growth in P_t^* or in Y_t, the government would collect some seigniorage revenue in a fixed exchange rate regime, but it would not have control over the money supply.

5. Drazen and Helpman (1987), as well as others, have proposed a different rule for the government's behavior: Fix future monetary policy and allow the central bank to borrow as much as possible, provided the present-value budget constraint of the government is not violated. This rule ends up being equivalent to a threshold rule. See van Wijnbergen (1991) and Burnside, Eichenbaum, and Rebelo (2001) for a discussion.

6. Rebelo and Végh (2002) show that this rule for abandoning the peg is optimal when the fiscal shock that makes the fixed exchange rate regime unsustainable is of moderate size, and either there are significant real social costs associated with a devaluation (such as loss of output or firm bankruptcy) or, while the exchange rate is fixed, a fiscal reform may arrive according to a Poisson process that restores the sustainability of the fixed exchange rate regime.

7. Proceeding as in the literature, it is assumed that the exchange rate must be a continuous function of time. So, the exchange rate is the same just before and after the collapse of the fixed exchange rate regime. If this were not the case, agents could take advantage of jumps in the exchange rate to make infinite profits.

8. See Flood and Garber (1984), Blanco and Garber (1986), Drazen and Helpman (1988), Cumby and van Wijnbergen (1989), and Goldberg (1994) for stochastic versions of speculative attack models.

9. Corsetti, Pesenti, and Roubini (1999) also discuss the possible role played by expectations of future seigniorage revenues in the Asian currency crises.

10. See Burnside, Eichenbaum, and Rebelo (2003) for a discussion.

11. See Corsetti, Pesenti, and Roubini (1999) and Kaminsky and Reinhart (1999).

References

Blanco, Herminio, and Peter M. Garber. 1986. "Recurrent Devaluation and Speculative Attacks on the Mexican Peso." *Journal of Political Economy* 94 (1): 148–66.

Burnside, Craig, Martin Eichenbaum, and Sergio Rebelo. 2001. "Prospective Deficits and the Asian Currency Crisis." *Journal of Political Economy* 109 (6): 1155–98.

———. 2003. "On the Fiscal Implications of Twin Crises." In Michael P. Dooley and Jeffrey A. Frankel, eds. *Managing Currency Crises in Emerging Markets*. Chicago: University of Chicago Press.

Cagan, Phillip. 1956. "Monetary Dynamics of Hyperinflation." In Milton Friedman, ed. *Studies in the Quantity Theory of Money*. Chicago: University of Chicago Press.

Corsetti, Giancarlo, Paolo Pesenti, and Nouriel Roubini. 1999. "Paper Tigers: A Model of the Asian Currency Crisis." *European Economic Review* 43 (7): 1211–36.

Cumby, Robert E., and Sweder van Wijnbergen. 1989. "Financial Policy and Speculative Runs with a Crawling Peg: Argentina 1979–1981." *Journal of International Economics* 27 (1–2): 111–27.

Drazen, Allan, and Elhanan Helpman. 1987. "Stabilization with Exchange Rate Management." *Quarterly Journal of Economics* 102 (4): 835–56.

———. 1988. "Stabilization with Exchange Rate Management under Uncertainty." In Elhanan Helpman, Assaf Razin, and Efraim Sadka, eds. *Economic Effects of the Government Budget*. Cambridge, MA: MIT Press.

Easterly, William, Paolo Mauro, and Klaus Schmidt-Hebbel. 1995. "Money Demand and Seigniorage-Maximizing Inflation." *Journal of Money, Credit, and Banking* 27 (2): 583–603.

8

Flood, Robert, and Peter Garber. 1984. "Collapsing Exchange Rate Regimes: Some Linear Examples." *Journal of International Economics* 17 (1-2): 1–13.

Goldberg, Linda. 1994. "Predicting Exchange Rate Crises: Mexico Revisited." *Journal of International Economics* 36 (3-4): 413–30.

Kaminsky, Graciela, and Carmen Reinhart. 1999. "The Twin Crises: The Causes of Banking and Balance-of-Payments Problems." *American Economic Review* 89 (3): 473–500.

Krugman, Paul. 1979. "A Model of Balance of Payments Crises." *Journal of Money, Credit, and Banking* 11 (3): 311–25.

Rebelo, Sergio, and Carlos Végh. 2002. "When Is It Optimal to Abandon a Fixed Exchange Rate?" Northwestern University. http://www.kellogg.nwu.edu/faculty/rebelo/htm/rebelo-vegh1may02.pdf.

Sargent, Thomas J., and Neil Wallace. 1973. "The Stability of Models of Money and Growth with Perfect Foresight." *Econometrica* 41 (6): 1043–48.

———. 1981. "Some Unpleasant Monetarist Arithmetic." *Federal Reserve Bank of Minneapolis Quarterly Review* 5 (3): 1–17.

Wijnbergen, Sweder van. 1991. "Fiscal Deficits, Exchange Rate Crises, and Inflation." *Review of Economic Studies* 58 (1): 81–92.

8

Chapter 9

233 -70

$|LOG|$

$F3I$

$F32$

$H63 \; H62$

$O19$

$O23$

Financing the Costs of
Currency Crises

Craig Burnside, Martin Eichenbaum, and Sergio Rebelo

9

The discussion in chapter 8 considered the view that currency crises are caused by large ongoing or prospective government deficits. Models embodying this view typically adopt highly stylized representations of the government budget constraint. For example, the "first-generation" models of Krugman (1979) and Flood and Garber (1984) assume that deficits can be financed only by printing money. Consequently, these models predict that a currency crisis is followed by high rates of money growth and inflation. When coupled with the assumption of purchasing power parity (PPP), these models also predict that the rates of inflation and devaluation coincide. While "first-generation" models have proved useful in understanding currency crises, they suffer from an obvious shortcoming: Many large devaluations are followed by moderate rates of money growth and inflation. Moreover, these models provide no guidance about the efficacy of different strategies for financing deficits in the aftermath of a currency crisis.

This chapter addresses two questions. First, what are the strategies available to a government for financing the fiscal deficits associated with currency crises? Second, what are the implications of these strategies for post-devaluation inflation and depreciation rates?

To address these questions, the highly stylized representations of the government budget constraint that are typically used in the literature are replaced with a more realistic formulation. This allows consideration of the first question. To address the second question, the revised government budget constraint is embedded into a version of the model discussed in chapter 8. The analysis will show that extended versions of "first-generation" models can account for the low rates of money growth and inflation that follow in the wake of many large devaluations. But their ability to do so depends crucially on a realistic specification of the actual financing options open to a government.

As in chapter 8, it is assumed that a currency crisis is triggered by information that a government faces a large rise in its deficit. The government can finance this deficit using a variety of strategies, including those emphasized in the literature: explicit fiscal reforms involving increasing tax rates or reducing the quantity of public spending, explicit default on outstanding debt, and the printing of money. In addition, the government can use inflation-related strategies that have received substantially less attention in the literature. These include deflating the dollar value of outstanding debt denominated in local currency, and reducing the dollar value of government expenditures via an *implicit* fiscal reform. The latter means that the government can deflate the dollar value of outlays that are fixed, at least temporarily, in nominal terms or tied to the consumer price index (CPI) as opposed to the exchange rate (for example, civil servant wages or social security payments). Finally, if nontradable goods (expenditures on health and education, for example) are an important component of government spending, then a decline in the dollar price of nontradable goods *automatically* improves the government's fiscal situation. As discussed in section 1, such a decline often occurs after a currency crisis.[1]

The remainder of this chapter is organized as follows. Section 1 presents some key facts about how prices behave in post-crisis environments. These facts motivate the salient features of the framework presented here. Section 2 uses the government's intertemporal budget constraint to discuss the different financing strategies available to the government. Section 3 presents a basic model of crises. Section 4 discusses two extensions: incorporating government liabilities denominated in local currency and eliminating the purchasing power parity assumption. Section 5 presents some numerical examples to illustrate the implications of different financing strategies. Section 6 contains concluding remarks.

1 Prices and Currency Crises

In this analysis, two key distinctions will be made between (1) tradable and nontradable goods and (2) producer prices and consumer prices. The first distinction plays an important role in the government budget constraint. Both distinctions play a key role in shaping the model's predictions for post-crisis rates of inflation.

Burstein, Eichenbaum, and Rebelo (forthcoming) study the behavior of prices after large devaluations associated with significant declines in the growth rate of aggregate income. Table 9.1, taken from their study, summarizes the behavior of prices in the aftermath of currency crises in Brazil, Indonesia, Malaysia, Mexico, the Philippines, Republic of Korea, and Thailand. This table reveals three key facts that are relevant for the purposes of this analysis:

1. Rates of inflation, as measured by changes in consumer price indices, are very low relative to rates of exchange rate depreciation.
2. The rate of nontradable goods inflation is much lower than the rate of depreciation.
3. The prices of imports and exports move much more closely with the exchange rate than the CPI.

Figures 9.1 and 9.2 illustrate these facts for the Mexican and Korean cases. These figures display the behavior of the exchange rate relative to the

9

Table 9.1: Rates of Change for Prices and Exchange Rate in the First Year after the Devaluation

Country	S	P	P^N	P^I	P^E
Korea, Rep. of	41.2	6.6	5.1	16.5	22.6
Thailand	49.7	10.1	9.3	40.4	32.3
Malaysia	48.2	5.7	5.4	n.a.	n.a.
Philippines	42.6	10.1	10.1	26.1	43.1
Indonesia	171.1	44.9	n.a.	93.2	137.2
Mexico	80.0	39.5	31.6	70.6	61.7
Brazil	42.4	8.7	6.5	32.1	39.6

Source: Burstein, Eichenbaum, and Rebelo (forthcoming).

Notes: S, exchange rate versus the U.S. dollar; P, consumer price index; P^N, nontradables price index; P^I, imports price index; P^E, exports price index.

Figure 9.1: Price Indices in Mexico, 1993–2000
(1994 Q3 = 100)

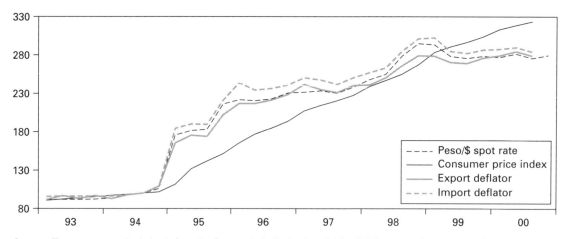

Sources: The consumer price index is from the Secretaría de Hacienda y Crédito Público, www.shcp.gob.mx. The import and export deflators are from the Mexican national accounts as published by the same agency.

Notes: All series are normalized so that their value in 1994Q3 = 100 by creating a new series $Q_t = 100 P_t / P_{1994Q3}$. The peso/$ spot rate is the IFS period-average market rate (AF...ZF).

Figure 9.2: Price Indices in Korea, 1996–2000
(1997 Q3 = 100)

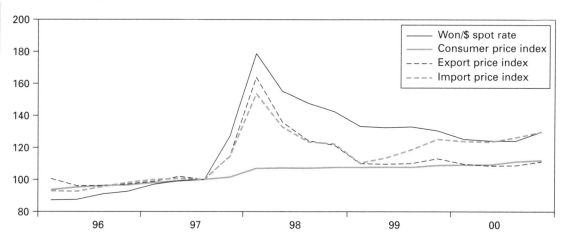

Sources: The consumer price index, export price index, and import price index are all from the Bank of Korea Web site.

Notes: All series are normalized so that their value in 1997Q3 = 100 by creating a new series $Q_t = 100 P_t / P_{1997Q3}$. The won/$ spot rate is the IFS period-average market rate (AF...ZF).

U.S. dollar, the CPI, the export deflator, and the import deflator after the Mexican and Korean currency crises.

To address these facts, two modifications are made to the basic model of chapter 8. First, a distinction is made between tradable and nontradable goods. Second, it is assumed that when tradable goods are sold at the retail level, they have an important distribution component involving nontradable goods.

To motivate the importance of distribution costs, consider the evidence in Burstein, Neves, and Rebelo (2003), who emphasize that such costs are large both in developed countries such as the United States and in emerging markets like Argentina. One way to assess the quantitative significance of distribution costs is to compute the distribution margin, defined as:

$$\text{Distribution Margin} = \frac{\text{Retail Price} - \text{Producer Price}}{\text{Retail Price}}.$$

Table 9.2, extracted from Burstein, Neves, and Rebelo (2003), displays distribution margins for different goods, computed using data from the 1992 U.S. Input-Output Table. The four expenditure categories considered are (1) personal consumption expenditures, (2) private gross fixed investment, (3) exports of goods and services, and (4) federal government consumption and gross investment. This table suggests that tradable consumption goods embody an important element of distribution services: These services represent 42 percent of the final price. In contrast, distribution services play a smaller role in investment, exports, and government spending.

Burstein, Neves, and Rebelo (2003) also use information on production and value added from Argentina's Census of Wholesale and Retail Commerce to compute the average distribution margin, which turns out to

9

Table 9.2: Distribution Margins by Expenditure Category

Statistic	Personal consumption expenditures	Private gross fixed investment	Exports of goods and services	Federal government consumption and gross investment
Weighted average	41.9	16.0	12.7	8.8
Standard deviation	13.0	10.1	7.0	10.7
Maximum	64.2	37.4	42.2	72.6
Minimum	0.0	0.0	0.0	0.0

Source: Burstein, Neves, and Rebelo (2003).

be very high—roughly 61 percent. Their view is that this margin reflects the inefficiencies that result from a system comprised of small retail stores and wholesalers. Argentina is probably not unusual relative to other emerging markets.

Motivated by the evidence discussed above, this model assumes that there are two types of consumption goods: tradables and nontradables. In addition, purchasing power parity is imposed at the level of the producer:

$$\overline{P}_t^T = S_t \overline{P}_t^{T*}.$$

Here $\overline{P}_t^T$ and $\overline{P}_t^{T*}$ denote the domestic and foreign producer price of tradable goods, respectively. Also, S_t is the exchange rate defined as units of domestic currency per unit of foreign currency. For convenience, assume throughout that $\overline{P}_t^{T*} = 1$ so that $\overline{P}_t^T = S_t$.

Proceeding as in Burstein, Neves, and Rebelo (2003), assume that selling tradable goods requires the use of distribution services.[2] In particular, selling one unit of a tradable good requires δ units of nontradable goods. As a result, purchasing power parity does not hold at the retail level. Perfect competition in the retail sector implies that the retail price of tradable goods is given by:

$$P_t^T = S_t + \delta P_t^N. \tag{1.1}$$

Here P_t^N and P_t^T denote the price of nontradable goods and the retail price of tradable goods, respectively. The CPI in this economy is given by:

$$P_t = \left(P_t^T\right)^\omega \left(P_t^N\right)^{1-\omega}, \tag{1.2}$$

where ω is the weight of tradable goods in the index.

To see how allowing for distribution services helps account for the three facts listed above, note that the dollar retail price of tradables is given by $P_t^T/S_t = 1 + \delta P_t^N/S_t$. If nontradable goods prices are sticky, then P_t^N will remain constant for some time after a crisis. Thus, when the exchange rate depreciates, P_t^N/S_t falls. So do the dollar retail price of tradables and the ratio of the CPI to the exchange rate: $P_t/S_t = (1 + \delta P_t^N/S_t)^\omega (P_t^N/S_t)^{1-\omega}$.

Notice that while the price of nontradables remains fixed at its pre-crisis level, P^N, the CPI inflation rate is given by

$$\frac{\dot{P}_t}{P_t} = \omega \frac{1}{1 + \delta P^N/S_t} \frac{\dot{S}_t}{S_t}. \tag{1.3}$$

This equation implies that the rate of CPI inflation, $\dot{P}_t/P_t$, must be lower than the rate of devaluation, $\dot{S}_t/S_t$. The wedge between these two objects is increasing in the distribution parameter, δ, and the share of nontradables in the CPI, $1 - \omega$.

Price stickiness is one explanation for why P_t^N/S_t falls after crises. A complementary reason why P_t^N/S_t might fall is a perceived decline in aggregate wealth following a currency crisis. Burstein, Eichenbaum, and Rebelo (forthcoming) argue that after such a decline, agents reduce the production and consumption of nontradable goods. Because certain factors like capital are fixed in the short run, the marginal dollar cost of producing nontradable goods is an increasing function of total output. So, like sticky prices, a negative wealth effect causes the dollar price of nontradable goods to decline after a devaluation.

2   The Government Budget Constraint

Now consider a version of the government budget constraint that takes into account the extensions to the basic model discussed in section 1. As in chapter 8, assume a perfect foresight economy populated by an infinitely lived representative agent and a government. All agents, including the government, can borrow and lend in international capital markets at a constant real interest rate r.

Suppose that before time zero, the economy under consideration is in a sustainable fixed exchange rate regime. That is, the exchange rate is fixed at the level S and the government can satisfy its intertemporal budget constraint without resorting to inflation. At time zero the economy learns that there will be an increase in government transfers starting at date T' that will be financed by inflation-related revenues. These transfers could, for example, represent payments made by the government to bail out failing banks.

The government purchases constant quantities of goods, g^T units of tradables and g^N units of nontradables, and makes its purchases at producer prices. Hence, the dollar value of government purchases is given by

$$g_t = \left(\overline{P}_t^T g^T + P_t^N g^N\right)/S_t = g^T + g^N P_t^N/S_t. \tag{2.1}$$

The government makes two types of transfers to domestic households: transfers denominated in units of local currency, $\hat{V}_t$, and transfers indexed to the exchange rate, $\tilde{v}_t$. The government also transfers v_t^* dollars to foreigners. Given these assumptions, total government transfers, measured in dollars, are

$$v_t = \hat{v}_t + \tilde{v}_t + v_t^*, \tag{2.2}$$

where $\hat{v}_t = \hat{V}_t/S_t$.

The government can raise resources by borrowing abroad, printing money, and collecting taxes. One can denote by τ^T and τ^N the tax rates on the output of the tradables and nontradables sectors, respectively. The dollar value of tax revenues at time t, τ_t, is given by

$$\tau_t = \tau^T y^T + \tau^N y^N P_t^N/S_t, \tag{2.3}$$

where y^T and y^N denote, respectively, constant endowments of tradable and nontradable goods. One can allow for different tax rates on the two sectors to account for the fact that (1) some nontradable goods (health care and education) are often provided by the government and are only partially taxed, and (2) in many countries it may be easier to evade paying taxes on nontradable goods and services.

For simplicity, assume that $\tilde{v}_t$ and v_t^* are equal to zero prior to $t = 0$. At time T' these transfers increase permanently. The present value of the new transfers is given by

$$\phi = \int_{T'}^{\infty} e^{-rt}(\tilde{v}_t + v_t^*)\,dt. \tag{2.4}$$

Before time zero the government issued nonindexed government consols (consolidated annuities) with a face value of B units of local currency and coupon rate r. Since expected inflation was zero before $t = 0$, the nominal value of these consols is equal to B. To simplify, assume that no new consols are issued after time zero.[3] The government also issues dollar-denominated bonds. Denote by b_t the stock of dollar denominated debt at time t.

The government's flow budget constraint is

$$\dot{b}_t = rb_t + g_t + v_t + rB/S_t - \tau_t - \dot{M}_t/S_t. \tag{2.5}$$

Here M_t denotes the period t stock of base money, while a dot over a variable denotes its time derivative. As discussed in chapter 8, there is a set of points in time, denoted by I, at which there are discrete jumps in the money supply and debt levels. At these points the change in government debt is given by: $\Delta b_t = -\Delta(M_t/S_t)$.

9

The flow budget constraint, (2.5), together with the condition $\lim_{t\to\infty} e^{-rt} b_t = 0$, implies the following intertemporal budget constraint for the government:

$$b_0 = \int_0^\infty e^{-rt}(\tau_t - g_t - v_t - rB/S_t)\, dt + \int_0^\infty (\dot{M}_t/S_t)e^{-rt}\, dt$$
$$+ \sum_{t\in I} \Delta(M_t/S_t)e^{-rt}. \tag{2.6}$$

Prior to time zero, the economy is in a steady state of a fixed exchange rate regime, with $\tilde{v}_t = v_t^* = 0$, $\hat{V}_t = \hat{V}$, $P_t^N = P^N$, $S_t = S$, and $M_t = M$, implying that seigniorage revenues, $\dot{M}_t/S_t$, equal zero. Therefore, in the steady state, the government's intertemporal budget constraint becomes

$$r(b_0 + B/S) = \tau - g - v, \tag{2.7}$$

where $g = g^T + g^N P^N/S$, $v = \hat{v} = \hat{V}/S$, and $\tau = \tau^T y^T + \tau^N y^N P^N/S$. According to equation (2.7), the primary fiscal surplus, $\tau - g - v$, is equal to the flow of interest payments on the government's debt.

To see the impact of the time zero information about prospective fiscal deficits on the government's intertemporal budget constraint, one can use (2.7) to rewrite (2.6) as

$$\phi + \int_0^\infty (\tau - \tau_t)e^{-rt}\, dt = \int_0^\infty (g - g_t)e^{-rt}\, dt + \int_0^\infty (\hat{v} - \hat{v}_t)e^{-rt}\, dt$$
$$+ \int_0^\infty \left(\frac{rB}{S} - \frac{rB}{S_t}\right)e^{-rt}\, dt$$
$$+ \int_0^\infty (\dot{M}_t/S_t)e^{-rt}\, dt + \sum_{t\in I} \Delta(M_t/S_t)e^{-rt}. \tag{2.8}$$

The left-hand side of equation (2.8) consists of the present value of the rise in government transfers, ϕ, and any shortfall in tax revenues that occurs after the crisis, $\int_0^\infty (\tau - \tau_t)e^{-rt}dt$. To understand this shortfall, recall that tax revenues from nontradable goods are given by $\tau^N y^N P_t^N/S_t$. A decline in P_t^N/S_t implies that the dollar value of tax revenues from the nontradable sector falls. So

$$\int_0^\infty (\tau - \tau_t)e^{-rt}\, dt = \int_0^\infty \tau^N y^N \left(P^N/S - P_t^N/S_t\right)e^{-rt}\, dt. \tag{2.9}$$

241

This effect is potentially quite important in practice since, as shown earlier, there is often a large decline in P_t^N/S_t in the aftermath of currency crises. There is an additional tax shortfall that has not been modeled: In many currency crises—particularly those associated with banking crises—output of both tradable and nontradable goods declines. Under these circumstances the dollar value of tax revenues would fall even holding relative prices fixed. One can abstract from this output effect for expositional purposes, but in practice it can also be very important.

Explicit fiscal reforms are ones that change the quantities of goods purchased by the government, g^T and g^N, tax rates, τ^T and τ^N, or the size of transfer payments, $\hat{V}$. Equation (2.8) implies that, absent explicit fiscal reforms, the *only* way that the government can satisfy its intertemporal budget constraint is to use monetary policy to generate a present value of seigniorage revenues and implicit fiscal reform equal to $\phi + \int_0^\infty e^{-rt}(\tau - \tau_t)\,dt$. To see this, suppose for a moment that the fixed exchange rate could be sustained once new information about higher deficits arrived. Then the money supply would never change and the government could not collect any seigniorage revenues, represented by the last two terms on the right-hand side of (2.8). This, in conjunction with the fact that the price level and exchange rate would remain fixed at their pre-crisis levels, would imply that the first three terms on the right-hand side of (2.8) would also equal zero.[4] But if all terms on the right-hand side of (2.8) were zero, then the government's budget constraint would not hold and this would contradict the assumption that the fixed exchange rate regime was sustainable. One can conclude that the government *must* at some point abandon the fixed exchange rate.

According to (2.8), the present value of the increase in transfers, ϕ, plus the change in tax revenue $\int_0^\infty (\tau - \tau_t)e^{-rt}\,dt$, must be financed from a combination of the following sources:

1. Seigniorage revenues: $\int_0^\infty (\dot{M}_t/S_t)e^{-rt}\,dt + \sum_{t \in I}\Delta(M_t/S_t)e^{-rt}$;
2. A reduction in the real value of local currency debt: $\int_0^\infty (rB/S - rB/S_t)e^{-rt}\,dt$;
3. A decrease in the real value of the local currency transfers: $\int_0^\infty (\hat{V}/S - \hat{V}_t/S_t)e^{-rt}\,dt$; and
4. A reduction in the dollar cost of government purchases of nontradable goods: $\int_0^\infty g^N(P^N/S - P_t^N/S_t)e^{-rt}\,dt$.

The first source, seigniorage revenues, is the one traditionally empha-sized in the literature. Seigniorage revenues have played an important role in countries such as Indonesia, Israel, Mexico, and Turkey. But there are other countries in which money growth was quite moderate after large cur-rency crises (Brazil, Finland, Korea, Sweden, and Thailand, for example). The second source of financing, a reduction in the real value of nonindexed debt, arises to the extent that a government was able to issue debt denomi-nated in domestic currency at interest rates that were lower than r plus the ex post devaluation rate. Such debt is often held by domestic agents, while dollar-denominated debt is often held by foreigners.

The third source of financing is a reduction in the real value of govern-ment transfers. In practice, many government transfers such as social secu-rity, transfers to regional governments, welfare, and unemployment benefits are not indexed to the dollar. The nominal value of these transfers is often large, so that a devaluation can generate a substantial decline in their dol-lar value. Note that this effect can still be important even when transfers are not literally fixed in nominal terms. If indexed to the CPI (since domestic inflation is typically much lower than the rate of depreciation), transfers will still fall substantially in dollar terms.

The fourth source of financing is a reduction in the dollar value of gov-ernment spending on goods and services. This effect arises because most government spending is directed toward nontraded goods such as health, education, and the labor services of civil servants. To the extent that a devaluation results in a decline in P_t^N/S_t, it reduces the dollar value of gov-ernment purchases. Later, the third and fourth sources of financing will be referred to as *implicit fiscal reforms*.

The inflationary consequences of a currency crisis depend on the financ-ing mix chosen by the government. For example, the government could pay for most of the rise in its deficits by reducing the real value of outstanding nominal debt or government outlays with a devaluation at time zero. Under these circumstances, the currency crisis would be followed by low rates of money growth and inflation. This scenario is closely related to the work of Cochrane (2001), Sims (1994), and Woodford (1995) on the fiscal theory of the price level.[5] In contrast, if the government does not have any nonin-dexed liabilities, purchases of nontradable goods or nonindexed transfers, then it must rely entirely on seigniorage revenues. This would have poten-tially very different implications for money growth and inflation. To more

9

carefully analyze the implications of different financing strategies, the extended government budget constraint is now embedded into a suitably modified version of the model discussed in chapter 8.

Equivalent to the assumptions made in chapter 8, the demand for money takes the form

$$M_t = \theta P_t y e^{-\eta R_t}. \tag{2.10}$$

Here θ is a positive constant, $y = y^T + y^N P^N/S$ is a constant dollar measure of real activity, and $R_t = r + \dot{S}_t/S_t$ is the nominal interest rate, consistent with uncovered interest parity. The fixed exchange rate regime is abandoned when the amount of domestic money sold by private agents in exchange for foreign reserves exceeds χ percent of the initial money supply. As for post-crisis monetary policy, again assume that in period $T \leq T'$ the government engineers a one-time increase in the money supply of γ percent relative to its pre-crisis level, M. Thereafter the money supply grows at μ percent per year. The behavior of the money supply can be summarized as follows:

$$M_t = \begin{cases} e^{-\chi}M, & \text{for } t^* \leq t < T \\ e^{\gamma+\mu(t-T)}M, & \text{for } t \geq T. \end{cases} \tag{2.11}$$

Given T, the pair (γ, μ) must be such that the government's budget constraint is satisfied.

3   A Benchmark Model

In this benchmark model, a number of the features described above are removed. In particular, assume that there are no nontradable goods, so set $\omega = 1$, $\delta = 0$, $g^N = 0$, and $y^N = 0$. Hence, $P_t = S_t$ and $y = y^T$. Set nominal debt, B, and the level of nominal transfers, $\hat{V}_t$, equal to 0. As a result, the government's lifetime budget constraint reduces to

$$\phi = \int_0^\infty (\dot{M}_t/S_t)e^{-rt}dt + \sum_{t \in I} \Delta(M_t/S_t)e^{-rt}.$$

Since $P_t = S_t$, the money demand function reduces to $M_t = \theta P_t y^T e^{-\eta(r+\pi_t)}$, where $\pi_t = \dot{P}_t/P_t$.

A Crisis in the Benchmark Model

Assume that prior to time zero, agents anticipate zero inflation and the economy is in a steady state with $\tilde{v}_t = v_t^* = 0$ and constant debt $b_0 = (\tau^T y^T - g^T)/r$. Consequently, all prices and quantities are constant. Since the economy is in a fixed exchange rate regime, inflation is zero and the money supply is given by $M = e^{-\pi r} \theta y^T S$. Proceeding as in chapter 8, it can be shown that the time of the speculative attack is given by:

$$ t^* = T - \eta \ln\left(\frac{\chi + \gamma + \mu\eta}{\chi} \right). \qquad (3.1) $$

Also, the lifetime budget constraint can be rewritten as

$$ \phi = e^{-rt^*} \frac{Me^{-\chi} - M}{S} + e^{-rT} \frac{Me^{\gamma} - Me^{-\chi}}{S_T} + e^{-rT} \frac{\mu e^{-\eta\mu}}{r} \frac{M}{S}, \qquad (3.2) $$

where $S_T = e^{\gamma + \eta\mu} S$. Given values of T, χ, and γ, (3.1) and (3.2) can be solved simultaneously for t^* and μ.

A Numerical Example

To discuss the properties of the model, it is useful to present a series of numerical examples. The following parameter values, discussed in greater detail in Burnside, Eichenbaum, and Rebelo (2003b), are loosely based on Korean data. First, normalize tradables output, y^T, and the initial exchange rate, S, to 1. Set the semi-elasticity of money demand with respect to the interest rate, η, equal to 0.5. This value of η is consistent with interest elasticities for emerging markets estimated by Easterly, Mauro, and Schmidt-Hebbel (1995). Set the real interest rate, r, to 4 percent. Then set the constant $\theta = 0.06$ so that the monetary base in the initial steady state, M, is about 6 percent of GDP, as in Korea.

The parameter ϕ was set to 0.24, a conservative estimate of the fiscal cost of Korea's banking crisis relative to its GDP.[6] It is difficult to calibrate χ, the decline of the monetary base during the crisis; so instead, assume that $t^* = 0.5$ and set χ consistent with this. Take t^* to be 0.5, as Korea's crisis in late 1997 took place about six months after the beginning of the Thai crisis, in mid-1997, which might be reasonably thought of as time zero. Set $\gamma = 0.12$ to match the ratio of the average values of the monetary base in 1998 and 1999. Then set $T = 1$. The qualitative characteristics of the

Table 9.3: Results for Numerical Examples

| | Inflation | | Devaluation | | Financing (% of total) | | |
Model variant	Year 1	Long run	Year 1	Seigniorage	Nominal debt deflation	Implicit fiscal reform
(a) Benchmark	35.3	20.0	35.3	100	0	0
(b) Nominal debt	29.7	15.0	29.7	78.7	21.3	0
(c) Implicit reform	18.4	5.0	18.4	30.6	16.0	53.5
(d) Sticky P^N	17.2	4.0	34.8	23.5	16.1	60.4
(e) Distribution costs	14.2	1.3	66.9	5.8	14.3	79.9

Source: Authors' calculations.

Notes: Row (a) represents results for the benchmark model in which all debt is dollar denominated, all transfers are indexed to the dollar, and there are no nontraded goods. Case (b) modifies case (a) by introducing nominal debt, as described in the text. Case (c) modifies case (b) by introducing transfers that are not indexed to the dollar, as described in the text. Case (d) modifies case (c) by introducing nontraded goods with sticky prices, as described in the text. Finally, case (e) modifies case (d) by introducing the concept of distribution costs in the retailing of traded goods.

results presented here are robust to reasonable perturbations of these benchmark parameters.

The first row of table 9.3 summarizes the implications of the benchmark model for inflation and the rate of devaluation. The properties of this model were discussed in chapter 8. Here there are two obvious shortcomings of the model. First, it predicts counterfactually large rates of inflation after a crisis. In this example, inflation is 35.3 percent in the year of the crisis and 20 percent in the steady state. This is inconsistent with the post-crisis inflation experience of countries like Mexico and Korea. Table 9.1 shows that post-crisis inflation was 6.6 percent in Korea and 39.5 percent in Mexico. Second, the model implies that the rate of inflation coincides with the rate of exchange rate depreciation. This, too, is inconsistent with evidence that rates of devaluation are typically much larger than rates of inflation after crises.

4   Model Extensions

This section incorporates four extensions of the framework taken from Burnside, Eichenbaum, and Rebelo (2003b). These extensions are designed to address the shortcomings of the benchmark model. First, government debt denominated in local currency is introduced. Then, government transfers that are not fully indexed to the exchange rate are introduced. These two extensions of the model partially address the first shortcoming of the benchmark model: that it predicted counterfactually high inflation in the post-crisis period. These modifications help because the government is able to finance part of its increased liabilities without printing money. However, these modifications do not address the second shortcoming: that inflation and depreciation are equal. To address this issue, eliminate the assumption of purchasing power parity by introducing nontradable goods with sticky prices. When also allowing for distribution costs, one ends up with a model roughly consistent with the empirical regularities mentioned earlier. The model can generate rates of devaluation that are large and CPI inflation rates that are small. Furthermore, the government can finance its new liabilities without printing much money.

Government Debt in Units of Local Currency

To assess the impact of local currency debt on the model's implications for inflation and devaluation rates, consider the following numerical example in which nonindexed debt is equal to 5 percent of GDP ($B = 0.05Py$). No other changes are made to the benchmark model. As with other parameter values, the value of B is loosely motivated by the Korean experience. Recall that nominal debt in the model is a perpetuity, so its duration is different from that of Korea's debt. For this reason, it is not appropriate to use the measured stock of nonindexed debt on the eve of the crisis to calibrate B. Choose B so that the amount of revenue from debt deflation in the final example, shown later, is roughly consistent with the evidence from Korea presented in Burnside, Eichenbaum, and Rebelo (2003a).

Table 9.3 shows that introducing nonindexed debt lowers the growth rate of money, μ, that is necessary to pay for the government's new liabilities, ϕ. This allows steady-state inflation to decline from 20 percent in the benchmark model to 15 percent. Obviously, the larger the initial stock of local currency debt the less need there is to finance the crisis with explicit seigniorage. For example, if B equaled $0.5Py$, the rate of inflation would be 15.1 percent in the first year after the currency crisis and 2.1 percent thereafter. The government would raise only 14.7 percent of the fiscal cost of the crisis from seigniorage revenues. The balance would come from debt deflation. So, in principle, allowing for nonindexed debt can reconcile the basic model with the observation that inflation is often quite moderate after a

9

currency crisis. But most emerging market country governments typically borrow mainly in U.S. dollars and other foreign currencies. To the extent that this is true, the amount of resources that can be gained from debt deflation will be small. Indeed, Burnside, Eichenbaum, and Rebelo (2003b) argue that, for the countries involved in the Asian crisis of 1997 as well as Mexico, there was not enough nonindexed debt for this to be a complete resolution of the model's counterfactual inflation predictions.

Implicit Fiscal Reform

Now allow for an implicit fiscal reform as a source of revenue for the government. Specific information on the size of nonindexed transfers in Korea is not available. So instead, assume that $\hat{V} = 0.025Py$; that is, nonindexed government transfer spending is about 2.5 percent of GDP. One can take this as a benchmark assumption. In addition, assume that $\hat{V}$ is fixed in nominal terms for roughly 2.5 years after the crisis and then starts to grow at the rate of inflation. So, in this example, the implicit fiscal reform amounts to a permanent reduction in the real value of government transfer spending relative to GDP.

Table 9.3 makes clear that allowing for an implicit fiscal reform has a significant impact on the model's predictions. Notice that, compared to the previous scenario, where the only nonindexed spending was interest payments on the government's local currency consols, year one inflation falls from 29.7 percent to 18.4 percent. Steady-state inflation declines from 15 percent to 5 percent. The percentage of the total fiscal cost paid for with seigniorage revenue falls from 78.7 percent to 30.6 percent, while the importance of debt deflation falls from 21.3 percent to 16.0 percent of total financing. Even though nonindexed government spending represents only 2.5 percent of GDP, the implicit fiscal reform pays for over half the cost of the crisis.

To understand this result, note that the currency crisis generates a permanent rise in the rate of inflation. In the example this inflation generates a permanent decline in the value of government expenditures. The present value of this decline is substantial. To take an example, suppose that nonindexed government spending fell permanently by 1 percentage point of GDP. Given a 4 percent dollar interest rate, the present value of this implicit fiscal reform would equal 25 percent of GDP. So here, an implicit fiscal reform would more than cover the entire cost associated with the currency crisis.

Allowing for debt deflation and implicit fiscal reforms can render the model consistent with the observation that inflation rates are often moderate after a currency crisis. However, these extensions cannot explain the other shortcoming of the benchmark model: Actual inflation is often much lower than the rate of depreciation associated with a currency crisis. One can now turn to this challenge.

Deviations from Purchasing Power Parity: Nontradable Goods with Sticky Prices

Up to this point in this analysis, it has been assumed that purchasing power parity holds. So, by construction, the rate of inflation coincides with the rate of devaluation. Now break the link between domestic inflation and exchange rate depreciation by introducing departures from purchasing power parity into the benchmark model. One can begin by introducing nontradable goods with sticky prices.

In the presence of nontradable goods, the CPI, P_t is given by:

$$P_t = \left(P_t^T\right)^\omega \left(P_t^N\right)^{1-\omega}. \tag{4.1}$$

Recall that P_t^N denotes the price of nontradable goods and P_t^T the price of tradable goods. By assumption, purchasing power parity holds for tradable goods, so $P_t^T = S_t$ for all t. Absent an explicit model of the nontradable goods sector, assume that P_t^N remains fixed for the first five months after the currency crisis. Thereafter, P_t^N moves one-to-one with the exchange rate. Consequently, a currency crisis is associated with a permanent decline in the relative price of nontradable goods. This assumption is motivated by the Korean experience. The price of nontradables in Korea increased by only 4.8 percent between October 1997 and April 1998, while it increased by only 5.6 percent between October 1997 and October 1998.

To solve a numerical version of the model with nontraded goods, modify the model of the previous section as follows. One can set $P^N = S = 1$, and maintain the assumption that $y = 1$. Set $\omega = 0.5$, which corresponds to the share of tradables in Korea's CPI.[7] Finally, as the annex to this chapter shows, to assess the magnitude of the implicit changes in government purchases, net of taxes, which are given by $\int_0^\infty (g^N - \tau^N y^N)$ $(P^N/S - P_t^N/S_t)e^{-rt}dt$, one needs to calibrate $(g^N - \tau^N y^N)P^N$. This is the nominal value of the government's purchases of nontradable goods net of its revenue derived from taxes on the nontraded goods sector. Burnside,

Eichenbaum, and Rebelo (2003a) estimate that $(g^N - \tau^N y^N)P^N \approx -0.006Py$ or –0.6 percent of GDP, so this value is used in the numerical example. One can include the magnitude of any implicit changes in government purchases, net of taxes, in this measure of total implicit fiscal reforms, which also, of course, includes the effect on transfers discussed earlier.

Table 9.3 indicates that allowing for these modifications of the model has two effects. First, there is a relatively small decline in the amount of inflation. Inflation is 17.2 percent in the first year after the crisis, while steady-state inflation is 4 percent. Second, and more important, the model now generates a large wedge between the initial rate of inflation and the rate of depreciation. Specifically, the currency crisis is now associated with a 34.8 percent rate of depreciation in the first year. The effect of the changes in the model on the sources of financing is relatively small: Seigniorage is less important, again, while implicit fiscal reforms become somewhat more important as a source of financing.

Deviations from Purchasing Power Parity: Distribution Costs

To induce an even larger wedge between inflation and depreciation, now allow for distribution costs in tradable goods. These are modeled as described earlier, so that the retail price of tradable goods and the CPI are given by (1.1) and (1.2). The last line of table 9.3 displays results for this version of the model under the assumption that it takes one unit of non-tradable goods to distribute one unit of tradable goods ($\delta = 1$). This value of δ corresponds to a distribution margin of 50 percent, which is consistent with the evidence presented in Burstein, Neves, and Rebelo (2003).

Notice the stark difference between this model and the benchmark model. In the benchmark model, inflation in the first year after the crisis is about 35 percent and declines to 20 percent in steady state. In addition, the rate of devaluation coincides with the rate of inflation. In contrast, the modified model implies first year inflation roughly equal to 14 percent, while the currency devalues by about 67 percent. Moreover, steady-state inflation is only 1.3 percent. Clearly, this version of the model can account for large devaluations without generating grossly counterfactual implications for inflation.

It is also striking that the government gets almost none of its additional revenue from seigniorage. Almost 80 percent of the government's financing comes from implicit fiscal reforms, while a further 14 percent of the financing

9

comes from debt deflation. The latter is roughly consistent with evidence for Korea, from Burnside, Eichenbaum, and Rebelo (2003a).

5 Tax Revenues and Currency Crises

In many cases, currency crises are followed by substantial reductions in the level of output. Table 9.4, taken from Burstein, Eichenbaum, and Rebelo (forthcoming), summarizes the decline in output in various countries after their currency crisis. For example, real GDP declined by 7 percent in Korea and 6 percent in Mexico in the first year after their crises. Argentina's recent experience was similar but more dramatic.

Not surprisingly, the dollar value of tax revenues also declines in the aftermath of a currency crisis. Other things equal, this leads to a deterioration of the government's financial situation and makes it more difficult to satisfy its intertemporal budget constraint. This model ignores this effect.

Here, two important countervailing effects to this phenomenon are incorporated, which can, in practice, be very important. The first effect is the decline in the dollar cost of government expenditures on nontradable goods. As emphasized earlier, in many countries nontradables such as health and education are publicly provided—and constitute an important component of government expenditures. To the extent that the relative price of nontradable goods falls, this makes it easier for the government to satisfy its intertemporal budget constraint. The fact that the cost of nontradable goods in local currency may be constant or even rise, is not relevant for the government's overall fiscal situation. What matters is the dollar cost, and this typically falls. The importance of this effect depends on the percentage of

Table 9.4: Rates of Growth of Real GDP in the First Year after a Crisis

Country	Year of crisis	Growth rate of real GDP
Korea, Rep. of	1997	−6.9
Thailand	1997	−10.7
Malaysia	1997	−7.7
Philippines	1997	−0.5
Indonesia	1997	−14.1
Mexico	1994	−6.4
Brazil	1998	0.7

Source: Burstein, Eichenbaum, and Rebelo (forthcoming).

the government budget devoted to nontradable goods and the decline in the dollar price of nontradable goods. The authors do not know of any studies that have documented the composition of government spending in terms of tradables and nontradables. They do, however, know that the dollar price of nontradable goods falls dramatically following many currency crises. Table 9.1 illustrates this fact for various countries. For example, in Korea the price of nontradable goods rose 5.1 percent, while the *won*-to-dollar exchange rate rose 41.2 percent, implying that the dollar price of nontradable goods fell by 25.6 percent in the first year after the crisis. The analogous number for Mexico is 26.9 percent.

The second effect results from the fact that, in some countries, tax revenues emanate primarily from taxes on tradable goods. An obvious example is Mexico, where the government derives substantial revenues from exports of oil. These revenues are not affected by the devaluation of the local currency. Other countries, like Turkey, have less access to dollar-based tax revenues. Other things equal, the post-crisis deterioration in the dollar value of tax revenue in these countries is expected to be much larger. Neither the first nor the second effect has received much attention in the literature, although research on the magnitude of these effects might go a long way toward explaining the differences in the post-crisis inflation rates across various episodes.

Does this abstraction from the output effects of currency crisis matter quantitatively? Certainly, if one were to calibrate the model to take into account lost revenue from a post-crisis recession, this would tend to increase the amount of seigniorage the government would need to raise, thus raising post-crisis inflation and depreciation. But post-crisis explicit fiscal reforms have also been neglected. Burnside, Eichenbaum, and Rebelo (2003a) estimate that post-crisis explicit fiscal reforms were bigger than the amount of revenue lost from the post-crisis recessions in Korea, Mexico, and Turkey. In principle, one should take both into account; but for the example based on Korea, if one were to do so, ϕ should also be made smaller, not larger.

6   Case Studies of Mexico, Korea, and Turkey

The previous sections have argued that because government budgets are sensitive to changes in the relative price of nontradables, stickiness in nontradable goods prices can have important implications for (1) the size of implicit fiscal reforms in the wake of a currency crisis and (2) the equilibrium outcomes for prices and the exchange rate. The question is whether implicit reforms were relevant in any recent crisis episodes.

This section examines the fiscal accounts of three countries that experienced twin banking and currency crises after 1990: Mexico (1994), Korea (1997), and Turkey (2001). It will show that each of these countries experienced dramatic changes in government revenue and expenditure as the result of changes in relative prices. Thus, the model, in which implicit fiscal reforms play an important role, is highly relevant.

To assess the importance of implicit fiscal reforms is difficult. From the perspective of the model, one would like to use data for each country to measure the cost of the banking sector bailout, ϕ, and the ways in which the bailout was financed: through additional seigniorage, debt deflation, implicit and explicit declines in government purchases of goods and services, implicit and explicit declines in government transfers, and implicit and explicit changes in government revenue. There are at least two problems with attempting to do this. First, only actual outcomes are observed. There is not a counterpart to the model scenario in which the fixed exchange rate regime is sustained through explicit fiscal reform. Second, the post-crisis economy has been observed for a finite period of time and, therefore, the picture of how the government will pay for costs of the crisis is incomplete.

In Burnside, Eichenbaum, and Rebelo (2003a), the first problem is avoided by constructing counterfactuals; that is, for each crisis episode, paths are constructed for what the relevant variables would have been equal to in the absence of the crisis. For the most part, these counterfactuals involve making simple forecasts of price, output, and budget variables based on projections of pre-crisis trends. All variables are then measured relative to these forecasts in assessing the changes in government finance after the crisis. This allows one to explicitly estimate the magnitude of additional seigniorage revenue, debt deflation, implicit reform, and explicit reform. Since describing the entire method for constructing these estimates is beyond the scope of this chapter, the simpler approach of presenting raw data from government accounts is used.

Mexico 1994

Table 9.5 shows how the behavior of macro variables and the government's budget changed after the crisis occurred in December 1994. After rising at an average rate of 6.6 per year in the period 1992–4, the ratio of the GDP

Table 9.5: Pre- and Post-crisis Data for Mexico
(percent)

Variable	Annual average growth rate	Cumulative growth between 1994 and			Deviation from projected path		
	1992–4	1995	1996	1997	1995	1996	1997
P_t/S_t	6.6	−27.5	−20.0	−9.6	−32.0	−29.6	−25.4
Real GDP	3.3	−6.2	−1.3	5.4	−9.2	−7.6	−4.5
Government purchases	14.8	−40.4	−34.6	−20.5	−45.9	−46.2	−40.6
Government transfers	43.3	−40.4	−28.6	0.1	−48.1	−43.6	−28.3
Government revenue	9.1	−32.0	−20.3	−3.6	−38.3	−34.4	−28.0

Sources: National income accounts data are from INEGI (Instituto Nacional de Estadística, Geografía e Informática), http://www.inegi.gob.mx. Data on the fiscal accounts of the government are from Banco de México, http://www.banxico.org.mx/. Statistics are based on authors' calculations.

Notes: P_t/S_t is the GDP deflator divided by the spot peso/dollar exchange rate. Real GDP is measured in constant 1993 pesos. Government purchases, transfers, and revenue are measured in U.S. dollars.

deflator to the spot exchange rate, P_t/S_t, fell 27.5 percent in 1995, and remained well below its 1994 value in 1997. If one were to assume that absent the crisis the value of P_t/S_t would have continued to rise, then the post-crisis data on P_t/S_t would be even more remarkable. Notice that by 1997, P_t/S_t remained 25.4 percent below its projected path.[8] Notice, also, that although the real *peso* value of output fell 6.2 percent in 1995, by 1997 real activity had actually risen above its 1994 level and was within a few percentage points of its projected path in a no-crisis scenario. This suggests that, consistent with the model in section 4, the changes in P_t/S_t may have had a much longer lasting impact on the budget than the changes in output.

The other data in table 9.5 are highly suggestive that the model is relevant for Mexico. Government purchases of goods and services, transfer payments, and tax revenue all declined sharply in dollar terms in 1995, and remained well below their 1994 values in 1996. By 1997, government purchases were still well below their pre-crisis value, though taxes and transfers had almost recovered to their pre-crisis levels. However, if one compares pre-crisis trends to the post-crisis data, the picture is quite different. In this case, all three components of the government's budget were well below their expected paths in 1997. Because P_t/S_t remained well below its projected path in 1997, Burnside, Eichenbaum, and Rebelo (2003a) attribute a large fraction of the changes in g_t, τ_t, and v_t in Mexico between 1994 and 1997, to implicit fiscal reforms. Of course, this assessment depends on what one assumes the path of P_t/S_t would have been absent a crisis. Nonetheless, the data seem to be consistent with the model presented earlier.

Seigniorage revenue and debt deflation have not been discussed, but both of these must have been small for Mexico. For example, seigniorage averaged about 1 percent of GDP in the period 1995–7. Regardless of the pre-crisis pattern of seigniorage, this suggests that the government did not finance a significant part of the banking sector bailout by printing money.

Debt deflation was also relatively modest for Mexico. As Burnside, Eichenbaum, and Rebelo (2003a) suggest, Mexico had relatively modest amounts—perhaps 5 percent of GDP—of outstanding nonindexed debt at the time of the crisis. Given the size of the depreciation that Mexico experienced, it is likely that revenue from debt deflation amounted to less than 2 percent of GDP.

Korea 1997

Table 9.6 shows how the behavior of macro variables and the government's budget changed after the crisis that occurred in late 1997. After rising at an average rate of 6.1 per year in the period 1994–6, the ratio of the GDP deflator to spot exchange rate P_t/S_t, fell 28.7 percent in 1998, and remained well below its 1997 value in 2000. If one were to assume that absent the crisis the

Table 9.6: Pre- and Post-crisis Data for Korea
(percent)

Variable	Annual average growth rate 1994–6	Cumulative growth between 1997 and			Deviation from projected path		
		1998	1999	2000	1998	1999	2000
P_t/S_t	6.1	−28.7	−17.6	−14.4	−43.4	−38.4	−39.7
Real GDP	8.0	−6.7	3.5	13.1	−13.0	−10.0	−8.2
Government purchases	14.4	−28.0	−13.2	−2.7	−45.0	−41.7	−42.6
Government transfers	14.3	−19.0	12.8	23.8	−34.6	−19.9	−22.8
Government revenue	18.0	−31.0	−10.8	12.2	−39.7	−31.5	−24.3

Sources: National income accounts data and the fiscal accounts of the government are from the Bank of Korea, http://www.bok.or.kr. Statistics are based on authors' calculations.

Notes: P_t/S_t is the GDP deflator divided by the spot won/dollar exchange rate. Real GDP is measured in constant 1995 won (official currency of Korea). Government purchases, transfers, and revenue are measured in dollars.

value of P_t/S_t would have continued to rise, then, as in the Mexican case, the post-crisis data on P_t/S_t would be more striking. Notice that by 2000, P_t/S_t remained almost 40 percent below its projected path. Notice, also, that although the real *won* value of output fell 6.7 percent in 1998, by 2000 real activity was well above its 1997 level and was within 8 percentage points of its projected path in a no-crisis scenario. Again, this suggests that the changes in P_t/S_t probably had a much longer lasting impact on the budget than the changes in output.

The other data in table 9.6 are highly suggestive that the model is relevant for Korea. Government purchases of goods and services, transfer payments, and tax revenue all declined sharply in dollar terms during 1998. In 1999 and 2000, government purchases remained below their pre-crisis value, though taxes and transfers surpassed their pre-crisis levels in 2000 and 1999, respectively. However, if one compares pre-crisis trends to the post-crisis data, the picture is quite different. In this case, all three components of the government's budget remained well below their expected paths in 2000. It makes sense to consider outcomes relative to pre-crisis trends, because output and the real exchange rate rose throughout 1996.

Because P_t/S_t remained well below its projected path in 2000, Burnside, Eichenbaum, and Rebelo (2003a) attribute a large fraction of the changes in g_t, τ_t, and v_t in Korea between 1998 and 2000 to implicit fiscal reforms. As for Mexico, this assessment depends on what one assumes the path of P_t/S_t would have been absent a crisis. Nonetheless, the data seem to be consistent with the model presented earlier.

As for Mexico, seigniorage revenue must have been relatively unimportant for Korea. For example, seigniorage averaged about 0.4 percent of GDP in the period 1998–2000. Regardless of the pre-crisis pattern of seigniorage, this suggests that the government did not finance a significant part of the banking sector bailout by printing additional money.

Debt deflation was probably more significant for Korea than for Mexico. Korea had about 16 percent of GDP in outstanding nonindexed debt at the time of the crisis. The *won* depreciated sharply after the crisis but rebounded significantly in value prior to the maturity of much of this debt. Given the nominal depreciation that Korea experienced, Burnside, Eichenbaum, and Rebelo (2003a) estimate that revenue from debt deflation was likely about 3.5 percent of GDP. This remains small, however, compared to the cost of bailing out the banks in Korea.

Table 9.7: Pre- and Post-crisis Data for Turkey
(percent)

Variable	Annual average growth rate 1998–2000	Cumulative growth between 2000 and		Deviation from projected path	
		2001	2002	2001	2002
P_t/S_t	−0.2	−21.0	−10.9	−21.0	−10.9
Real GDP	1.8	−7.5	−0.9	−10.5	−7.2
Government purchases	5.5	−27.8	−5.3	−30.2	−11.5
Government transfers	0.3	−24.6	2.7	−27.2	−4.0
Government revenue	12.6	−23.1	−7.7	−25.6	−13.6

Sources: National income accounts data and the fiscal accounts of the government are from the Bank of Turkey's Electronic Data Delivery System (EDDS) Web site, http://tcmbf40.tcmb.gov.tr/cbt.html. Statistics are based on the authors' calculations.

Notes: P_t/S_t is the GDP deflator divided by the spot TL/dollar exchange rate. Real GDP is measured in constant 1987 TL. Government purchases, transfers, and revenue are measured in dollars. TL, Turkish lira.

Turkey 2001

Table 9.7 shows how the behavior of macro variables and the government's budget changed after the crisis occurred in Turkey during February 2001. After staying roughly constant in the period 1998–2000, the ratio of the GDP deflator to spot exchange rate, P_t/S_t, fell 21 percent in 2001, and remained almost 11 percent below its 2000 value in 2002. The real Turkish lira (TL) value of output fell 7.5 percent in 2001, but by 2002 real activity was near its 2000 level. However, it remained a little more than 7 percentage points below its projected path in a no-crisis scenario. Here it is less clear that the changes in P_t/S_t will have a longer-lasting impact on the budget than the changes in output.

The other data in table 9.7 are highly suggestive that the model is relevant for Turkey. Government purchases of goods and services, transfer payments, and tax revenue all declined sharply in dollar terms during 2001. In 2002, government purchases and tax revenues remained below their pre-crisis value, although spending on transfers slightly surpassed its pre-crisis level. Nonetheless, if one compares pre-crisis trends to the post-crisis data, all three components of the government accounts remained below their expected paths in 2002.

Because P_t/S_t was well below its projected path in 2001 and 2002, Burnside, Eichenbaum, and Rebelo (2003a) attribute a large fraction of the

9

changes in g_t, τ_t, and v_t in Turkey in 2001–2 to implicit fiscal reforms. Implicit in this assessment is the assumption that P_t/S_t was expected to remain stable before the crisis occurred.

Seigniorage revenue is more important in Turkey than in Korea and Mexico. For example, in the period 2001–2, seigniorage averaged about 3 percent of GDP per year. However, what is relevant for the model is how much seigniorage increased in Turkey during the post-crisis period, relative to what was expected. Since Turkey has a history of raising significant amounts of revenue through printing money, it is not clear that unanticipated increases in seigniorage revenue have played a significant role in financing the costs of bailing out the banks in Turkey.

Debt deflation was almost certainly more significant in Turkey than in Korea and Mexico. Turkey had close to 25 percent of GDP in outstanding nonindexed debt at the time of the crisis. Given the sharp and continued depreciation of the TL in the wake of the crisis, Burnside, Eichenbaum, and Rebelo (2003a) estimate that revenue from debt deflation was likely about 6.2 percent of GDP. This is between one-third and one-fourth of typical estimates of the cost of bailing out the banking system in Turkey as a result of the 2001 crisis.

7   Governmental Benefits of Crises

These results may seem puzzling, because crises appear to benefit the government's finances. First, this is not really the case. The banking crisis imposes a cost, ϕ, on the government—so the crisis is costly. However, it is true that in the calibrated model presented in section 4, there is a sense in which the government benefits from a currency devaluation. Apart from dollar transfers to domestic and foreign agents (which increase), the net impact of the crisis on the rest of the government budget constraint (which occurs through implicit fiscal reforms and debt deflation) is positive. The government needs to print only a small amount of money to close its budget constraint.

This may seem puzzling given the analysis of debt dynamics presented in chapter 3. There it appeared that a devaluation, or more precisely a real devaluation, hurt the government because it made foreign currency debt larger in domestic currency terms.

To understand that there is no lack of consistency between the results in this chapter and the results in chapter 3, it is useful to rewrite the government's flow budget constraint, (2.5), while assuming that the stock of nominal debt is zero:

$$\dot{b}_t = rb_t - x_t - \dot{M}_t/S_t, \tag{7.1}$$

where b_t is the government's debt, denominated in dollars; r is the dollar interest rate; $x_t = \tau_t - g_t - v_t$ is the primary balance, measured in dollars; M_t is the monetary base, measured in units of local currency; and S_t is the local currency-dollar exchange rate.

Notice that if the *constant* local currency unit (LCU) value of government debt is defined as $\bar{b}_t = S_t b_t/P_t$ it is clear, by definition, that

$$\partial \bar{b}_t/\partial t = (d_t + \dot{b}_t/b_t - \pi_t)\bar{b}_t, \tag{7.2}$$

where $d_t \equiv \dot{S}_t/S_t$ and $\pi_t \equiv \dot{P}_t/P_t$. Solving (7.2) for $\dot{b}_t$, notice that

$$\dot{b}_t = \frac{\partial \bar{b}_t}{\partial t}\frac{b_t}{\bar{b}_t} + (\pi_t - d_t)b_t = \frac{\partial \bar{b}_t}{\partial t}\frac{P_t}{S_t} + (\pi_t - d_t)b_t. \tag{7.3}$$

Combining (7.3) with (7.1),

$$\frac{\partial \bar{b}_t}{\partial t}\frac{P_t}{S_t} + (\pi_t - d_t)b_t = rb_t - x_t - \frac{\dot{M}_t}{S_t}.$$

Multiplying through by S_t/P_t,

$$\frac{\partial \bar{b}_t}{\partial t} = r\bar{b}_t - \bar{x}_t - \frac{\dot{M}_t}{P_t} + (d_t - \pi_t)\bar{b}_t. \tag{7.4}$$

Notice that the first term on the right-hand side of (7.4), $r\bar{b}_t$, is interest payments expressed in constant LCUs (the equivalent of $\bar{\iota}_t$ in chapter 3). The second term, $\bar{x}_t = x_t S_t/P_t$, is the primary balance expressed in constant LCUs. The third term, $\dot{M}_t/P_t$, is seigniorage in constant LCUs. The fourth term is the revaluation effect discussed in chapter 3.

When purchasing power parity holds, there are no revaluation effects because $\pi_t = d_t$. In the models with sticky prices, there are revaluation effects. To see this, but to keep things simple, consider the model with sticky prices, but without distribution costs, described in section 4. Notice that during the interval of time in which nontraded goods prices are sticky, the price level is given by $P_t = S_t^\omega (P^N)^{1-\omega}$, so that the inflation rate is $\pi_t = \omega d_t$ and the revaluation effect is $(1 - \omega)d_t\bar{b}_t$. So the revaluation effect is implicit in this chapter's accounting—since (7.4) is derived from (7.1)—even though the accounting is done in dollars.

It also turns out that local currency accounting has no impact on the interpretation of where the government's additional financing comes from. To see this, consider the lifetime budget constraints derived from (7.1) and (7.4):

$$b_0 = \int_0^\infty x_t e^{-rt}\, dt + \int_0^\infty \frac{\dot{M}_t}{S_t} e^{-rt}\, dt, \qquad (7.5)$$

$$\bar{b}_0 = \int_0^\infty \bar{x}_t e^{-D_t}\, dt + \int_0^\infty \frac{\dot{M}_t}{P_t} e^{-D_t}\, dt, \qquad (7.6)$$

where the discount factor is defined as

$$D_t \equiv \int_0^t (r + d_s - \pi_s)\, ds. \qquad (7.7)$$

For convenience, the "jump" seigniorage terms in (2.6) have been ignored, since they do not affect the point being made here.

Suppose that one begins in a sustainable fixed exchange rate regime where $S_t = S$, $M_t = M$, $\tau_t = \tau$, $g_t = g$, $v_t = v$, and, hence, $x_t = x$ for all t. In this case $d_t = \pi_t = 0$ for all t, $D_t = rt$, (7.5) implies that $b_0 = x/r$, and (7.6) implies that $\bar{b}_0 = \bar{x}/r = (xS/P)/r$. Since $\bar{b}_0 = b_0 S/P$, the two results are obviously equivalent.

Now suppose that a crisis is considered as an event at time zero, which causes the government to acquire new debt valued at ϕ dollars. Now the government's lifetime budget constraint in dollars becomes

$$b_0 + \phi = \int_0^\infty x_t e^{-rt}\, dt + \int_0^\infty \frac{\dot{M}_t}{S_t} e^{-rt}\, dt,$$

which, given the result that $b_0 = x/r$, implies that

$$\phi = \int_0^\infty (x_t - x)e^{-rt}\, dt + \int_0^\infty \frac{\dot{M}_t}{S_t} e^{-rt}\, dt. \qquad (7.8)$$

But the government's lifetime budget constraint in constant local currency units becomes

$$\bar{b}_0 + \phi S/P = \int_0^\infty \bar{x}_t e^{-D_t}\, dt + \int_0^\infty \frac{\dot{M}_t}{P_t} e^{-D_t}\, dt,$$

which implies that

$$\phi S/P = \int_0^\infty \bar{x}_t e^{-D_t}\, dt - \frac{\bar{x}}{r} + \int_0^\infty \frac{\dot{M}_t}{P_t} e^{-D_t}\, dt. \qquad (7.9)$$

At first it appears that (7.8) and (7.9) are very different. But notice that (7.7) implies that $e^{-D_t} = e^{-rt}(S/S_t)(P_t/P)$. This allows one to write $\int_0^\infty \bar{x}_t e^{-D_t}\,dt$ as $\int_0^\infty (x_t S_t/P_t)e^{-rt}(S/S_t)(P_t/P)\,dt = (S/P)\int_0^\infty x_t e^{-rt}\,dt$ and $\int_0^\infty (\dot{M}_t/P_t)e^{-D_t}\,dt$ as $(S/P)\int_0^\infty (\dot{M}_t/S_t)e^{-rt}\,dt$. This means that (7.9) can be rewritten as

$$\phi S/P = S/P \int_0^\infty (x_t - x)e^{-rt}\,dt + S/P \int_0^\infty \frac{\dot{M}_t}{S_t}e^{-rt}\,dt. \qquad (7.10)$$

This shows that the changes in financing in constant LCUs are the same as the ones in dollars, scaled up by a factor of S/P.

If x_t is broken into its components, the story does not change. Take, for example, government purchases, defined as $G_t = \bar{P}_t^T g^T + P_t^N g^N$ in local currency units. In dollars one has

$$g_t = \left(\bar{P}_t^T g^T + g^N P_t^N\right)/S_t = g^T + g^N P_t^N/S_t,$$

while in constant local currency units one has

$$\bar{g}_t = \left(\bar{P}_t^T g^T + g^N P_t^N\right)/P_t = g^T S_t/P_t + g^N P_t^N/P_t.$$

Notice that this means that the change in the present value of government purchases (measured in constant LCUs) induced by the crisis is given by

$$\int_0^\infty \bar{g}_t e^{-D_t}\,dt - \frac{gS/P}{r} = \int_0^\infty \left(g^T \frac{S_t}{P_t} + g^N \frac{P_t^N}{P_t}\right)e^{-rt}\left(\frac{S}{S_t}\frac{P_t}{P}\right)dt - \frac{gS/P}{r}$$

$$= \int_0^\infty \left[g^T\left(\frac{S}{P}\right) + g^N \frac{P_t^N}{S_t}\left(\frac{S}{P}\right)\right]e^{-rt}\,dt - \frac{(g^T S + g^N P^N)/P}{r}.$$

Notice that the terms involving g^T cancel out, and that the change in government purchases can be rewritten as

$$\int_0^\infty \bar{g}_t e^{-D_t}\,dt - \frac{gS/P}{r} = \frac{S}{P}\left(\int_0^\infty g^N \frac{P_t^N}{S_t}e^{-rt}\,dt - \frac{g^N P^N/S}{r}\right).$$

This, of course, corresponds to S/P times the expression for the change in the dollar cost of government purchases of nontradable goods.

Although the constant LCU value of government purchases of tradables, $g^T S_t/P_t$, increases after the crisis if S_t/P_t rises, the rate at which these flows are discounted, $r + d_t - \pi_t$, increases as well. These two effects cancel each other out. The constant LCU value of government purchases of tradables,

$g^T P_t^N / P_t$, falls after the crisis, assuming that P_t^N / P_t falls. However, given that these flows are also discounted at the rate $r + d_t - \pi_t$, they fall even more in present-value terms.

The only alternative explanation of these results that seems plausible is one that does not focus on the government's lifetime budget constraint at date zero. Suppose, instead, that one focuses on the government's lifetime budget constraint at the first date $\bar{t}$ beyond which nontraded goods prices are no longer sticky, and nominal transfers are reindexed to the price level. Given these assumptions, at any date $t \geq \bar{t}$, $S_t/P_t = S_{\bar{t}}/P_{\bar{t}} > S/P$, $P_t^N/P_t = P_{\bar{t}}^N/P_{\bar{t}} < P^N/P$, and $\hat{V}_t/P_t = \hat{V}_{\bar{t}}/P_{\bar{t}} < \hat{V}/P$. In the end the model is fully consistent with chapter 3, in the sense that a real depreciation hurts the government. The government budget constraint, (7.4), makes very clear that absent significant changes in real seigniorage, $\dot{M}_t/P_t$, or the government's primary surplus measured in constant LCUs, $\bar{x}_t$, the government's debt measured in constant LCUs, $\bar{b}_t$, rises as real depreciation occurs.[9] Once this real depreciation stops happening, one might think that the government would be in extremely bad financial shape because its debt had increased substantially; that is, $\bar{b}_{\bar{t}} > \bar{b}_0$. But this will be true only if the future primary surpluses, $\bar{x}_t$, remain invariant to the real depreciation that has occurred. What the model suggests, however, is that $\bar{x}_t$ is unlikely to be invariant to a crisis in which real depreciation occurs. For $t \geq \bar{t}$, the primary surplus, excluding dollar transfers, is given by

$$\bar{\tau}_{\bar{t}} - \bar{g}_{\bar{t}} - \bar{v}_{\bar{t}} = \bar{\tau} - \bar{g} - \bar{v} + (\tau^T y^T - g^T)\left(\frac{S_{\bar{t}}}{P_{\bar{t}}} - \frac{S}{P}\right)$$

$$+ (\tau^N y^N - g^N)\left(\frac{P_{\bar{t}}^N}{P_{\bar{t}}} - \frac{P^N}{P}\right) + \frac{\hat{V}}{P} - \frac{\hat{V}_{\bar{t}}}{P_{\bar{t}}}. \qquad (7.11)$$

In the long run, the effect of the crisis is to make this component of the primary balance improve. The first term is positive because $S_{\bar{t}}/P_{\bar{t}} > S/P$, and this calibration implies that the government gets more revenue from taxing the tradable sector than it spends on tradable goods, that is, $\tau^T y^T - g^T > 0$. The second term is also positive, because $P_{\bar{t}}^N/P_{\bar{t}} < P^N/P$; but the government gets less revenue from taxing the nontraded goods sector than it spends on nontraded goods, that is, $\tau^N y^N - g^N < 0$. Finally, the third term is also positive, because the government doesn't fully index local currency transfers to the price level, that is, $\hat{V}_{\bar{t}}/P_{\bar{t}} < \hat{V}/P$. If it were to do so, however, the third term would be zero. The government's lifetime budget constraint in constant LCUs, at date $\bar{t}$, is

$$\bar{b}_{\bar{t}} = \frac{\bar{\tau}_{\bar{t}} - \bar{g}_{\bar{t}} - \bar{v}_{\bar{t}}}{r} + \mu \frac{M_{\bar{t}}}{P_{\bar{t}}} \frac{1}{r}. \tag{7.12}$$

Debt is greater than it would have been in the absence of the crisis, but so is $\bar{\tau}_{\bar{t}} - \bar{g}_{\bar{t}} - \bar{v}_{\bar{t}}$, due to implicit fiscal reforms, and so is seigniorage.

If the accounting is done in dollars,

$$\tau_{\bar{t}} - g_{\bar{t}} - \hat{v}_{\bar{t}} = \tau - g - \hat{v} + \left(\tau^N y^N - g^N\right)\left(P_{\bar{t}}^N/S_{\bar{t}} - P^N/S\right) + \hat{V}/S - \hat{V}_{\bar{t}}/S_{\bar{t}}. \tag{7.13}$$

The primary balance written this way also improves as a result of the crisis, although the improvement does not seem to stem from exactly the same sources. For example, traded goods do not appear in (7.13), and transfers will matter in (7.13) even if they are indexed to the price level, as long as a real depreciation occurs. The lifetime budget constraint in dollars at date $\bar{t}$ is

$$b_{\bar{t}} = \frac{\tau_{\bar{t}} - g_{\bar{t}} - \hat{v}_{\bar{t}}}{r} + \mu \frac{M_{\bar{t}}}{S_{\bar{t}}} \frac{1}{r}. \tag{7.14}$$

Since $\bar{b}_t = S_t b_t / P_t$, this suggests that for (7.12) and (7.14) to be consistent, one must have

$$\frac{S_{\bar{t}}}{P_{\bar{t}}} \frac{\tau_{\bar{t}} - g_{\bar{t}} - \hat{v}_{\bar{t}}}{r} + \frac{S_{\bar{t}}}{P_{\bar{t}}} \mu \frac{M_{\bar{t}}}{S_{\bar{t}}} \frac{1}{r} = \frac{\bar{\tau}_{\bar{t}} - \bar{g}_{\bar{t}} - \bar{v}_{\bar{t}}}{r} + \mu \frac{M_{\bar{t}}}{P_{\bar{t}}} \frac{1}{r}$$

or, equivalently, that

$$\frac{S_{\bar{t}}}{P_{\bar{t}}}(\tau_{\bar{t}} - g_{\bar{t}} - \hat{v}_{\bar{t}}) = \bar{\tau}_{\bar{t}} - \bar{g}_{\bar{t}} - \bar{v}_{\bar{t}}. \tag{7.15}$$

Of course, (7.15) is true. Even though the right-hand sides of (7.11) and (7.13) do not appear to be proportional to each other, by the definitions of $\bar{\tau}_t$, $\bar{g}_t$ and $\bar{v}_t$, they are.

8   Conclusion

Chapter 9 has explored the implications of different strategies for financing the fiscal costs of twin crises for inflation and depreciation rates. This was done using an extended version of the model in chapter 8, in which a crisis is triggered by a rise in prospective fiscal deficits. The extended model has three key features. First, the government has outstanding nonindexed debt whose real value can be reduced through a devaluation. Second, a portion of the government's liabilities is not indexed to the exchange rate. Third, there are nontradable goods whose prices are sticky and there are costs of distributing tradable goods, so that purchasing power parity does not hold at the level of the CPI.

The chapter argued that the strategy pursued by the government for covering the fiscal costs associated with a currency crisis plays a crucial role in determining post-crisis rates of devaluation. In the presence of significant nonindexed debt and government liabilities, it is feasible to finance large prospective deficits with moderate rates of money growth and low inflation rates, but at the same time experience rapid depreciation of the local currency.

9   Annex: Solving the Model

The Baseline Model

The baseline model is summarized by the equations (3.1) and (3.2), which can be solved simultaneously for t^* and μ given values of T, χ, and γ. An algorithm that begins with a guess for μ and solves (3.1) for t^* is used. The right-hand side of (3.2) is then evaluated. If it exceeds ϕ, the guess for μ is reduced; otherwise, the guess for μ is increased. The algorithm converges if the right- and left-hand sides of (3.2) are approximately equal within some chosen tolerance.

The Extended Model with Nominal Debt

When nominal debt is added to the model, but the other assumptions of the baseline model are kept, the only change is to the budget constraint. Equation (3.2) must be augmented with a term that computes revenue from debt deflation:

$$\int_0^\infty \left(\frac{rB}{S} - \frac{rB}{S_t} \right) e^{-rt} dt = \int_{t^*}^\infty \left(\frac{rB}{S} - \frac{rB}{S_t} \right) e^{-rt} dt. \qquad (9.1)$$

In the model with no price stickiness, the result from chapter 8, $S_t = Se^{\gamma + \eta\mu + \mu(t-T)}$ for $t \geq T$, can be used so that we may simplify further to

$$\frac{B}{S}[e^{-rt^*} - e^{-rT}] - rB \int_{t^*}^T S_t^{-1} e^{-rt} dt + \frac{B}{S} \frac{\mu + r(1 - e^{-\gamma - \mu\eta})}{\mu + r} e^{-rT}. \qquad (9.2)$$

Here the first integral may be evaluated numerically using the fact that

$$\ln S_t = \ln S - \chi + (\mu\eta + \gamma + \chi)e^{(t-T)/\eta}, \tag{9.3}$$

for $t^* < t < T$.

The Extended Model with Nominal Transfers

When adding nominal transfers to the model (but maintaining the assumptions of the previous section), assume that $\hat{V}_t = \hat{V}$ until some time $T_V \geq T$. After time T_V, assume that transfers increase at the same rate as the exchange rate, so that $\hat{V}_t = \hat{V}S_t/S_{T_V}$. Equation (3.2) must be augmented with a term that computes implicit revenue from the reduction in the dollar value of transfers:

$$\int_0^\infty (\hat{v} - \hat{v}_t)e^{-rt}\,dt = \int_{t^*}^{T_V} (\hat{v} - \hat{V}/S_t)e^{-rt}\,dt + \int_{T_V}^\infty (\hat{v} - \hat{V}/S_{T_V})e^{-rt}\,dt. \tag{9.4}$$

In the model with no price stickiness, this simplifies further to

$$\frac{\hat{v}}{r}(e^{-rt^*} - e^{-rT_V}) - \hat{V}\int_{t^*}^T S_t^{-1}e^{-rt}\,dt + \hat{v}\,\frac{e^{-rT_V+\mu(T-T_V)} - e^{-rT}}{(\mu + r)e^{\gamma+\mu\eta}}$$

$$+ \left(\hat{v} - \frac{\hat{V}}{S_{T_V}}\right)\frac{1}{r}e^{-rT_V}, \tag{9.5}$$

where the first integral may be evaluated numerically using (9.3).

The Extended Model with Sticky Nontradables Prices

First, consider the case where $\delta = 0$, so that there are no distribution costs. Then assume that the price of nontradable goods remains fixed at its pre-crisis level until time T, and thereafter grows at the same rate as the price on tradables.

Finding t*

The same rule can no longer be used for determining t^*. The key equation in determining the time of the speculative attack is the money demand function, (2.10): $M_t = \theta P_t y \exp[-\eta(r + \dot{S}_t/S_t)]$. When $\delta = 0$, $P_t = S_t^\omega(P_t^N)^{1-\omega}$. So

$$M_t = \theta S_t^\omega (P_t^N)^{1-\omega} y \exp[-\eta(r + \dot{S}_t/S_t)]. \tag{9.6}$$

This means that in the initial steady state we have M $= \theta S^{\omega}(P^N)^{1-\omega}ye^{-\eta r}$.

The assumptions made about P_t^N imply that $P_t^N/S_t = P^N/S_T$ for $t \geq T$. Hence, for $t \geq T$ one obtains

$$M_t = \theta S_t(P^N/S_T)^{1-\omega}y \exp[-\eta(r + \dot{S}_t/S_t)], \qquad (9.7)$$

which can be rewritten as a differential equation in $s_t = \ln S_t$:

$$s_t = \eta r - \ln \theta - (1-\omega)\ln(P^N) + (1-\omega)s_T + \ln(M_t/y) + \eta \dot{s}_t. \quad (9.8)$$

It follows that

$$s_t = \eta r - \ln \theta - (1-\omega)\ln(P^N) + (1-\omega)s_T$$
$$+ \frac{1}{\eta}\int_t^{\infty} \ln(M_s/y)e^{-(s-t)/\eta}ds, \qquad t \geq T. \qquad (9.9)$$

Since $M_t = e^{\gamma+\mu(t-T)}M$ for $t \geq T$, (stgT1) implies

$$s_t = \eta r - \ln \theta - (1-\omega)\ln(P^N) + (1-\omega)s_T$$
$$+ \gamma + \mu(\eta + t - T) + \ln(M/y) \qquad t \geq T. \qquad (9.10)$$

Using the expression for M, notice that this means

$$s_t = \omega s + (1-\omega)s_T + \gamma + \mu(\eta + t - T) \qquad t \geq T. \qquad (9.11)$$

Hence, $S_T = Se^{(\gamma+\mu\eta)/\omega}$ and $S_t = Se^{(\gamma+\mu\eta)/\omega+\mu(t-T)}$ for $t \geq T$.

For $t^* \leq t \leq T$, we have $M_t = \theta S_t^{\omega}(P^N)^{1-\omega}y \exp[-\eta(r + \dot{S}_t/S_t)]$ so that

$$s_t = [\eta r - \ln \theta - (1-\omega)\ln(P^N)]/\omega + (1/\omega)\ln(M_t/y) + (\eta/\omega)\dot{s}_t. \quad (9.12)$$

Since $M_t = Me^{-\chi}$ for $t^* \leq t \leq T$, one obtains

$$s_t = [\eta r - \ln \theta - (1-\omega)\ln P^N + \ln(M/y) - \chi]/\omega + (\eta/\omega)\dot{s}_t. \quad (9.13)$$

Hence, for $t^* \leq t \leq T$, $s_t = [\eta r - \ln \theta - (1-\omega)\ln(P^N) + \ln(M/y) - \chi]/\omega + e^{\omega t/\eta}C$, where C is a constant of integration. Using the expression for M, this means $s_t = s - \chi/\omega + e^{\omega t/\eta}C$ for $t^* \leq t \leq T$. Since one already has an expression for $s_T = s + (\gamma + \mu\eta)/\omega$, this means that $C = e^{-\omega T/\eta}(\gamma + \mu\eta + \chi)/\omega$. And since one must also have $s_{t^*} = s$, this means

$$t^* = T - \frac{\eta}{\omega}\ln\left(\frac{\chi + \gamma + \mu\eta}{\chi}\right). \qquad (9.14)$$

Notice that this is a slightly modified version of (3.1).

Satisfying the Government's Lifetime Budget Constraint

The expressions for seigniorage on the right-hand side of (3.2) are unchanged, except that $S_T = Se^{(\gamma+\mu\eta)/\omega}$ and $M = \theta S^\omega (P^N)^{1-\omega} y e^{-\eta r}$.

Since $S_t = Se^{(\gamma+\mu\eta)/\omega+\mu(t-T)}$ for $t \geq T$, the expression for debt deflation becomes

$$\frac{B}{S}[e^{-rt^*} - e^{-rT}] - rB\int_{t^*}^T S_t^{-1} e^{-rt} dt + \frac{B}{S}\frac{\mu+r\left[1-e^{-(\gamma+\mu\eta)/\omega}\right]}{\mu+r}e^{-rT}. \quad (9.15)$$

Here the first integral may be evaluated numerically using the fact that

$$\ln S_t = \ln S + \left[(\mu\eta + \gamma + \chi)e^{\omega(t-T)/\eta} - \chi\right]/\omega \quad (9.16)$$

for $t^* < t < T$.

The expression for the reduction in the dollar value of transfers becomes

$$\frac{\hat{v}}{r}(e^{-rt^*} - e^{-rT_V}) - \hat{V}\int_{t^*}^T S_t^{-1} e^{-rt} dt + \hat{v}\frac{e^{-rT_V+\mu(T-T_V)} - e^{-rT}}{(\mu+r)e^{(\gamma+\mu\eta)/\omega}}$$

$$+ \left(\hat{v} - \frac{\hat{V}}{S_{T_V}}\right)\frac{1}{r}e^{-rT_V}, \quad (9.17)$$

where $S_{T_V} = Se^{(\gamma+\mu\eta)/\omega+\mu(T_V-T)}$. The first integral may be evaluated numerically using (9.16).

On the left-hand side of the government budget constraint, one has the tax revenue component:

$$\int_0^\infty e^{-rt}(\tau - \tau_t)dt = \int_0^\infty \tau^N y^N \left(P^N/S - P_t^N/S_t\right)e^{-rt} dt$$

$$= \tau^N y^N P^N\left[\frac{e^{-rt^*}}{rS} - \left(\int_{t^*}^T S_t^{-1} e^{-rt} dt + \frac{1}{rS_T}e^{-rT}\right)\right]. \quad (9.18)$$

The integral may be evaluated numerically using (9.16).

Finally, on the right-hand side of the budget constraint, one has the government purchases component:

$$\int_0^\infty (g - g_t)e^{-rt} dt = \int_0^\infty g^N\left(P^N/S - P_t^N/S_t\right)e^{-rt} dt$$

$$= g^N P^N\left[\frac{e^{-rt^*}}{rS} - \left(\int_{t^*}^T S_t^{-1} e^{-rt} dt + \frac{1}{rS_T}e^{-rT}\right)\right]. \quad (9.19)$$

Distribution Costs

Solving the model is more difficult when $\delta > 0$. To see why, notice that when $\delta > 0$, $P_t = (S_t + \delta P_t^N)^\omega (P_t^N)^{1-\omega}$ so that $M_t = \theta(S_t + \delta P_t^N)^\omega$ $(P_t^N)^{1-\omega} y \exp[-\eta(r + \dot{S}_t/S_t)]$. This complicates solving the model for $t^* \le t \le T$ because in this case one has $M_t = \theta(S_t + \delta P^N)^\omega (P^N)^{1-\omega} y$ $\exp[-\eta(r + \dot{S}_t/S_t)]$, which is no longer a linear differential equation in $s_t = \ln S_t$. Rather than solve the model exactly, which would require one to solve the differential equation numerically, instead approximate the model for the case of $\delta > 0$. Notice that when $\delta = 0$, then $P_t = S_t^\omega (P_t^N)^{1-\omega}$, so that the inflation rate was $\pi_t = \omega \dot{S}_t/S_t + (1-\omega)\dot{P}_t^N/P_t^N$. When $P_t = (S_t + \delta P_t^N)^\omega (P_t^N)^{1-\omega}$, the inflation rate is

$$\pi_t = \omega \frac{S_t}{S_t + \delta P_t^N}\frac{\dot{S}_t}{S_t} + \left[\omega \frac{\delta P_t^N}{S_t + \delta P_t^N} + (1-\omega)\right]\frac{\dot{P}_t^N}{P_t^N}.$$

The two expressions for the inflation rate are similar, except that the weight put on the rate of depreciation in the expression for inflation is smaller. The model is solved with $\delta > 0$ approximately by letting $\tilde{\omega} = \omega S/(S + \delta P^N)$. The same solution technique is used here as for $\delta = 0$, using $\tilde{\omega}$ in place of ω.

Notes

1. The fiscal costs of a crisis could also be paid for with international aid, namely, through subsidized loans granted by institutions such as the International Monetary Fund (IMF). Jeanne and Zettelmeyer (2000) argue that the subsidy element of IMF lending is small. For Korea and Mexico they estimate that this subsidy amounted to less than 1 percent of GDP.
2. Distribution services have not been required for the consumption of nontradables. The most important nontradables are housing, health, and education expenditures, which are sectors where wholesaling, retailing, and transportation do not play a significant role.
3. This is an innocuous assumption, because after time zero there is no uncertainty. So new local currency-denominated debt would be equivalent to new dollar-denominated debt.
4. To see this, notice that the first term on the right-hand side of (2.8) is $\int_0^\infty (g - g_t)e^{-rt}dt = \int_0^\infty g^N(P^N/S - P_t^N/S_t)e^{-rt}dt$, and the second term is

$\int_0^\infty (\hat{v} - \hat{v}_t) e^{-rt} dt = \int_0^\infty \hat{V}(1/S - 1/S_t) e^{-rt} dt$. These terms and the third term, $\int_0^\infty rB(1/S - 1/S_t) e^{-rt} dt$, are clearly zero if P_t^N and S_t remain fixed at their pre-crisis levels.

5. See Dupor (2000), Daniel (2001), and Corsetti and Mackowiak (forthcoming) for open-economy applications of the fiscal theory.

6. See Burnside, Eichenbaum, and Rebelo (2000) for a discussion.

7. See Burnside, Eichenbaum, and Rebelo (2003b).

8. See Burnside, Eichenbaum, and Rebelo (2003a) for details of the calculations.

9. It is conceivable that changes in $\dot{M}_t/P_t$ and $\bar{x}_t$ between dates zero and $\bar{t}$ would be significant enough that the government's debt might not rise between dates zero and $\bar{t}$, but this does not occur in our calibrated examples with sticky prices.

References

Burnside, Craig, Martin Eichenbaum, and Sergio Rebelo. 2000. "Understanding the Korean and Thai Currency Crises." *Federal Reserve Bank of Chicago Economic Perspectives* 24 (3): 45–60.

———. 2003a. "Government Finance in the Wake of Currency Crises." NBER Working Paper 9786, National Bureau of Economic Research, Cambridge, MA.

———. 2003b. "On the Fiscal Implications of Twin Crises." In Michael P. Dooley and Jeffrey A. Frankel, eds. *Managing Currency Crises in Emerging Markets.* Chicago: University of Chicago Press.

Burstein, Ariel, Martin Eichenbaum, and Sergio Rebelo. Forthcoming. "Large Devaluations and the Real Exchange Rate." *Journal of Political Economy.*

Burstein, Ariel, Joao Neves, and Sergio Rebelo. 2003. "Distribution Costs and Real Exchange Rate Dynamics during Exchange-Rate-Based Stabilizations." *Journal of Monetary Economics* 50 (6): 1189–214.

Cochrane, John. 2001. "Long-Term Debt and Optimal Policy in the Fiscal Theory of the Price Level." *Econometrica* 69 (1): 69–116.

Corsetti, Giancarlo, and Bartosz Mackowiak. Forthcoming. "Nominal Debt and the Dynamics of Currency Crises." *European Economic Review.*

Daniel, Betty. 2001. "A Fiscal Theory of Currency Crises." *International Economic Review* 42 (4): 969–88.

9

Dupor, William. 2000. "Exchange Rates and the Fiscal Theory of the Price Level." *Journal of Monetary Economics* 45 (3): 613–30.

Easterly, William, Paolo Mauro, and Klaus Schmidt-Hebbel. 1995. "Money Demand and Seigniorage-Maximizing Inflation." *Journal of Money, Credit, and Banking* 27 (2): 583–603.

Flood, Robert, and Peter Garber. 1984. "Collapsing Exchange Rate Regimes: Some Linear Examples." *Journal of International Economics* 17 (1-2): 1–13.

Jeanne, Olivier, and Jeromin Zettelmeyer. 2000. "International Bailouts, Financial Transparency, and Moral Hazard." Manuscript, Research Department, International Monetary Fund, Washington, DC.

Krugman, Paul. 1979. "A Model of Balance of Payments Crises." *Journal of Money, Credit, and Banking* 11 (3): 311–25.

Sims, Christopher. 1994. "A Simple Model for the Determination of the Price Level and the Interaction of Monetary and Fiscal Policy." *Economic Theory* 4 (3): 381–99.

Woodford, Michael. 1995. "Price Level Determinacy without Control of a Monetary Aggregate." *Carnegie-Rochester Conference Series on Public Policy* 43: 1–46.

9

Index

Boxes, figures, notes, and tables are indicated by b, f, n, and t, respectively.

I

I

I

I

I

I

I

I